"Learning to Write and Loving It! offers a comprehensive review of current research on early writing instruction compiled to provide practical strategies including technology tips to develop writers in your classroom. A must-have writing resource for early childhood teachers!"

—Sue Haas, Kindergarten Teacher
Alpha School, Morristown, TN

"This book is a first of its kind—full of ideas for developmentally appropriate writing activities teachers can immediately use in the classroom—a terrific resource."

—Susan B. Neuman, Professor
University of Michigan Educational Studies Department
Ann Arbor, MI

Learning to Write and LOVING IT!

Preschool–Kindergarten

MIRIAM P. TREHEARNE

Foreword by
Timothy Shanahan

CORWIN
A SAGE Company

CORWIN
A SAGE Company

FOR INFORMATION:

Corwin
A SAGE Company
2455 Teller Road
Thousand Oaks, California 91320
www.corwin.com

SAGE Ltd.
1 Oliver's Yard
55 City Road
London EC1Y 1SP
United Kingdom

SAGE India Pvt. Ltd.
B 1/I 1 Mohan Cooperative Industrial Area
Mathura Road, New Delhi 110 044
India

SAGE Asia-Pacific Pte. Ltd.
33 Pekin Street #02-01
Far East Square
Singapore 048763

Acquisitions Editor: Jessica Allan
Associate Editor: Allison Scott
Editorial Assistant: Lisa Whitney
Production Editor: Veronica Stapleton
Illustrator: Mark Mason
Typesetter: C&M Digitals (P) Ltd.
Proofreader: Wendy Jo Dymond
Indexer: Sheila Bodell
Cover Designer: Rose Storey
Permissions Editor: Karen Ehrmann
Photographers: Bob Hart and Patrick Trehearne

Library of Congress Cataloguing-in-Publication Data

Trehearne, Miriam P.
Learning to write and loving it! preschool-kindergarten / Miriam P. Trehearne; foreword by Timothy Shanahan.

p. cm.
Includes bibliographical references and index.

ISBN 978-1-4522-0313-3 (pbk. w/cd)

1. Language arts (Preschool)—United States. 2. Language arts (Kindergarten)—United States. 3. English language—Composition and exercises—Study and teaching (Preschool) 4. English language—Composition and exercises—Study and teaching (Elementary)—United States. I. Title.

LB1140.5.L3T74 2011
372.6—dc23   2011019153

This book is printed on acid-free paper.

11 12 13 14 15 10 9 8 7 6 5 4 3 2 1

Contents

Foreword

Once upon a time encouraging—or even allowing—young children to write was considered ridiculous. Parents and teachers were loathe to introduce writing early and their excuses were legion: the kids might mark up the walls, hurt themselves with sharp pencils, waste paper by just scribbling, or, heavens to behaviorism, they could develop bad habits that would stay with them long into the future (like awkward penmanship or deficient spelling). Even some "scholars" got into the act with cautionary tales that claimed that if we involved young children in academic learning "too early" we would stultify their growing brains. Among the forbidding warnings, few parents or teachers could see any potential value worth the terrible risks. The message was clear: early writing was to be avoided.

Alas, even as those unsubstantiated fears have evaporated and the value of early writing has come into clearer relief, writing still has not gained much of a foothold in the early childhood curriculum. This continued neglect owes something to reading's "big shoulders." Early reading is now such a concern that it has made it difficult for teachers and parents to fit writing in among the phonological awareness exercises, letter and word cards, and decoding practices that are usually the purview of an early reading curriculum.

The publication of *Learning to Write and Loving It!* shows how times have changed, and it is a change for the good. Teachers, parents, theoreticians, and researchers have been shifting their positions on early writing, and thank goodness. Early writing doesn't have the portended bad consequences: it doesn't harm children's small muscles, if anything, it provides valuable exercise; young children's writing practice doesn't lock them into early misspellings never to be forgotten, but instead helps to strengthen early understanding of spelling and decoding in ways that actually improve reading abilities. As a scholar, I can tell you that early writing helps children to develop literacy skills. Not surprisingly, writing bolsters early phonological development, strengthens phonics skills, and gives children greater purchase on their knowledge of the alphabet. This, of course, is all to the good.

However, as a parent and former child, I'd situate the value of early writing experience elsewhere. Having observed my own children when they were dictating their stories and keeping diaries of family trips and experiences, I gained a deep appreciation of the *real* value of their early writing. Sometimes these efforts to compose were easy and sometimes painstaking, but my daughters always emerged with a profound sense of accomplishment (writing, unlike reading, leaves a physical record) and they gained a more thorough grasp of the value of their ideas and a joy in being able to make themselves understood. Such experiences provide kids with insights into their potential power over memory and a greater awareness of the changes they themselves are going through. (You may be surprised at how quickly a piece of writing shifts, in the child's eyes, from being a proud accomplishment to nothing more than embarrassing baby work.)

I remember my own childish efforts to write as well. My grandmother would write letters to me and send them all the way from Florida (sometimes along with a handkerchief or a dime, and always ending with a series of Os and Xs symbolizing her grandmotherly hugs and kisses). Mom would read those letters to me, and I so wanted to write back that one day I gave it a try. I scribbled a "letter" (Gram's cursive looked like scribbles to me) and thought Mom would send it off with the postman, but scribbling isn't writing, and I was puzzled: how could Mom read grandma's letters, but not mine? My failure led to me think harder about the problem and to watch more closely to try to discern what I was missing. Nothing especially remarkable in any of that: writers know that writing always falls a bit short of our aspirations, but we gain deep moral and intellectual insights from those shortcomings (and such insights into communication, love, expression, and creativity are good to start on early, as humans have been known to struggle a bit with humility).

Miriam Trehearne's aspirations are very high. She encourages the teaching of early writing (and shows us some successful ways of encouraging it and supporting it) and she obviously does so for the love of children and the love of literacy—ultimately the only legitimate reasons.

Timothy Shanahan
University of Illinois at Chicago

Acknowledgments

Corwin wishes to acknowledge the following peer reviewers for their editorial insight and guidance.

Dorothea Flanagan
Kindergarten Teacher/Lead Teacher and Mentor
Oak Grove Elementary in NEISD
San Antonio, TX

Julie Frederick
Kindergarten Teacher
Broadview Thomson K-8 School
Seattle Public Schools
Seattle, WA

Iris Goldberg
Director of Early Childhood/Childhood Programs
Long Island University, Westchester Graduate Campus
Purchase, NY

Sue Haas
Kindergarten Teacher
Big Bend School
Big Bend, WI

Renee Ponce-Nealon
Kindergarten Teacher
McDowell Elementary School
Petaluma, CA

About the Author

Miriam P. Trehearne has been a classroom teacher, resource teacher, Program Specialist (exceptional needs students), coach, Literacy Specialist, and University Associate. As a Literacy and Early Childhood Specialist, she led a very successful research-based literacy initiative (Kindergarten to third grade) in a large urban school district (156 elementary schools) which focused on 56 high-needs schools. Due to her many and varied roles and experiences, Miriam has become passionate in her belief that preschool and kindergarten are the most important grades. She believes that effective, engaging early literacy programs are not only important but crucial. This belief is supported by highly credible research.

Miriam presently devotes much of her time to researching literacy best practices and presenting to teachers, literacy coaches, paraprofessionals, school administrators, and parents, nationally and internationally. Miriam has keynoted at the ASCD Kindergarten Conference in Chicago and cochaired a one-day Institute with renowned literacy expert Regie Routman at the IRA in San Antonio. She can be found speaking regularly at early childhood conferences such as NAEYC, ECEC, and the Annual ASCD Pre-kindergarten/Kindergarten Conference as well as the Annual International Reading Association Conference, the World Congress, and the European Reading Conference.

Miriam also writes books, journal articles, and literacy materials for classroom use. *Learning to Write and Loving It!* is Miriam's fifth book. Three have been translated into French. Her books include *The Comprehensive Literacy Resource for Kindergarten Teachers,* the 2006 AEP award-winning *Comprehensive Literacy Resource for Grade 1–2 Teachers,* and *The Comprehensive Literacy Resource for Preschool Teachers. The Comprehensive Literacy Resource for Grade 3–6 Teachers* was a finalist for the AEP Award 2007. *Center Stage Literacy,* engaging and developmentally appropriate literacy focus centers for K–2 classrooms, won the 2008 Teachers' Choice Award for Classroom Materials.

Introduction

Learning to write assists children in their reading; in learning to read, children also gain insights that help them as writers. But writing is more than an aid to learning to read; it is an important curricular goal. Through writing children express themselves, clarify their thinking, communicate ideas, and integrate new information into their knowledge base.

—Centre for the Improvement of Early
Reading Achievement (CIERA) 1998b

The single most important thing you can do to help young children become writers is to provide them with time to write, materials with which to write, and to demonstrate the process and the importance of writing to them.

—Cunningham and Allington 1994, 88

Showing students how to write makes more sense to them when they understand and value why they are writing. Certainly, effective writing defies a cookie-cutter model, but our students do need to see and experience the thinking that goes into producing effective writing. Be explicit-show students how.

—Routman 2005, 15

Figure Intro 1
A real reason to write!

A Note From Miriam

Teachers of young children know that no two days are the same and that young children never cease to amaze. Recently I visited a high-needs kindergarten class just outside Chicago, Illinois. The teacher has the children write a great deal from the first day. By spring she has many very skilled and engaged writers in her classroom. The day I arrived she introduced me as an author. She held up my *Kindergarten Teacher's Resource Book* and showed the children my picture on the back. She asked the children if they had any questions for me, the author.

Meredith: Where did you get all the paper? (The book is 500+ pages!)

José: How long did it take you to write? (5 years)

And the question that stopped me in my tracks . . .

Christian: Where do you get your ideas?

Clearly, these children are developing writing skills and understandings and see themselves as writers. That this is happening is no accident. The children write from day one. They are frequently encouraged to self-select their own writing topics. They are taught that their art is also very important. They are taught to look carefully so that they can include lots of details when they draw. Additionally, they are writing across the curriculum—in science, social studies, and math. And through the use of mentor texts and mini-lessons, the children are learning the craft of writing (see Figure 6.32 and Figure 6.33 on page 179). This is but one example of the many exciting and effective classrooms in which I have had the pleasure of participating. The children in Jo Simpson's class are learning literacy and loving it!

I would also like to acknowledge all of the other amazing preschool and kindergarten teachers across Canada and throughout North America with whom I have had the pleasure of working. You have supported me in many ways in writing this book. Your love of young children and your dedication to joyful literacy learning make me your biggest fan! One can never get old teaching young children . . . exhausted, but not old.

A special thank you to Heather Jelley and Colleen Drautz at Jersey Public School (York Region District School Board, Keswick, Ontario), Diana Bruni at Transfiguration of Our Lord Catholic School (Toronto Catholic District School Board, Toronto, Canada), and Jo Simpson from Boulder Hill Elementary (Oswego 308, Oswego, Illinois) for opening your Kindergarten (Prek–JK and K) classrooms to me. By allowing me to spend time and capture your exemplary literacy practice in this book, you have benefited fellow teachers, administrators, and coaches across North America. Even though you may not realize it, your kindergarten classrooms, with all of their ups and downs, are like poetry in motion!

Thanks as well to Karen Frick, Laura Ferguson, and their principal Joan Green, Radisson Park School (Calgary Board of Education, Calgary, Alberta), for allowing a professional photographer to invade your space to capture joyful and playful but intentional literacy learning. The authentic photos bring the book to life.

In a book on writing, it is the authentic writing samples that really bring the instructional strategies, mini-lessons, and activities to life. Thank you to the many teachers across North America who provided me with such great examples of early writing . . . from scribbles to conventional text.

Thanks also to all of the kindergarten teachers, Public, Catholic, Private, and Charter, who I continue to have the privilege of working with across Canada and the United States. A special thank you to Laura Devitt and Joan Green and many other wonderful teachers and administrators in the Calgary Board of Education. You taught me so much.

A word of thanks to the many early childhood and literacy consultants who work tirelessly to support the work of preschool and kindergarten teachers. And to the principals who realize that preschool and kindergarten are the most important grades and who go above and beyond the call of duty to support their teachers and students. You are ALL my heroes!

And finally thank you to wonderful educators, authors and researchers such as Donald Graves, Barbara Bowman, Lucy Calkins, Marie Clay, David Dickinson, Shelley Harwayne, Judy Harris Helm, Georgia Heard, Don Holdaway, Lillian Katz, Lesley Mandel Morrow, Susan Neuman, David Pearson, Katie Wood Ray, Kathleen Roskos, Regie Routman, Timothy Shanahan, Catherine Snow, Vicki Spandel, Dorothy Strickland, Elizabeth Sulzby, Sharon Taberski, and William Teale, and Canadians Andy Biemiller, David Booth, Jim Cummins, Christine Gordon, and Keith Stanovitch, among others, who have taught us so much about early literacy and specifically how to most effectively support young literacy learners.

Dr. Tim Shanahan is professor of urban education at the University of Illinois at Chicago (UIC) and director of the UIC Center for Literacy. His research emphasizes reading-writing relationships, reading assessment, and improving reading achievement. Tim is former president of the International Reading Association and former chair of the National Early Literacy Panel. He was inducted into the Reading Hall of Fame in 2007. But most importantly to me, Tim always makes time to help out fellow educators all around the world. He is just an email away. Thank you Tim for the ongoing support you provide and for writing the foreword to this book. I am very honored!

And finally, thank you to the International Reading Association and the National Association for the Education of Young Children for leading the way. You have my greatest respect and appreciation!

Squiggles on a Page

By Colleen Drautz, Kindergarten Teacher

Jersey Public School, York Region District School Board, Keswick, Ontario

What is my teacher looking at?

Whatever can it be?

I wonder what is over there?

Some paper's all I see.

I think I'll take a closer look . . .

Huh!

Some funny squiggles, that is all

    A loop around,

       A little snake,

         A dot,

           A line,

             A ball.

My teacher comes and talks to me.

I tell her about my cat.

She smiles, picks up her marker

and makes more squiggles—- just like that!

Now she's pointing to the marks she made

I hear my words out loud again.

You can read those marks? I can, too?

Will they always sound the same?

I think I'd like to do that, too.

I could practice every day.

I need squiggles to tell my story

I have so much to say.

Welcome to *Learning to Write and Loving It!*

Early childhood is unique. Early Childhood teachers need and deserve their own professional books geared specifically to literacy learning. This is the goal of *Learning to Write and Loving It!:* to help preschool and kindergarten teachers, teachers of 3-, 4-, and 5-year-olds, get children off to a strong start. Although this book targets our youngest writers and readers, first grade teachers will also find many of the instructional strategies, assessment tools, mini-lessons and engaging activities both appropriate and valuable. "I believe that teaching a child to learn, to love learning, and to feel successful and joyful are among the most worthwhile of all endeavors" (Regie Routman, 2008 and 2009). That is what *Learning to Write and Loving It!* is all about.

Michael – Once upon a time there was a king who lived in a castle that had water all around, trees and bushes beside it, flags on the top, and it had a blue jewels above the door that was a crystal. It was a beautiful land with birds and clouds. The king always left the lights on in the castle.

Figure Intro 3
Look at the details in the drawing and in the scribed text. Notice the lights on!

Writing From 2000 to Today:
Some Things Have Changed!

My first professional book appeared in June 2000: *Kindergarten Teacher's Resource Book* (Nelson Thomson Learning). I wrote from the perspective of a kindergarten teacher. My goal was to provide a practical research-based book on literacy teaching and learning for kindergarten teachers. Judging by the responses from kindergarten teachers around the world, it appears that I succeeded. I am pleased to say that more than 10 years later the content of that book is still valid. However, the research data on literacy, kindergarten teaching, and learning have provided some additional insights.

Educators now know, for example, that writing in preschool and kindergarten is extremely important. In fact, the quality of writing support for 4-year-olds is highly related to their language and literacy growth at the end of kindergarten and Grade 1 (Dickinson and Sprague 2001). Many preschoolers and kindergarteners are writing before they are reading! In fact, the long-awaited US Report of the National Early Literacy Panel, released in January 2009, indicates that writing that develops from birth to age 5 is one of six variables that predict later literacy development.

Preschool and Kindergarten teachers have been so focused on reading that not enough attention has been given to writing. The irony is that supporting writing also supports reading! There is no doubt that early childhood teachers deserve a book to help them use developmentally appropriate and engaging assessments, activities, and approaches to support writing in preschool and kindergarten.

Research Base, Beliefs, and Understandings for *Learning to Write and Loving It!*

There are no more important *grades* than preschool and kindergarten. Literacy learning at this time can change lives. Research indicates that what happens in school and at home with 3-, 4-, and 5-year-olds has a long-lasting and powerful impact. All children deserve a strong start.

In a joint position statement issued by the International Reading Association (IRA) and the National Association for the Education of Young Children (NAEYC), "One of the best predictors of whether a child will function competently in school and go on to contribute actively in our increasingly literate society is the level to which the child progresses in reading and writing" (1998, 30).

Research Base, Beliefs, and Understandings		Learning to Write and Loving It!
"Excellent teachers know it's both what you teach and how you teach" (Copple and Bredekamp 2009b, 48).	→	shares both the *what* and the *how* of effective literacy teaching and learning
Research consistently points to the importance of ensuring that children enter first grade with the attitudes and knowledge about literacy that will enable them to succeed (Snow, 1998).	→	provides the skills, strategies, engaging mini-lessons, activities, and assessment tools to make this happen
Play and literacy learning naturally support each other (Copple and Bredekamp 2009b; Bodrova and Leong 2004; Elementary Teachers' Federation of Ontario 2011).	→	provides many excellent examples of teachers scaffolding effective play-based literacy activities, both spontaneous and planned
"A balanced developmentally appropriate language and literacy curriculum is not only beneficial but perhaps crucial in these early years" (Neuman 1998, x–xi).	→	supports such a curriculum
The latest research on early childhood literacy learning not only stresses the importance of writing for its own sake but also supports early reading (both decoding and meaning), phonological awareness and concepts of print, and the reading–writing connection (Harrison et al. 2008; Shanahan, 1984, 2006; Snow, 1998; Dickinson and Sprague, 2001).	→	provides motivating and engaging writing activities as well as mini-lessons to scaffold learning
Young children construct knowledge, but they also need direct teaching involving much scaffolding through modeling, demonstrating, explaining and guided practice (McGee and Richgels 2003; Schickedanz, 2004; Routman, 2005).	→	supports the Gradual Release of Responsibility Model as one example of focused teaching
Children must be provided with opportunities to apply the strategies they are taught by doing interesting activities that make sense to them. They learn best when they see a specific purpose for what they are learning (Routman, 2005; Copple and Bredekamp 2009; Helm and Katz 2010).	→	provides engaging, interesting, and purposeful activities

Differentiation or "embracing" the individual child (Tomlinson 2010) is key to both academic success and happiness in early childhood.	→	provides a variety of assessment tools to help drive instruction; supports many instructional approaches and materials; engaging activities and projects provide managed choice (Allington 2002) for the students.
Literacy learning occurs across the preschool-kindergarten day, across the curriculum. Integration is natural for teachers. Through cross-curricular integration and inquiry in areas such as social studies and science, young children are able to develop literacy skills while acquiring important "big ideas" involving hands-on activities (Copple and Bredekamp 2009b).	→	provides many examples of integrated cross-curricular projects and activities that celebrate the inquiry approach and project-based learning
The home plays a key role in emergent/early literacy development (National Early Literacy Panel Report 2009; Bennett-Armistead, Duke, and Moses 2005; Gullo, 2006).	→	includes many examples of practical and easy-to-implement home literacy activities

Research

Assessment

Instruction

How to Effectively Use This Resource

As with all of my professional books, *Learning to Write and Loving It!* enables you to quickly access specific content or topics using the detailed table of contents in conjunction with the index. However, you may prefer to read through the entire resource in order to gain a more complete picture of writing development in preschool and kindergarten. Reputable research, developmentally appropriate and easily implemented assessment tools, instructional strategies, samples of children's work, and descriptions of what some of the samples reveal are key components of this resource. The diagnostic assessments featured in this resource are both formative (assessment for learning) and summative (assessment of learning).

Also included are proven teaching and organizational strategies, mini-lessons, and activities that effectively support writing. Frequently a series of mini-lessons that may extend over several days is listed as one lesson. It is important to follow the particular children and their needs. Limit mini-lesson time, at any one time, to what is appropriate for the individual or group. The Window on the Classroom feature brings the early childhood experience to life. Some of the vignettes exemplify strong classroom practice while others describe specific situations that you may connect with personally. All of the accounts come from actual classrooms and are included to make you think.

Rounding out the contents is a list of recommended professional books, reports, CDs, and DVDs, and a comprehensive bibliography. The reproducibles, which are conveniently packaged in an accompanying modifiable CD, include literacy assessments, observation checklists, assessment summaries, literacy home–school links, and more.

Learning to Write and Loving It! consists of nine chapters and can be thought of as being written in two parts that work together to provide the big picture:

PART 1: The Introduction and Chapters 1 through 3 provide the background, research base, and user-friendly assessment tools to support effective early childhood writing.

PART 2: Chapters 4 through 9 and the Closing Thoughts *link assessment to instruction* by providing the practical *how-to* of daily effective literacy practice in preschool and kindergarten.

- **Chapter 1: Literacy Learning in Preschool and Kindergarten** provides the necessary background to teach literacy including writing, reading, speaking, listening, viewing, and representing. The chapter includes predictors of early literacy success, important literacy skills and understandings, a continuum of children's development in early reading and writing, an explanation of the term *developmentally appropriate,* a list of developmentally appropriate literacy expectations, and a clarification of the role of play in supporting literacy learning.

- **Chapter 2: Research on Writing in Preschool and Kindergarten** provides a description of writing stages, categories, goals, skills, and understandings. It also details spelling development in early childhood (the five stages of spelling development, the pros and cons of invented spelling, and the pros and cons of underwriting). Finally, it describes some effective writing tools (including technology) and outlines the high-yield strategies for successfully supporting young writers.

- **Chapter 3: Assessing Writing in Preschool and Kindergarten** describes ways to assess and document student writing and to effectively implement writing portfolios. Suggestions for determining each child's

The following symbols are used throughout the book:

Easy-to-implement and effective strategies for involving parents/caregivers in their child's learning

Recommended read-alouds and other great resources to support literacy development

User-friendly tips for incorporating technology to enhance literacy development in your classroom

Suggestions for when to use think-alouds to support literacy learning

Opportunities to scaffold learning through play-based literacy activities

Reproducibles found on the accompanying CD

writing category and spelling stage are also provided, as is support for children learning to assess themselves as writers. Trait-based scoring scales, spelling stages, and writing exemplars are also included, in addition to a reproducible Writing Checklist (Reproducible 2.1 on the accompanying CD).

- **Chapter 4: Effective Instructional Approaches** includes a description of instructional approaches to teach writing and proven implementation strategies for each approach.

- **Chapter 5: Writing Workshop** describes the four stages of writing workshop. Stage 1 provides practical examples of important procedural and skill and strategy mini-lessons. Stage 2 outlines strategies for implementing sustained writing. Stage 3 describes different kinds of writing conferences and provides step-by-step implementation guidelines. Stage 4 outlines the importance and how to of author share.

- **Chapter 6: Writing Fiction and Nonfiction Genres** provides an understanding of preschool and kindergarten children's typical aptitude for and interest in writing fiction (narrative) and nonfiction (including informational text). The chapter shares practical mini-lessons and activities to support writing both genres.

- **Chapter 7: Writing Songs and Poetry** provides easy-to-implement mini-lessons for writing and enjoying songs and poetry.

- **Chapter 8: Play Plans Before and After Centers** describes the purpose of play plans and mini-lessons to scaffold play-plan writing before centers and writing after centers.

- **Chapter 9: Writing Messages and Using Interactive Journals** provides descriptions of many different kinds of authentic messages that students can write along with the mini-lessons to scaffold implementation. Based on research done in kindergarten classrooms, interactive journals provide an alternative to the regular journal writing typically seen in kindergarten.

Chapter 1

Literacy Learning in Preschool and Kindergarten

Preschool and kindergarten are the most important grades! I say this to preschool, kindergarten, primary, middle school, junior high, and high school teachers. I passionately share this with administrators, parents/caregivers, and politicians. I want to yell it from the rooftops! The research is clear. School systems working with families have a small window of opportunity in which to get children off to a strong start. Research indicates that children who begin third grade struggling in reading and writing rarely catch up with their age-appropriate peers and tend to struggle all the way through high school (Snow 1998). All children deserve a strong start. Early childhood is crucial to later success in school and in life.

Literacy Learning in Preschool and Kindergarten Can Change Lives

Emerging literacy results at the end of kindergarten are very predictive of reading and writing achievement levels at the end of Grade 1. This finding is extremely important because research indicates that there is close to a 90 percent probability that children struggling with reading (and often writing) at the end of Grade 1 will remain poor readers (and often writers) by the end of Grade 4 (Allington, 1998, 12). Kindergarten teachers can predict at the end of the kindergarten year where most of the children will be in literacy learning by the end of Grade 1. The good news is that teachers, beginning in preschool, can prevent this negative spiral from occurring for at least 95 percent of young learners. What preschool and kindergarten teachers (and other primary teachers) do or do not do really makes a difference.

> All I really need to know I learned in kindergarten.
> (Robert Fulghum, 1988)

> Although first-grade interventions are necessary for some children, the best intervention is well-designed kindergarten instruction (CIERA 1998a).

> Research indicates that preschool education is a sound investment academically, socially, and economically. (Barnett and Hustedt, 2003).

Figure 1.1

In fact, research indicates that what happens in preschool and kindergarten is long lasting and powerful. Kindergarten literacy learning even affects classroom achievement in middle and high school. Longitudinal research by Ralph Hanson and Diane Farrell (1995) tracked close to 4,000 students from kindergarten to Grade 12. Approximately one-third of the students had been taught to read in kindergarten. The other two-thirds had not learned to read in kindergarten. Reading had not been a kindergarten focus area in their classrooms. "The major finding of this study is that students who learned to read in kindergarten were found to be superior in reading skills and all other educational indicators as measured as seniors in high school. This finding held up across districts and schools, as well as ethnic, gender and social class groups. Also, there was absolutely no evidence of any negative effects from learning to read in kindergarten" (p. 929). These students not only displayed higher grades but also had better attendance in school. The study concludes, "Any school district with a policy that does not support kindergarten reading should be ready to present new and compelling reasons to explain why not . . . !" (929).

Other research also confirms that children's language and literacy skills in preschool and in kindergarten are strongly related to later academic success. "The receptive vocabulary scores of kindergarten students near the end of kindergarten were strongly related to the end of seventh grade vocabulary and reading comprehension" (Dickinson and Sprague 2001, 273). Additionally, the quality of writing support given to 4-year-olds is highly related to their literacy growth at the end of kindergarten and Grade 1. And of course the children's vocabulary levels and background knowledge have a significant impact on their writing.

Develop Strong Readers and Writers

The landmark work of Catherine Snow, Susan Burns, and Peg Griffin (1998) indicates that young children develop into strong readers and writers when their teachers focus on these foundational areas of literacy development:

- Alphabet letter knowledge/letter recognition
- Phonological (including phonemic) awareness
- Letter–sound correspondence (phonics)
- Concepts about print and books
- Oral comprehension and vocabulary (listening and speaking, receptive and expressive language)

Receptive vocabulary refers to words that are understood by a reader or a listener. Expressive vocabulary refers to the words that one uses to communicate as a speaker or a writer.

The IRA and NAEYC Joint Position Statement states that "Failing to give children literacy experiences until they are school age can severely limit the reading and writing levels they ultimately attain" (1998, 6).

Oral Language is the foundation of literacy learning.

Figure 1.2

This is an important message!

Predictors of Literacy Success

As stated earlier, kindergarten teachers can predict at the end of the kindergarten year where most of the children will be in literacy learning by the end of Grade 1.

According to Marilyn Jager Adams, prereaders' ability to recognize and name letters (letter knowledge) is "the single best predictor of first-year [Grade 1] reading achievement, with their ability to discriminate phonemes auditorily ranking a close second. Furthermore, these two factors were the winners regardless of the instructional approach used" (1990, 36). However, "it is not simply the accuracy with which children can name letters that gives them an advantage in learning to read [and write], it is the ease or fluency [speed] with which they can do so. . . . A child who can recognize most letters with thorough confidence will have an easier time learning about letter sounds and word spellings than a child who still has to work at remembering what is what" (p. 43).

According to research, knowing letter names is important because they contain a sound typically represented by the letter. For example, recognizing a *d* helps the reader to remember that its sound is /d/. The more time children have to spend on figuring out letters, the less time and energy they will have available to use other strategies to decode print and to write. Thus, letter recognition must become automatic.

PREDICTORS OF EARLY LITERACY SUCCESS

1. *Letters*
2. *Phonological/ Phonemic Awareness*
3. *Oral Language*

The second best predictor of reading success is the child's ability to discriminate between phonemes (individual letter sounds). Phonemic awareness is one aspect of phonological awareness. It involves

- an understanding that oral language is composed of a series of individual sounds, and
- the ability to play with these sounds.

"Enhancing children's letter knowledge and phonological awareness skills should be a priority goal in the kindergarten classroom" (Snow 1998, 188). However, no matter how skilled the child is in alphabet letter knowledge and phonological awareness, he or she still needs a strong understanding of both the concepts about books and about print, and a strong foundation in oral language. Oral language proficiency (receptive and expressive), which includes vocabulary knowledge, is a third strong predictor of future literacy success that lasts well into high school.

Figure 1.3

Turn and talk develops both oral language and comprehension.

Literacy Experiences and the Emergent/Early Reader and Writer

Much of the landmark research on emergent literacy development comes from the work of Dolores Durkin in the 1960s. Durkin studied the home environments of many children who had learned to read before entering kindergarten. She found that these children received on average 1,000 to 1,500 hours of preschool literacy experiences.

These home experiences included

- frequent read-alouds and discussion
- the teaching of alphabet letters and their sounds
- the teaching of "sight words" or high-frequency words
- providing help to the child based on the child's questions and requests for assistance

- making rhymes with words
- reading-related activities (for example, playing with magnetic letters on the fridge to create some words or "writing" a letter to someone)
- providing many opportunities to write
- listening to the child "read"
- engaging in literacy activities "on the run" (for example, reading signs and food labels)

Early childhood teachers need to provide intentional literacy experiences similar to what the children in Durkin's research were exposed to at home. For example, they need to
- read to the children and discuss what was read
- provide many shared reading experiences
- engage the children in many intentional activities to support oral language development
- teach alphabet letter names and sounds
- point out "sight words" (high-frequency words)
- develop phonological awareness (an ability to play with language)
- provide many opportunities to model writing and frequently engage children in motivating writing experiences using both invented (temporary) spelling and *for-sure words,* such as their names (see page 38 for more information on *for-sure words*)
- listen to each child "read" (books, environmental print, and even their own writing) and provide instruction and modeling
- support their play

When preschool and kindergarten teachers provide the intentional literacy activities listed above, most children will exhibit the seven signs of emergent literacy cited by Patricia Cunningham and Richard Allington in their well-loved book *Classrooms that Work: They Can All Read and Write* (New York: HarperCollins, 1994).

Seven Signs of Emergent Literacy

The child

1. can "pretend read" favorite books and poems/songs/chants
2. can "drite" and can read what he or she has written even if no one else can
3. can "track print" (that is, show you what to read and point to the words using left–right/top–bottom conventions)
4. knows critical jargon (for example, she or he can point to a specific word, the first word in a sentence, one letter in a word, the first letter in a word, the longest word in a sentence, and so on)

drite = draw and write

5. recognizes some concrete words (for example, his or her name, the names of other children, favorite words from books, poems, and chants, and so on)

6. recognizes if words rhyme and can make up rhymes

7. can name many letters and can tell you words that begin with the common initial sounds (Cunningham and Allington 1994, 143)

"Although it may seem as though some children acquire these understandings magically, or on their own, studies suggest that they are the beneficiaries of considerable, though playful and informal, adult guidance and instruction" (IRA and NAEYC 1998, 32). As much as it is true that young children play and discover many things on their own, it also is true that they need adult assistance and guidance (Schickedanz 1994, 46). Unfortunately, not all children receive the preschool support described by Dr. Durkin.

At Risk in Preschool and Kindergarten

Large numbers of children arrive in preschool or kindergarten behind before they even start.

The research indicates that children who are most likely to have difficulty with literacy learning are those who begin school with less prior knowledge and skill in areas such as oral language and background knowledge, phonological awareness, alphabet letter knowledge, print awareness, and writing. What is most important for all children is that schools provide strong kindergarten literacy programs and effective intervention in kindergarten. The gift of time (waiting) is generally no gift at all.

To determine if a child is at risk, teachers need to know what specific literacy skills and understandings they should expect of students by the end of kindergarten.

Literacy Skills and Understandings in Kindergarten

Research consistently points to the importance of ensuring that children enter Grade 1 with the attitude toward and knowledge about literacy that will enable them to succeed (Snow, Burns, and Griffin 1998).

"More than one in four children in Ontario Canada who enter Grade 1 are significantly behind their peers" (Dr. Charles Pascal 2009, 4). Ontario is not alone.

Figure 1.4
Giving children many opportunities to sit together to look at and discuss books is very important.

Children develop literacy from birth and excel as they

- develop both a rich vocabulary and a deep understanding of many concepts and language structures. Developing reasoning, creative and critical thinking, and inquiry skills is crucial.
- learn that written language is a system for representing oral language.
- learn concepts about print (what is a letter, what is a word, directionality) and concepts about books (the purpose of a book, book features).
- learn that speech can be segmented into small units of sound and learn how to play with language (phonological awareness) by rhyming, segmenting, and blending for example.
- learn to recognize alphabet letters and their corresponding sounds.
- learn how to print most letters (when provided with letter names, sounds, pictures, or key words) and a few words (using invented spelling and a few *for-sure words,* such as their names and other familiar and high-frequency words).
- see a purpose for writing and want to write.
- recognize their own names in print in addition to a few other familiar and high-frequency words.
- see a purpose for reading and want to read.
- enjoy being read to.
- are able to listen to and understand stories and informational books. Their retellings must include important information or ideas.
- choose to look at books independently.
- begin to see themselves as readers and writers.

Develop Vocabulary, Concepts, and Reasoning

Understand Concept of Written Language
Understand Concepts About Print and About Books

Develop Phonological Awareness

Learn Letter Names and Sounds
Print Letters and Words

See a Purpose for Writing and Want to Write
Recognize Words

See a Purpose for Reading and Want to Read
Enjoy Being Read To

Listen With Understanding

Choose to Look at Books
See Oneself as a Reader and a Writer

Continuum of Children's Development in Early Reading and Writing

Tables 1.1 through 1.3 list the end-of-year literacy skills and understandings for preschool, kindergarten, and Grade 1 children. This list is intended to be illustrative, not exhaustive. Children at any grade level will function at a variety of phases along the reading–writing continuum. Since it is important for kindergarten teachers to be aware of developmentally appropriate expectations before and after preschool and Grade 1, goals for those levels have also been included.

Table 1.1   Continuum of Literacy Skills: Phase 1

PHASE 1: Awareness and exploration (goals for preschool)		
Children explore their environment and build the foundations for learning to read and write.		
Preschoolers . . .	*So preschool teachers . . .*	*And family members should be encouraged to . . .*
• enjoy listening to and discussing storybooks • understand that print carries a message • engage in reading and writing attempts • identify labels and signs in their environment • participate in rhyming games • identify some letters and make some letter–sound matches • use known letters or approximations of letters to represent written language (especially meaningful words like their name and phrases such as *I love you*)	• share books with children (including Big Books) and model reading behaviors • talk about letters by name and sounds • establish a literacy-rich environment • reread favorite stories • engage children in language games • promote literacy-related play activities • encourage children to experiment with writing	• engage their child in conversation, provide the names for things, and show interest in what their child says • read and reread stories with predictable texts • encourage their child to recount experiences and describe ideas and events that are important • visit the library regularly • provide opportunities to draw and print using markers, crayons, and pencils

PHASE 2: Experimental reading and writing (goals for kindergarten)
Children develop basic concepts of print and begin to engage in and experiment with reading and writing.

Kindergarteners . . .	So kindergarten teachers . . .	And family members should be encouraged to . . .
• enjoy being read to and can retell simple narrative stories and nonfiction text	• encourage children to talk about reading and writing experiences	• read and/or reread narrative stories and nonfiction texts to their child daily
• use descriptive language to explain and explore	• provide many opportunities for children to explore and identify sound–symbol relationships in meaningful contexts	• encourage their child's attempts at reading and writing
• recognize letters and letter–sound matches		• allow their child to participate in activities that involve reading and writing (for example, cooking, making grocery lists)
• show familiarity with rhyming and beginning sounds	• help children to segment spoken words into individual sounds and blend the sounds into whole words (for example, by slowly writing a word and saying its sound)	
• understand left-to-right and top-to-bottom orientation and familiar concepts of print		• play games with their child that involve specific directions (such as Simon Says)
• match spoken words with written words	• frequently read aloud interesting and conceptually rich stories	• have conversations with their child during mealtimes and throughout the day
• begin to write letters of the alphabet and some high-frequency words	• provide daily opportunities for children to write	
• begin to see themselves as writers and illustrators	• help children to build a sight vocabulary	
	• create a literacy-rich environment for children to engage independently in reading and writing	

(Continued)

Table 1.1 (Continued)

PHASE 3: Early reading and writing (goals for Grade 1)
Children begin to read simple stories and can write about a topic that is meaningful to them.

Grade 1 children . . .	So Grade 1 teachers . . .	🏠🔁🔤 And family members should be encouraged to . . .
• read and retell familiar stories • use strategies (rereading, predicting, questioning, contextualizing) when comprehension breaks down • use reading and writing for various purposes on their own initiative • orally read with reasonable fluency • use letter–sound correspondence, word parts, and context to identify new words • identify an increasing number of words by sight • sound out and represent all substantial sounds in spelling a word • write about topics that are personally meaningful • attempt to use some punctuation and capitalization • see themselves as writers and illustrators	• support the development of vocabulary by reading daily to the children, transcribing their language, and selecting materials that expand children's knowledge and language development • model strategies and provide practice for identifying unknown words • give children opportunities for independent reading and writing practice • read, write, and discuss a range of different text types (poems, informational books) • introduce new words and teach strategies for learning to spell new words • demonstrate and model strategies to use when comprehension breaks down • help children build lists of commonly used words from their writing	• talk about favorite storybooks • read to their child and encourage the child to read to them • suggest that their child write to friends and relatives • bring to a parent–teacher conference evidence of what their child can do in writing and reading • encourage their child to share what he or she has learned about writing and reading

Source: Adapted from "Learning to Read and Write: Developmentally Appropriate Practices for Young Children." *The Reading Teacher* 52 (1998): 193–216. Copyright 1998 International Reading Association. This is a joint position statement of the International Reading Association and the National Association for the Education of Young Children.

Figure 1.5

Making Your Program Developmentally Appropriate

The International Reading Association and the National Association for the Education of Young Children (1998, 38) defines *developmentally appropriate* as the goals and expectations for young children's achievement, which are challenging but achievable, with sufficient adult support. *Developmentally appropriate* not only refers to what teachers should expect children to be able to learn but also how best to support this learning. (For examples of developmentally appropriate literacy expectations for preschool and kindergarten children, see pages 18–20.)

Early childhood teachers set developmentally appropriate goals and expectations based on
- their understanding of child development,
- their understanding of literacy learning, including current research in the areas of assessment and instruction, and
- their knowledge of the children's strengths, interests, and needs.

An activity is developmentally appropriate if
- the child is able to do the task, and
- the task is worthwhile (effective) in moving the child toward a particular goal (supports a goal).

According to Sue Bredekamp (1997), former director of professional development for NAEYC, "Too many preschool and kindergarten teachers, perceiving themselves as advocates of developmentally appropriate practice, fear pushing children too much academically and fail to teach them the knowledge and skills they need" (p. 38).

It is clear that children need focused teaching, but they also need spontaneous and planned play experiences during language arts and across the day.

"Excellent teachers know it's both what you teach and how you teach" (Copple and Bredekamp 2009, 48).

Literacy Learning and Play

Young children are meant to play and literacy learning naturally supports play. "Children benefit both from engaging in self-initiated spontaneous play and from teacher-planned and structured activities, projects and experiences" (Copple and Bredekamp 2009b, 49). "Rather than detracting from academic learning, play appears to support the abilities that underlie such learning and thus to promote school success" (Copple and Bredekamp 2009b, 15). There are many reasons why children should play at home and at school. Play develops:

- Social skills and self-regulation
- Abilities to problem solve
- Oral language
- Creativity
- Knowledge and skills

Teacher scaffolding of *mature* (imaginative, creative) *play* supports specific literacy skill development such as oral language and phonological awareness. It also supports student self-regulation and successful school adjustment (Bodrova and Leong, 2004). See Chapter 8, page 205, "Play Plans Before and After Centers."

Judith Schickedanz says it best: "We will not have done our best for young children if we deny them the path to learning they seek through play. But, we also will not have done our best if we fail to provide instruction. As much as it is true that young children play and discover many things on their own, it is also true that children need adult assistance or guidance. It is possible to preserve childhood and to give children access to academic skills" (1994, 46).

Figure 1.6
Warming our hands over the campfire at the camping center.

Check It Out!

"Chopsticks and Counting Chips: Do Play and Foundational Skills Need to Compete for the Teacher's Attention in an Early Childhood Classroom?" by Elena Bodrova and Deborah J. Leong in *Beyond the Journal: Young Children on the Web* (Washington, DC: National Association for the Education of Young Children, 2004), 1–7. Also see *Spotlight on Young Children and Play*, edited by Derry Koralek (Washington, DC: National Association for the Education of Young Children, 2004). "The Importance of Being Playful," by Elena Bodrova and Deborah J. Leong in *Educational Leadership* 60, no. 7 (2003): 50–53.

Play-based learning and focused teaching are NOT mutually exclusive. Young children need both!

Check It Out!

Playing is Learning is a great pamphlet for parents of preschool and kindergarten children (http://www.etfo.ca/ELKP/PlayingisLearning/Documents/PlayingisLearning.pdf).

Many examples of effective play-based literacy activities are embedded throughout this book. Also see Chapter 8, "Play Plans Before and After Centers." Look for this icon that indicates opportunities to scaffold learning through play-based literacy activities.

Literacy Learning Across the Day

Literacy learning occurs across the day. Writing occurs during writing workshop (see Chapter 5) and during play at centers. It also occurs across the day, across the curriculum. Integration is a natural approach for early childhood teachers. Through cross-curricular integration in areas such as social studies and science, young children are able to develop literacy skills while acquiring important "big ideas" involving hands-on activities. Children learn best when the concepts, vocabulary, and skills they encounter are related to things they know and care about and when the new learnings are interconnected (Copple and Bredekamp 2009b).

Figure 1.7

Watching the butterflies hatching leads to drawing and writing the lifecycle of the butterfly, part of the science unit, living things.

Chapter 2

Research on Writing in Preschool and Kindergarten

The research is clear. It is not only developmentally appropriate but also crucial to support writing in preschool and kindergarten. Children typically arrive in preschool or kindergarten believing that they are already writers or at least that they will become writers. It is important that their expectation becomes a reality beginning the first day. Additionally, writing is a prerequisite to developing the whole child: heart, mind, and soul. This is because writing allows children to express themselves, clarify their thinking, communicate ideas, and integrate new information into their knowledge base (CIERA 1998b). Writing (including drawing) helps children to make sense of their world. It also develops skill in letter recognition, phonics, print awareness, phonological awareness, oral language, and comprehension. As mentioned in the introduction, the quality of writing support for 4-year-olds is highly related to their language and literacy growth at the end of kindergarten and Grade 1 (Dickinson and Sprague 2001).

The Reading–Writing Connection

In her landmark research, Dr. Dolores Durkin (1966) discovered that the parents and caregivers of children who had learned to read before coming to kindergarten had read with their children. However, they did more than this. They did "literacy on the run" on a regular basis. They sang with their children, rhymed, pointed out letters on signs, and wrote to and with their children. They also gave their children many writing opportunities. It became clear that early readers generally are very interested in writing and many write long before they read.

Canadian researchers reviewed K–3 studies conducted in Canada, the United Kingdom, and the United States on early writing. The findings, published in a paper titled "The Influence of Early Writing Instruction on Developing Literacy" (Harrison et al. 2008), indicated that writing instruction should begin at the outset of formal schooling, which is usually kindergarten (either prekindergarten and kindergarten or junior kindergarten and senior kindergarten). They also discovered that early writing

- enhances early reading (word identification, decoding, passage comprehension, and word reading)
- supports the development of phonological awareness, the alphabetic principle, and phonics

Check It Out!

Two excellent teacher resources are *Already Ready: Nurturing Writers in Preschool and Kindergarten* by Katie Wood Ray and Matt Glover (Portsmouth, NH: Heinemann, 2008) and *Never Too Early to Write: Adventures in the K-1 Writing Workshop* by Bea Johnson (Gainesville, FL: Maupin House Publishing, Inc., 1999). Why do these authors use the terms *already ready and never too early?* They are making a point: preschool and kindergarten children are ready to write when they walk through the door on the first day of school. In fact many of them have been "writers" for a very long time.

Writing and reading develop reciprocally, but more emphasis has gone into the teaching of reading than writing in many classrooms. In reality, learning to write often precedes learning to read (McGill-Franzen 2006), even though learning to write is in many ways more difficult than learning to read. To write, young children

- need to understand and apply the concepts of print, such as where on the page to start writing and directionality
- have something that they want to say
- have the background knowledge and vocabulary to be able to express themselves
- have skill in both phonics and phonological awareness
- have the necessary fine motor skills and knowledge of letter formation

In addition, young children have to feel that they have something worth sharing and be confident to share. This can be challenging because writing reveals the writer's inner and sometimes private thoughts. That is why an accepting and encouraging risk-taking atmosphere is so crucial in all grades, but especially in preschool and kindergarten.

Randy Bomer, on the other hand, feels that writing is in some ways easier than reading. "A blank page presents children with an invitation to make meaning, while reading presents them with an expectation to figure out someone else's meaning" (Ray and Glover 2008, 13). Bomer suggests that the big difference lies in the terms *invitation* versus *expectation*. Writing allows the children some freedom to create, while reading requires them to "get it right." Whether reading is more difficult than writing, is open to debate. What is known is that effective classrooms reveal a balance of reading, writing, speaking, listening, viewing, and representing, and fitting it all in is a very challenging undertaking, especially in a half-day preschool or kindergarten program.

Writing: The Stages, Categories, Goals, Skills, and Understandings

Kindergarten and preschool children are typically described as both emerging and early writers. In her pioneering work in emergent literacy, Elizabeth Sulzby defined seven broad categories of writing used by emergent and early writers. In addition, there are four major writing goals and many specific writing skills and understandings.

Writing Stages

A child may move back and forth between the emergent and early writer stage depending on the day and what he or she chooses to write.

Writing is a kindergarten activity that promotes both alphabet letter knowledge and phonological awareness. Writing also helps children to understand concepts of print, including the fact that the end of a line is not always the end of a thought (Snow, Burns, and Griffin 1998).

"Writing has long been recognized as a valuable way for children to learn to focus on how sounds map onto print (phonics)." (Dickinson and Sprague 2001, 269)

Writing Behaviors	Literacy Knowledge
Emergent Writers	
The term *emergent literacy* comes from the work of Marie Clay (1966). It is a landmark term that says to parents/caregivers and teachers that literacy begins at birth and is constantly emerging. There is no magic age or developmental level when children are deemed ready to write. They begin to write as soon as they can think and have the ability to scribble.	• know that writing communicates an idea • rely primarily on pictures (without print) to convey meaning • use squiggles, sticks, wavy lines, and scribbles • draw pictures with recognizable shapes • create letterlike units or forms • use an individual letter only (may be repeated) • use random, nonphonetic strings of letters • copy print (not necessarily correctly) • may print own name so that it is recognizable • use one letter to represent a word • can describe their own writing and drawing • may see themselves as writers although some do not consider themselves writers until they know how to write the alphabet

Figure 2.1

I can write my name.

Invented or temporary spelling, writing letters backwards, using a mix of upper and lowercase letters, and not consistently leaving spaces between words are all characteristics of *kid writing*, a term coined by Eileen Feldgus and Isabell Cardonick (1999).

Writing Behaviors	Literacy Knowledge
Early Writers	
Early writers are developing more consistency in their appropriate use of concepts of print and sound–symbol correspondence. They use invented spelling and their approximations become more accurate as the year goes on. Early writers are more successful with many initial consonants and a few final consonants, and occasionally even find success with the middle of a word. Totally random strings of letters rarely appear as early writers know that not just anything goes. Their repertoire of high-frequency words is growing, both in reading and writing. These words are often called glue words, islands of certainty in a sea of print; *for-sure words,* or *pop-up words* and they generally appear on word walls. Use of upper- and lowercase letters becomes more appropriate. Typically by the end of kindergarten early writers can write at least one complete sentence or thought using invented spelling and appropriate closing punctuation.	• understand that print is functional—it can be used to get things done in everyday life • use pictures with print • create words regardless of spelling • know directional pattern on the page (left to right, top to bottom) • leave spaces between words • use some initial consonants correctly while using invented spelling • use some final consonants correctly while using invented spelling • can correctly print their own name • can spell a few other words conventionally • create phrases (two or more words) • use a pattern • begin labeling and using titles • create a sentence (a complete thought) leaving spaces between words, regardless of spelling • begin to use uppercase letters at the beginning of proper names and sentences • begin to more consistently use upper- and lowercase letters appropriately • write some high-frequency words (may be copied) • begin to experiment with closing punctuation (period, question mark, exclamation mark) • create several sentences about a subject • may create their own "books" • are able to read some of their own writing, even after a few days • see themselves as writers

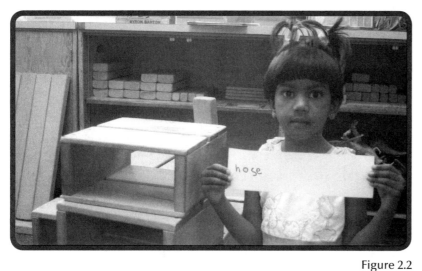

Figure 2.2

A label for the house I built.

Figure 2.3

This writer uses a writing pattern
I love . . . to support her drawings.

The Categories of Writing

Writing is developmental. Most children progress through seven broad categories as they learn, from the least mature to the most mature forms of writing. However, not all children pass through each and every category, and many go back and forth between or among categories as they develop. Most kindergarten children reach the invented spelling category by the end of the year, with some words written conventionally, such as their names, the names of others, and a few high-frequency words. To reach this level requires many opportunities to write and mini-lessons to scaffold learning. (For more information, see Spelling in Preschool and Kindergarten, page 35.)

Least Mature

1. drawing as writing

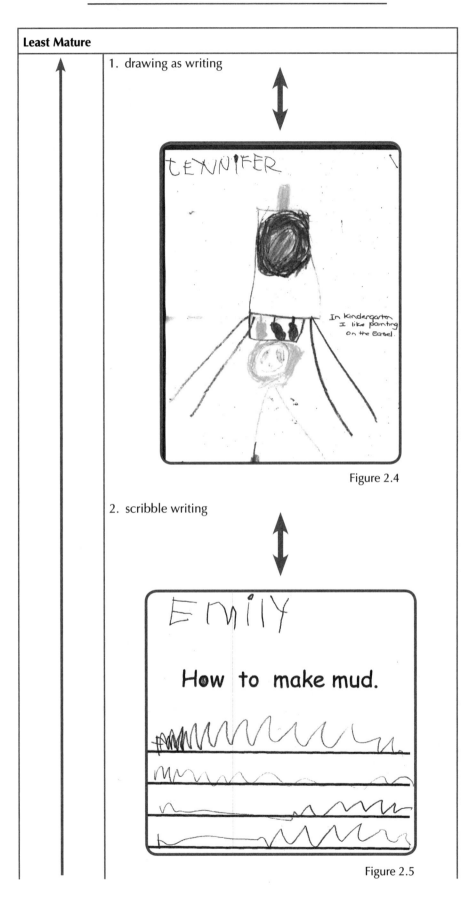

Figure 2.4

2. scribble writing

Figure 2.5

3. letterlike units or forms

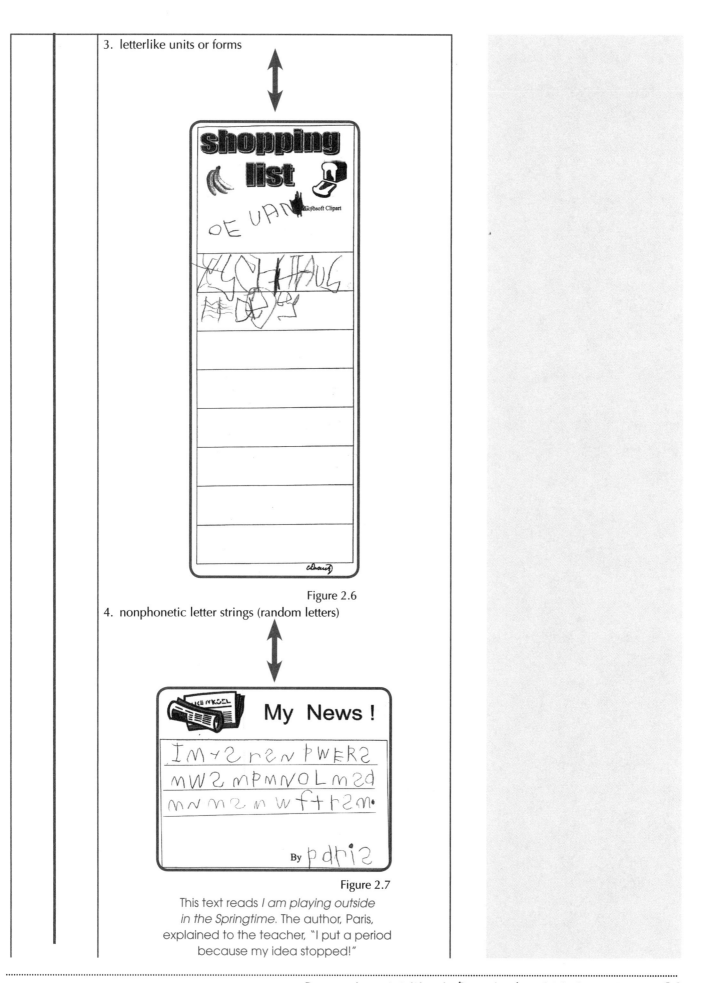

Figure 2.6

4. nonphonetic letter strings (random letters)

Figure 2.7

This text reads *I am playing outside in the Springtime.* The author, Paris, explained to the teacher, "I put a period because my idea stopped!"

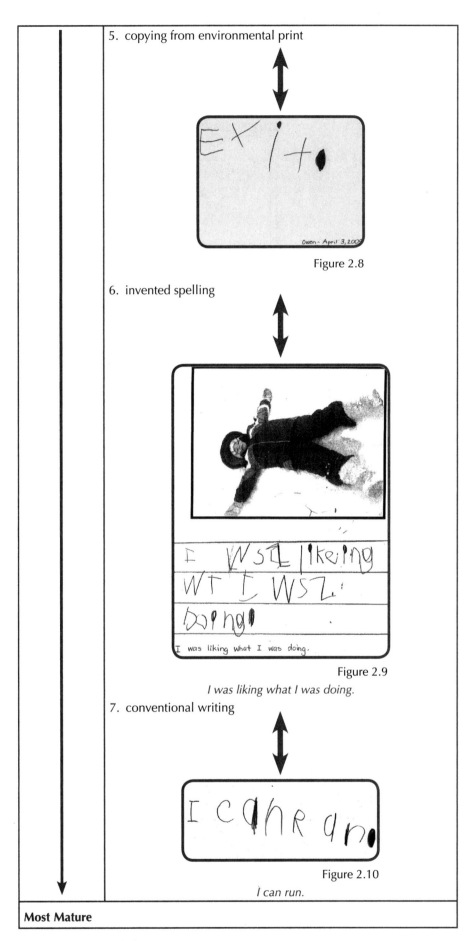

5. copying from environmental print

Figure 2.8

6. invented spelling

Figure 2.9

I was liking what I was doing.

7. conventional writing

Figure 2.10

I can run.

Most Mature

Source: Vukelich and Christie (2004), 7.

Children move back and forth through these categories of writing. On any one day, a child may draw, copy environmental print, use invented spelling, and then use a nonphonetic string of letters that do not seem to make any sense. Writing development is not a linear process; however, there is a developmental continuum of sorts, which moves from drawing and scribbling (least mature writing form) to conventional writing (most mature writing form). When assessing to determine the category into which each child falls, choose the highest stage typically evident.

The Goals of Kindergarten Writing

Beginning in preschool and kindergarten, children develop knowledge about the functions of writing. They use writing to label pictures, to further their pretend play, to take part in family uses of print, to experiment with composition, and to join in the literate communities around them, whether at home or in the classroom (Neuman and Roskos 1998).

By the end of kindergarten, children should
- develop an understanding that print is speech written down and that it conveys meaning
- develop the skill and confidence of a beginning writer and illustrator
- develop an interest in writing and a desire to write
- begin to recognize and use many types of writing for different purposes (for example, lists, letters, labels, personal recounts)

The Skills and Understandings of Kindergarten Writers

By the end of kindergarten, most children should
- understand that writing is speech written down and that it conveys meaning
- understand the many reasons why people write
- understand that speech (written and oral) is functional; it can be used to get things done in everyday life
- recognize and use different kinds of writing (for example, list, title, calendar, story, note or letter, label, sign, poster, survey, personal recount, nonfiction piece) and understand how one kind looks different from another
- see a purpose for writing and want to write often
- understand the concepts of print (including the concept of a sentence or a complete thought) and the concepts of author and illustrator in books
- write using a variety of tools and media (for example, crayons, paper, computer, chalkboard, colored markers, whiteboard)
- write their names and the names of some others
- frequently write their names on their papers

Should teachers refer to young children's drawings (without text) as writing? Research by Jerome Harste, Arlene Schulze, and others indicates that by age 3 children are distinguishing the difference between their drawings and written text and do not consider drawing alone writing.

"Young children must learn to think like writers, to think they are writers, and to believe that they have ideas to share with others" (CIERA 1998b).

If you don't know where you are going, any road will get you there.

Figure 2.11

- apply the concept of "rubber-banding" or stretching the sounds when trying to write words
- write simple messages using a combination of pictures, symbols, letters, phonetic spellings, familiar words, and two-word phrases (for example, a grocery list or labels for a sand or block construction, such as a zoo or a space station)
- frequently use some initial consonants correctly
- occasionally use some final consonants correctly
- occasionally use medial consonants correctly
- copy print so that it is recognizable
- contribute words or sentences to a class narrative (for example, an account of a class trip) that is written down as part of shared or interactive writing (see Chapter 4, pages 81–84)
- print the letters of the alphabet, some high-frequency words (for example, *it, in, to*), and short, phonically regular words (for example, *cat*)
- more consistently use upper- and lowercase letters appropriately,
- create a sentence (a complete thought) incorporating invented spelling, word spaces, and closing punctuation
- choose a writing topic independently. Here is the bat mobile.

Figure 2.12

Here is the bat mobile.

- use patterns as a writing base, such as developing vocabulary around ways to move (*I can run, I can jump, I can skip, I can waddle, I can stroll*)
- share their writing with others
- be able to read some of their own writing, even after a few days
- be risk takers (that is, be willing to reveal inner thoughts in their writing)
- see themselves as readers and writers

Spelling in Preschool and Kindergarten

Preschool and kindergarten children mainly use invented spelling when they write. Invented spelling occurs when young children spell words using their best judgment or make an educated guess based on their knowledge of early literacy concepts. To spell, one has to know letters, letter–sound correspondence (phonics), and concepts of print, and must have some degree of phonological awareness. For example, to spell the word *cat* conventionally requires one to know the letters and their sounds and be able to rubber-band the word or stretch the letters *c-a-t*. For young children, invented spelling helps them approximate the spelling of a word they do not know how to spell. For many kindergarten children, especially in the first half of the year, *cat* would appear as *CT or KT*. Invented spelling is truly something to celebrate.

> Invented spelling is meant to be temporary, diminishing in use over the course of Grades 1 and 2. By Grade 3, children should be using conventional spelling for the vast majority of their words.

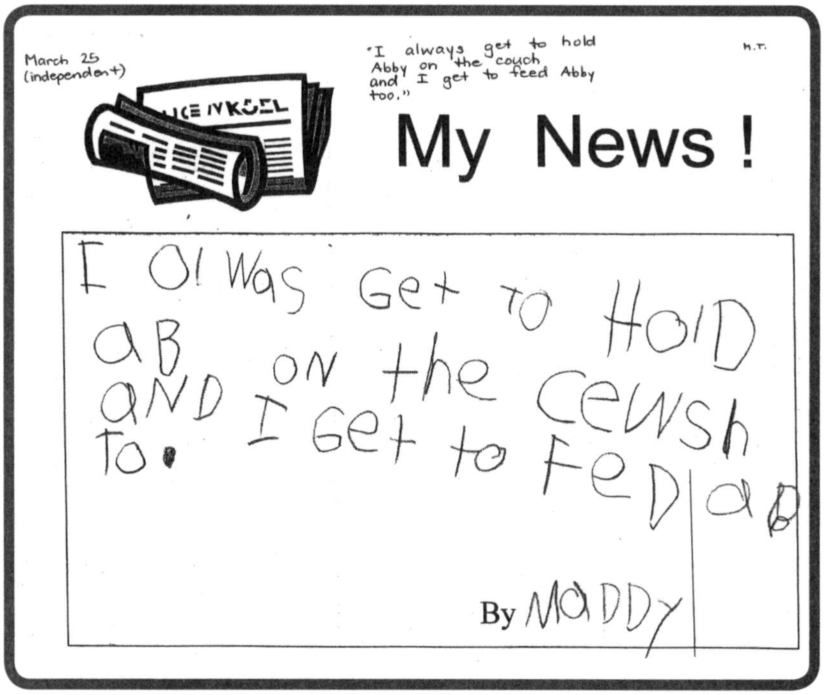

March 25
(independent)

"I always get to hold Abby on the couch and I get to feed Abby too."   h.t.

My News !

I OI WAS GET TO HOID aB AND on the ceWSh To. I Get to FeDIaB

By MADDY

Figure 2.13

I always get to hold Abby on the couch and I get to feed Abby too.

> Don Graves (1994) explained that the purpose of invented spelling is to allow children to make meaning before they know how to actually spell a word.

Why Promote Invented Spelling?

The promotion of invented spelling recognizes and respects that learners need lots of time and practice to take risks and make mistakes. However, invented spelling was never meant to be "anything goes." You should expect closer approximations as the year progresses.

There are many reasons to promote invented spelling. Invented spelling frees children to express themselves in writing without worrying about the exact spelling of a word. It gives them confidence and makes them think of themselves as writers. We know that for children to become strong writers they need to write a great deal. If they stopped to worry about the exact spelling of every word, they would become inhibited, write very little, write only simple or "safe" words, and progress very slowly. In addition, such writing would take a long time and would be very discouraging.

Invented spelling also helps children to understand the alphabetic principle, meaning that words are made up of letters and letters stand for sounds we make when we say the words. By putting the letters together in various ways we make different words (Bennett-Armistead, Duke, and Moses 2005). Invented spelling provides for authentic, hands-on practice in phonological awareness and phonics (letter–sound correspondence). This is very important since a child's level of phonological awareness at the end of kindergarten is one of the best predictors for how well the child will learn to read and write in Grade 1. Invented spelling also provides you with easily accessible information about the child's phonics and phonological awareness development.

It is also very important for teachers and parents/caregivers to understand the role of invented spelling and how to effectively support spelling development at school and at home. (see Reproducible 2.6: Spelling in Preschool and Kindergarten, on the CD).

Celebrate children's spelling approximations each day. Encourage the children to be "fearless spellers."

Figure 2.14

Used with permission from Sue Ann Goshima, Gustav H. Webling Elementary School

Figures 2.15 and 2.16 show one child's use of invented spelling, but look at the difference between the two samples!

(My dinky cars are little.)

Figure 2.15

My dinky cars are little.

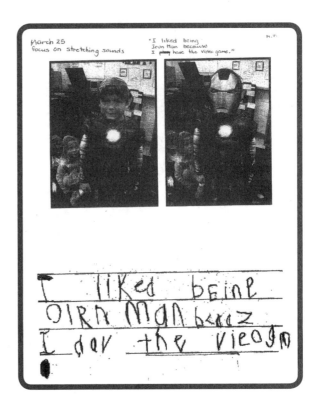

Figure 2.16

I liked being Ironman because
I have the video game.

Is There a Downside to Promoting Invented Spelling?

Some teachers believe that invented spelling will reduce the incentive for children to learn to spell conventionally; however, the research does not support this belief. In fact, through much invented spelling and many reading and writing mini-lessons, children learn phonics, including the ability to recognize patterns found in words and the ability to write high-frequency words correctly. This leads to conventional spelling.

Even by the spring in kindergarten, there is a core group of high-frequency words that children should be encouraged to at least copy correctly in their everyday writing. These words include the children's own names, the names of some of their classmates, and the following *for-sure* or *pop-up words* (since they pop up all the time):

For-Sure or Pop-Up Words			
a	and	he (she)	I
in	is	it	of
that	the	to	was

Surprisingly, these 12 simple words make up approximately 25 percent of the words children will encounter in their reading up to the end of Grade 3! (Note the word *she* has been added to make it 13.) All of these words should appear on the classroom word wall as they are important for children's writing.

The following 13 words, together with the 12 *for-sure words,* compose a list of 25 words that make up one-third of the materials typically written for adults: *are, as, at, be, for, from, had, his, on, or, they, with,* and *you.* These words are even more common to the reading and writing frequently done by young children. By the end of Grade 1, at least 70 percent of what children read and write is made up of approximately 100 words. For a list of these high-frequency or Pop-Up words, see Reproducible 2.2: High-Frequency or Pop-Up Words (End of Grade 1, on the CD).

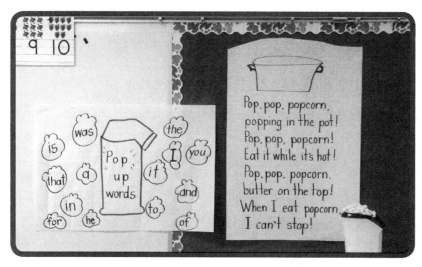

Figure 2.17

Source: Popcorn poem by Helen H. Moore.

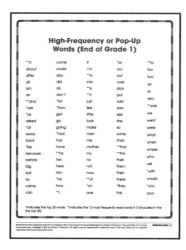

Invented spelling can be problematic if neither the author nor others can decipher the text. Invented spelling can also frustrate those very logical children who want to know the one correct spelling for a word. I have experienced such as scenario with regard to our son Colin. Colin would ask his teacher how to spell a difficult word (for example, *dinosaur*). When the teacher suggested to Colin to "give it a go," that he could do it, Colin was not impressed. He knew that he did not know how to spell *dinosaur,* but he also knew that there was one correct way to spell it. To avoid embarrassment, children like Colin simply stop writing or write only very safe words.

"Invented spelling not only allows children to write well before first grade, but it also builds essential literacy skills." (Neuman et al. in Bennett-Armistead, Duke, and Moses 2005, 146)

Children experiencing difficulties spelling a word should be encouraged to "give it a go," but they should also be given support. This is a perfect opportunity for interactive writing. Have the child write the part of the word he or she knows and then help with the conventional writing of the rest.

Assist the children with spelling by encouraging them to

- sub-vocalize or stretch out (rubber-band) the sounds as the word is said aloud (for example c_a_t)
- use magic lines (a line inserted for every sound the child hears, even if she or he does not know the corresponding letter) to represent unknown letters
- write the letters they hear clearly
- use word walls and other environmental print
- problem solve with a classmate or an adult

Learning word families (also called rimes or phonograms) is also important to early reading and writing. Children who can recognize and use word families will be able to read and write hundreds of words. There are 37 key word families for the primary grades. These 37 word families allow children to read and write nearly 500 primary-level words. Begin with a few in kindergarten.

Common Phonograms

-ack	-ain	-ake	-ale	-all	-ame	-an	-ank	-ap	-ash	-at	-ate	-aw
-ay	-eat	-ell	-est	-ice	-ick	-ide	-ight	-ill	-in	-ine	-ing	-ink
-ip	-it	-ock	-oke	-op	-ore	-ot	-uck	-ug	-ump	-unk		

Source: R. E. Wylie and D. D. Durrell, "Teaching Vowels Through Phonograms," *Elementary English* 47 (1970): 787–91.

Figure 2.18

Should Invented Spelling Ever Be Corrected or Discouraged?

Children should be encouraged to write, write, write. They should be encouraged to draw, as well as scribble, label, and write in whatever manner

Check It Out!

It is helpful to provide the children with a word and a picture to go with the phonogram or word family being introduced. Find all 37 downloadable word family cards, illustrations and corresponding word cards at http://www.etacuisenaire .com/miriamtrehearne/ miriam.jsp.

they can. Spelling is not a major focus. However, as children become more comfortable with recognizing and being able to write letters, and as high-frequency words are being introduced and practiced (generally in context and through games using the word wall and wall stories and through shared reading and writing), the concept of *for-sure words* should be introduced.

For-sure words are simply high-frequency words that the children use over and over again in their reading and writing. In Grade 1, there are 25 *for-sure words*, although by the end of Grade 1 many children are spelling many more words conventionally. By the end of Grade 2, there are 103 such words. In kindergarten there are typically 12 such words, 13 if *she* is added to the list (see page 38). It is important not to inhibit kindergarten writing by insisting that *for-sure words* be spelled conventionally. Instead, make it a game to find and copy these words correctly.

As Regie Routman (2005) and others have stressed in their work, allowing children to write these high-frequency words incorrectly using invented spelling over and over again does not help them to ultimately spell the words correctly. Furthermore, some of these words are not phonically regular (for example, *the* and *of*), meaning that the child may not even be able to use much invented spelling to "give it a go." The good news is that about half of the high-frequency words stressed in Preschool–Grade 2 follow a pattern or word family, such as -it (Cunningham 2000). By learning word families or rimes, kindergarten children are able to read and write hundreds of words.

You need to show children that you also use invented spelling when you do not know how to spell a word conventionally. Provide the children with examples of difficult words that you may struggle with. However, do not use invented spelling as a model of a word that most adults are likely to know how to spell. Provide an honest example. Also demonstrate for the children how you rubber-band or stretch a non-high-frequency word that you do not know how to spell to make an attempt at spelling it.

The Five Stages of Spelling Development

Richard Gentry (1993), among others, has named and defined five different stages of spelling. Stages 1, 2, and 3 deal with invented spelling and typically apply to preschool and kindergarten. It is important to note that the stages are developmental but that children can move back and forth across these spelling stages. Mini-lessons held during writing workshop (see Chapter 5) and across the day help the children to grow as writers.

Play the game Can You Read My Mind? with the children. Use only *for-sure words* or the children's names. Say, for example, "I am thinking of a word on the word wall. It is under the letter t. It is three letters long" *(the)*. Instruct the children to each write what they think the word is. Ask one child to then point to the word on the word wall. Once all the children agree that this is the word you were thinking of, spell the word together letter by letter as the children check what they have written.

During shared or interactive writing (see Chapter 4, pages 82 and 84) children often use invented spelling for non-high-frequency words. Invented spelling should be encouraged and approximations always celebrated. Praise how close the child has come to the conventional spelling. However, if the writing is going to be used by the children for rereading, such as reading around the room (reading environmental print in the classroom), the invented spelling, after being acknowledged for its merits, should be changed to conventional spelling.

Stages 1, 2, and 3 on the continuum of spelling development (the shaded areas of the adjacent chart) typically apply to preschool and kindergarten children. Most children should reach Stage 2, the semiphonetic stage, by the end of kindergarten, but many will be well into the phonetic stage.

Stages of Spelling Development	Mini-lessons during writing workshop and across the day should focus on . . .
Stage 1: Precommunicative	
Precommunicative spellers are at the babbling stage of spelling. They use scribbling, numbers, mock letters, and real letters to write words, but the letters are strung together randomly. They often repeat the same letter over and over. The letters do not correspond to the sounds (for example, they may write *OPSPS* for *eagle*). Uppercase letters are used more often than lowercase letters, but both are used indiscriminately. Generally, only the child can read his or her own writing and only sometimes.	• alphabet letter knowledge • letter–sound correspondence • phonological awareness • concepts of print, including the concepts of words and left–right directionality • many authentic reasons to write
Stage 2: Semiphonetic	
Semiphonetic spellers know that letters represent sounds and letter sounds can be used to make words. Spellings are often abbreviated and reflect initial and/or final sounds (for example, *E* for *eagle* or *MR* for *monster*). These spellers may also use the literal name of a letter to represent a word (*u* for *you* or *r* for *are*). Generally, the child can read her or his own writing more often than at Stage 1, and teachers can sometimes read the writing.	• concepts of print, including the concept of words • alphabet letter knowledge • letter–sound correspondence • beginning work with word families • lots of work with phonological awareness, including phonemic awareness • many authentic reasons to write
Stage 3: Phonetic	
Phonetic spellers spell words the way they sound. All the phonemes in a word are represented although not necessarily conventionally (for example, *EGL* for *eagle*, *BOTM* for *bottom*, and *STOPT* for *stopped*). Short vowels are often problematic. Generally, the child and teachers can read what has been written.	• more word families and short vowels • spelling patterns, phonics, and word structures (word parts, base words, and little words) • more segmenting and blending of phonemes • many authentic reasons to write

Stage 4: Transitional	
Transitional spellers think about how words appear visually (a visual memory of spelling patterns is apparent). Spellings exhibit conventions of English orthography, such as vowels in every syllable, e-marker (for example, *made, like*) and vowel digraph patterns (for example, *boat, each*), and correctly spelled inflectional endings (for example, *EGUL* for *eagle* and *BOTTUM* for *bottom*). To distinguish between phonetic spellings (influenced by sound) and transitional spellings (influenced by visual conventions), ask yourself, "Is this word spelled like it sounds (phonetic), or is its spelling more representative of a visually recalled spelling (for example, *BOTTUM* with the double *tt*)?	• commonly misspelled words, including homonyms and contractions • many authentic reasons to write
Stage 5: Conventional (Standard)	
Conventional or standard spellers continue to improve their spelling accuracy, spell a large body of words correctly, and know how to proofread (and hopefully do!). Typically, conventional spelling is most evident in Grade 3 and beyond.	• prefixes and suffixes • homonyms • contractions • possessives • irregular spelling patterns • many authentic reasons to write

Source: Adapted from Richard Gentry and Jean Wallace Gillet, *Teaching Kids to Spell* (Portsmouth, NH: Heinemann, 1993), 26–37.

Underwriting: Should Teachers Do It?

The term *underwriting* refers to transcribing writing in standard form using conventional spelling (Feldgus and Cardonick 1999). Typically, the teacher writes directly under or sometimes above what the child has written, or at the bottom of the page. The teacher may write a whole sentence or more typically just a word. The word may be a high-frequency word that the child should eventually learn to write correctly. The teacher may pick one word that is so far from conventional spelling that rereading it by anyone would likely be impossible. Or the word may be very close to conventional spelling and the underwriting highlights how close the child came.

The reasons for underwriting include

- providing the child with a correct model of writing that she or he may choose to refer to and use later
- responding to a child's request
- helping the child to read back (remember) what he or she has written
- helping you and parents/caregivers understand (and remember) what the child has written
- supporting a mini-lesson with the child during an individual conference
- celebrating strong approximations made by the child

Figure 2.19
Pictures were taken of the children in costume.
Each wrote something about the costume
experience. Owen wrote about showing off his
costume in a Grade 1 class. *I am the joker. I really
liked going to grade 1.*

The primary debate around underwriting is whether doing so reduces the child's ownership of the piece. According to Eileen Feldgus and Isabell Cardonick, underwriting is a positive tool, done for the purpose of teaching, not correcting. Typically, the child writes in bright marker while you write small and in pencil, usually at the bottom of the page. This sends the message that the child's writing is the focus. Children love to see how their writing compares to adult writing. Underwriting is a great teaching tool that allows you to reread what the child has written and track progress over time. Once underwriting is explained to parents/caregivers, they too appreciate the benefits of this kind of teacher support (see Reproducible 2.3: Kindergarten or *Kid* Writing, on the CD).

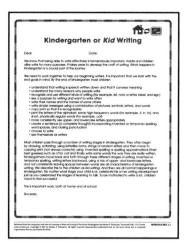

Writing Tools and Materials

Unlined paper is typically best to use at the beginning of the year. Many researchers, including Lucy Calkins and Lesley Mandel Morrow, believe that since children typically draw as a stimulus to write, lines simply get in the way. Other teachers prefer the children use half-and-half pages—plain at the top of the page for drawings and lined at the bottom for print. Thin markers are easy to handle and the children do not need to erase (Calkins, in Schulze 2006). However, as the year progresses, allowing the children to choose from a wide variety of paper (shapes, colors, and textures) and writing tools is a good idea.

Many teachers also wonder how important pencil hold and handwriting (letter formation) are and at what age it is developmentally appropriate to teach both.

Pencil Hold

It is important to teach young children, even before kindergarten, how to hold a pencil or marker so that they can write most effectively and enjoy writing. If children develop awkward pencil holds, their hands will easily tire and often their writing will be illegible. There are several awkward pencil holds. These include

- grasping the pencil with four fingers (including the ring finger and the little finger) rather than with two is common in kindergarten. This grasp may initially feel better to the child, but it often causes the hand to lift off the table.
- holding the middle finger on top of the pencil rather than under it.
- grasping the pencil either too high or too low. Holding the pencil too close to the tip does not allow the child to see the tip and therefore to write effectively.

Waiting until Grade 1 to teach these skills often results in habits that are very difficult if not impossible to break. Many children enter preschool already exhibiting these less effective habits.

The most effective pencil hold is the tripod. This hold allows for maximum stability and writing efficiency. It is important to model this grip and help those children who may be struggling to actually place their fingers and hands appropriately. The pencil is supported by the thumb, index, and middle fingers. The pencil rests on the middle finger. The ring finger and little finger curl in with the wrist and the side of the hand resting on the table.

But how does a teacher teach the child to use an effective pencil hold beyond modeling it? One teacher in Surrey, British Columbia, uses this method with great success:

1. Have the child put the pencil on table with the point pointing at him/her.

2. Have the child using the first finger and thumb (pincer) pick up the pencil.

3. Then ask the child to rock the baby (eraser end down).

4. The child then rocks the pencil up and over to rest on the hand (this is putting the baby to bed).

5. Finally have the child slide the 3rd finger under the pencil (and puts a pillow under the baby's head).

Figure 2.20
The most effective pencil hold
is the tripod, shown here.

One more key issue is hand dominance. Some children write with one hand and then switch to the other and back again. Watch to see if you can determine the hand with which the child has more success Some children might need

Consult an occupational therapist about any fine motor issues that might impact writing.

a bit of encouragement to determine a dominant hand; however, dominance should not be forced as not all dominances are determined in kindergarten. Most children will eventually establish dominance on their own.

Letter Formation

There are many programs and approaches available to support children who are learning letter formation, but you may wonder if there is a research-based, developmentally appropriate method or approach. Should you have the children simply copy letters? Should you think aloud as you model writing a letter for the children? For example, "To print an uppercase letter B, start at the top, go down, hop to the top, bump, bump" (Bergen 2008, 44) or "Line down, curve forward, curve forward" (McGee and Morrow 2005, 196). Or is there something else that you should do to support the children in learning to write letters? Should you spend time having the children trace, copy, and drill individual letters? Should time be spent simply on printing practice? Should upper and lowercase letters be taught at the same time?

The research of Marie Clay and Don Holdaway, among others, indicates that when children themselves decide to copy or trace letters, they learn more than writing lessons ever teach. The goal is readable letters not perfect letters. Readable letters occur when the child chooses to write rather than when the teacher pressures the child to write. Writing lessons taught separately from meaningful writing are boring and tedious. Children need to see themselves as writers and do lots of meaningful writing. The best way to learn to write is through lots of engaging writing activities.

So how do children learn to write letters without formal letter-writing lessons? Teachers need to model letter formation during modeled, shared, interactive, guided, and independent writing time. (See Mini-Lessons 5.2: Letter Formation on page 101 of Chapter 5.)

Technology as a Tool for Literacy Learning

There is no clear agreement as to exactly what technology looks like or should look like in preschool and kindergarten. Typically, one may see any of the following being used: computers and software programs, overhead projectors, digital cameras, document cameras, digital microscopes, CDs and tape recorders (such as at the Music/Listening Center), DVDs, talking word processors, the Internet along with e-books (with adult support), and interactive whiteboards (for example, SMART Boards).

Interactive whiteboards are gaining in popularity and frequency of use in elementary schools. In preschool and kindergarten they are typically used to support word work, modeled and shared reading, and modeled, shared, and interactive writing. They allow the children to interact with the print as they write (for example, find, circle, and manipulate words, letters,

Donald Graves reported that poor letter formation and handwriting improved in a little over a month when children were allowed to compose and share topics of their own choosing in a writing workshop approach (Schulze 2006, 31).

Talking word processors are great to use. They allow the children to hear a voice reading what they have created. It may be what has been scribed and/or what they have written. How exciting for them when they realize that the letters have turned into spoken words!

punctuation, and graphics). Interactive whiteboards also promote thinking skills as children can use them to solve problems and answer questions.

WINDOW ON THE CLASSROOM

In one classroom I visited, the kindergarten teacher used the SMART Board to help children write answers to questions related to a science unit. Using the shade screen in the SMART Notebook program, the teacher dragged it down to uncover just the question. What is in the egg? was revealed at the top of the page. She then pulled down the shade screen further to uncover both the question and the picture clue (a frog). The children wrote their answer(s) using invented spelling (A fg is in the ag.) before the teacher pulled down the shade screen to uncover the answer.

The SMART Board can also be used to make words available to build the same answer. The SMART Board provides the option of dragging words into place (A frog is in the egg.) before the shade screen is pulled down to reveal the answer. The children can then check to see if their answer(s) match the one provided.

Software can promote learning only to the extent that it engages children's attention—yet software that engages children's attention may or may not promote learning (Snow et al. 1998).

Technology may very well engage the children and there are many teacher testimonials to this effect. However, teachers are not always sure what the children are really engaged in doing, and simply being engaged using a software program does not necessarily result in learning.

Deciding on Technology Use

Children use technology to play, learn, and create. Technology has great potential to enhance literacy learning in preschool and kindergarten. That being said, it is important that teachers ask themselves several important questions before using technology in the classroom:

- Is the activity developmentally appropriate (i.e., is it consistent with how the child develops and learns and with the child's current developmental stage)?
- Will the activity benefit the child, or will it replace other, more meaningful learning activities?
- Is the choice of technology based on how well the tool supports both learning and teaching needs?
- Can technology deliver the same or better results in terms of literacy learning than more traditional approaches?
- Are there enough manipulatives, Little Books, Big Books, puppets, art materials, and other learning materials in the classroom? Teachers and administrators should weigh the costs of technology against the costs of other learning materials and program resources to arrive at an appropriate balance for classrooms.

Will the children have a healthy balance of the electronic world and the real world? Limit screen time (television, videos, and computers).

Source: Adapted from Van Scoter and Boss (2002).

What the Research Says about Technology Use in Preschool and Kindergarten

In the end, there is very little empirical research or hard data to show that current technologies have any effect, good or bad, on young children's literacy outcomes, any more than traditional approaches. Most of what is known about technology as a tool for literacy learning, especially in preschool and kindergarten, comes from the trenches—from teachers trying new technologies themselves and sharing with one another.

Teachers have shown that technology can be a powerful tool to support a project-based curriculum where children investigate big questions. For example, see Mini-Lessons 6.14: Writing a Question-and-Answer Report on page 180 of Chapter 6.

Computers

For many children, computers are an important part of their lives both at home and at school, and teachers frequently look for ways to use computers to enhance early literacy learning. There are differences of opinion about computer use with young children, however. Here are some of the research findings:

- Many early childhood educators question having children spend much solitary time in front of a computer screen, especially when the activity replaces more active play involving interaction, oral language and drawing, writing, and building. Others find computers a good tool to support kindergarten literacy.

Figure 2.21
Encourage the children to work together to problem solve and develop vocabulary when using technology. There is typically more conversation at computers when children are seated together than there is when assembling puzzles or interacting at the Block/Building Center. The more conversation the better! (Van Scoter et al. 2001)

Check It Out!

See "Using Technology with Kindergarten Students" by kindergarten teacher Chris Gathers (www.4teachers. org) for some best practice examples of exciting activities using technology to enhance learning in the kindergarten classroom.

"Teachers make thoughtful use of computers and other technologies in the classroom, not to replace children's experience with concrete objects and materials but to expand the range of tools with which children can seek information, solve problems, understand concepts . . . and move at their own pace." (Copple and Bredekamp 2009b, 315)

Check It Out!

Early Connections: Technology in Early Childhood Education (www.netc.org/ earlyconnections) is a great site to support teachers and parents/caregivers interested in effective technology use. Under Publications, see "Learners, Language, and Technology: Making Connections That Support Literacy" and "5 Effective Ways for Young Children to Use Technology."

Check It Out!

The International Children's Digital Library (www.icdlbooks .org) is a great resource for all teachers, but especially for ELL children and their families. Beautiful picture books for children aged three to five are available in such languages as English, Arabic, Chinese, Croatian, Filipino/Tagalog, Danish, French, German, Hebrew, Italian, Persian/Farsi, Portuguese, Russian, Spanish, and Thai. There are also chapter books, make-believe books, true books (informational text), fairy and folk tales, real animal characters, kid characters, and books about imaginary creatures. These books can be accessed through the Internet at no cost. (See Reproducible 2.5: Picture Books in Many Languages, on the CD.)

Research and common sense tell us that computers could be used more effectively if there were more than one of them in each classroom, more technical support, more time for teachers to examine software and determine how to effectively use it, and more adult support. Consider beginning the year with one or two computer programs. Identify peer "experts" who can help others.

- Including a computer (or other technologies) at existing centers, such as at the Restaurant/Pizza Parlor Center or Doctor's Office Center, demonstrates to children that it is a useful tool in real life.
- Interactive talking books, which allow children to participate in choral and echo reading; support comprehension, vocabulary, and fluency; and may stimulate writing.

- It can take hours to research, access, and get to know developmentally appropriate and effective software. Additionally, teachers must have the ability to introduce the software to the children and monitor its use. Before children use computer programs, teachers have to conduct hardware- and software-related lessons. Children have to be taught the concepts of screen along with the concepts of print. Many 5-year-olds are familiar with these concepts, but many others are not! Some children do not yet understand the concepts of top and bottom (whether page or screen), letter, and so on. Concepts of screen are multifaceted and include moving the mouse, matching the mouse and cursor, clicking in the right place, double-clicking to open icons, clicking and dragging, locating appropriate programs on the desktop, opening the program, closing the program, navigating using icons, directionality, and scrolling. Working with 20 or more 3- to 5-year-olds makes this very difficult without regular support from paraprofessionals and/or volunteers.
- Many very young children struggle with fine motor skills. Research indicates that keyboarding skills for children do not effectively develop until at least Grade 4. This is simply a reality.

Selecting Software for Young Children

For young children to use computers successfully, it is critical to select software that is developmentally appropriate (consistent with how children develop and learn). "Researchers agree that software for young children should

- encourage exploration, imagination, and problem solving
- reflect and build on what children already know
- involve many senses and include sound, music, and voice
- be open-ended, with the child in control of the pace and the path" (Van Scoter, Ellis, and Railsback 2001).

Open-ended software allows users to explore, discover, and make choices. It does not limit children with a set of predetermined options; rather, it encourages children to extend their imagination. For example, they can decide what to create in a picture, what ending to give a story, or in what direction to take an inquiry. Children learn by experiencing and benefit from discovering rather than being told. Appropriate open-ended software helps children reflect on what they already know and encourages creativity and engagement in learning. It is linked to improvements in measures of intelligence and nonverbal skills.

Programmed learning software, which offers drill-and-practice activities much like electronic worksheets or flashcards, often discourages creativity, imagination, and working together. These programs should not be the primary focus of computer use in the kindergarten classroom. Limiting the amount of time they are used is recommended (Van Scoter, Ellis, and Railsback 2001).

There are computer programs that support multi-sensory learning, which have prove helpful in supporting some struggling readers and writers. However, according to William Teale and Junko Yokota,

> Many of the reading and writing computer applications aimed at young children are little more than electronic worksheets. They may be effective for keeping records of the answers children get right and wrong, and they may amuse and engage children, but they teach little of what children need to become capable readers and writers. What is needed instead are computer-related activities that (1) provide authentic and meaningful literacy experiences and (2) are woven into the fabric of the curriculum, connected to thematic units and to the curriculum areas outlined above. (as cited in Strickland and Morrow 2000, 18)

In the end, there are two major points taken from the research of Elizabeth Sulzby and her colleagues about the value of computers in supporting early literacy teaching and learning:

> First, computer uses for reading and writing are only as strong as the off-computer reading and writing environment in the classroom. In other words, computer technology cannot substitute for a good early literacy program, it can only complement it. Second, computers contribute most to children's literacy development when children are able to create with them, rather than just "use" or "consume" ready-made programs (Nicholson et al. 1998). . . . In addition, we should always remember that the issue is not computer use but literacy. The computer is a tool that can help children achieve literacy, but it is not the end in itself. (Teale and Yokota as cited in Strickland and Morrow 2000, 18–19)

Effectively Supporting Young Writers

Much is known about how preschool and kindergarten teachers effectively support young writers. Emergent literacy research has shown that young

A touch-sensitive tablet or an adaptive device that takes the place of a mouse is useful for those children who have limited technology at home and/or those who have fine motor delays. For more information, visit Early Childhood Technology Integrated Instructional System (www.wiu.edu/ectiis). See also "Meaningful Technology Integration in Early Learning Environments" (in NAEYC's *Beyond the Journal: Young Children on the Web*, September 2008).

"(Y)oung children learn through exploration and play, through open-ended activities. This is true with software and technology as well as with blocks and dress-up clothes." (Van Scoter and Boss 2002, 33)

Technology is only as strong as the comprehensive literacy program in the classroom. Teachers know that technology is a tool . . . no more than that. The focus is the literacy learning, not the technology. Whichever materials, technology, and approaches are used, they simply have to work for the teacher and the children.

children learn many important concepts and develop the confidence that they can write when they are encouraged to write and when they are frequently engaged in writing. Children need to write daily and across the day. In fact, many writing experiences (often playful) are key to writing development. Young children thrive on routine. Daily writing time at centers and through writing workshop is crucial. However, writing alone is not enough. Children also need the support of mini-lessons as you model, demonstrate, explain, and bring to life the writing process.

When you think aloud as you write, you make the writing process more obvious. Through shared, modeled, interactive, guided, and independent reading and writing, children are given many opportunities to develop writing skills. Writing conferences, both in groups and one on one, also provide powerful teaching opportunities. (See Chapter 4 for information on effective instructional approaches to writing. See Chapter 5 for information on writing workshop, including the section on writing conferences beginning on page 118.)

Figure 2.22

I wonder what else I should write about Benji.

Writing must also be part of a comprehensive early childhood literacy program. Children cannot write what they cannot think or say, so there must be a strong focus first and foremost on oral language development and phonological awareness. Print awareness, alphabet letter knowledge, phonics, and word work are also important to writing.

The High-Yield Strategies of Effective Writing Programs

Learning to write is daunting to many 3-, 4-, and 5-year-olds, but there are a number of high-yield (or nonnegotiable) strategies you can use to help children develop both the skill and will to write. Perhaps the most important factor is the classroom environment.

- **Be enthusiastic about writing.** When teachers show excitement about writing and write with the children, the children will realize and respond to that energy (Polochanin 2004).

- **Write daily and often.** "We believe that if children (or adults for that matter) are to learn to write well, they need lots of experience with writing. There is no such thing as too much writing if you are trying to develop yourself as a writer. The more you do it, the easier it becomes for you to continue to do it and the more you learn about how it gets done" (Ray and Cleaveland 2004, 24). Children will write a great deal when the activities are engaging and when they see a purpose. Routines are also important. Children need to write daily not only during writing workshop but also across the day. (For more information on writing workshop, see Chapter 5.)

- **Establish developmentally appropriate goals and believe in the children.** You need to know what the developmentally appropriate writing expectations are. As with any area of the curriculum, when the children enter the classroom on the first day, there is great diversity of knowledge, skill, and interest in writing. By the end of kindergarten, however, it is realistic to expect that the children are able to move from being emergent writers to early writers. (See the descriptions of emergent and early writers on pages 27–28, The Categories of Writing on page 29, The Goals of Kindergarten Writing on page 33, and The Skills and Understandings of Kindergarten Writers on page 33. See also Trait-Based Scoring Scales: Early Beginning Writers on page 71 of Chapter 3 and Reproducible 2.1: Assessing Kindergarten Writing Checklist, on the CD.)

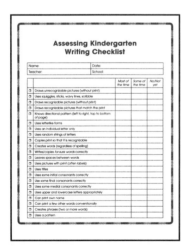

- **Use assessment to drive instruction.** Having developmentally appropriate goals and informally assessing the children's writing on a daily basis are crucial to effective instruction. It is important to look not only at what children write, but also how they write. Catch them in the act!

Assessment tools should be based on the four major goals for preschool and kindergarten writers (see page 33) and the specific writing skills and

"The single most important thing you can do to help students become writers is to provide them with time to write, materials with which to write and to demonstrate the process and the importance of writing to them." (Cunningham and Allington 1994, 89)

Teacher enthusiasm for writing goes a long way!

Young children need to write, write, write!

"Every child is entitled to excellent instruction that includes daily opportunities and teacher support to write many kinds of texts for different purposes, including stories, lists, messages to others, poems, reports and responses to literature." (IRA and NAEYC 1998, 42)

According to Mem Fox, "If you don't have clear expectations, how can children know what to aim for? If you don't have the highest expectations, how do you know if you're not underestimating what your students can do?" (Spandel 2001, 318).

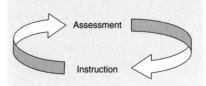

understandings expected by the end of kindergarten (see pages 33–35). (For more information on assessing writing in preschool and kindergarten, see Chapter 3.)

- **Use modeled and shared writing often.** There are numerous opportunities in every classroom for you to write as the children watch—and sometimes help—with suggestions of what to write. As children watch you write (modeled writing), they learn a great deal about writing. For example, they observe print conventions (writing starts in a certain place, goes in certain directions, has spaces between words). They also learn about topic and word choice.

Think-alouds while you write help children to understand what is going on in the writing process. Susan Neuman, Kathleen Roskos, and others have stated that the Language Experience approach, a form of shared writing, is a highly recommended strategy. As you transcribe the children's responses (shared writing), they are able to connect the abstract words to the real event, thus facilitating understanding about what writing really is: talk written down. But there is some debate over whether teachers should write down exactly what the child says even if it is grammatically incorrect or does not make sense (for example, *She eat spaghetti* rather than *She eats spaghetti*). For some of the arguments put forth in this debate, see Dictation: The Pros and Cons of Scribing on page 55.

Figure 2.23
Think aloud: "I put a question mark at the end of the sentence because I am asking you a question. Who can find the question mark?"

DICTATION: THE PROS AND CONS OF SCRIBING

Dictation (scribing what the child says) helps children to understand the purposes of writing and the speech–text connection (*What I think about, I can say, and what I can say, I can write*). Through dictation, children are also supported in learning phonics, the conventions of print, capitalization, and punctuation. But should you write down exactly what the child says during dictation? Some experts such as Lesley Mandel Morrow (2005) feel that what the child says should be scribed verbatim, meaning the dialect and vocabulary should be preserved exactly as spoken. This honors what the child has said and aids emergent readers when they attempt to read back what has been written. Others feel that rereading grammatically incorrect text does not support young readers and writers, especially if it is being displayed in the classroom for reading around the room. Ultimately, what is perhaps most important is that the children feel their responses, their ideas, are valued whether or not they are written down exactly as stated.

On the other hand, dictation provides limited value for teaching children to read and write. Few children are able to read back what they dictate because their oral language is generally at a much higher level than their reading and writing ability. A highly verbal child who is able to dictate very complex sentences may become frustrated when she or he is unable to read back the scribed sentences. This is problematic as many children learn to read, at least in part, by reading and rereading what they have written.

Scribing, therefore, must not be used to the exclusion of the child actually writing or minimize the child's writing in any way. Because many children are already writing when they arrive at school, they should be encouraged to be actively engaged in many forms of writing from the very first day. Modeled and shared writing as well as Language Experience (a form of shared writing) are all important forms of writing. However, independent writing is also crucial. Children need to write a great deal.

Try planned dictation while creating a message with the children based on a common experience. Write what each child has to say and place his or her name after the thought. Children love to go back and read their line and the lines of others.

"Pretend play is a valuable part of early literacy development. . . . In fact the amount of time children engage in pretend play is correlated to their performance on language and literacy assessments." (Van Scoter and Boss 2002, 6)

Kindergarten teachers can facilitate language and literacy development through play-based literacy instruction (Snow, Burns, and Griffin 1998).

Figure 2.24

- **Support play daily to develop writers.** Literacy learning and play support each other. Writing often emerges naturally as children play. Dramatic play at various classroom centers may lead children to write grocery lists, menus, receipts, and even a chart listing a patient's medications at the Hospital Center. However, children do not automatically choose to write. They often need to be nudged. One of the ways that you can nudge a young writer is to make sure appropriate resources are readily available, such as a notepad and pencil next to the telephone at the Restaurant/Pizza Parlor Center.

Other ways to link writing and play include having conversations with the children about their play before they begin and having them create play plans (see Chapter 8, page 205). Writing after centers encourages children to reflect on their play and to record or report their thoughts (see Writing after Centers: Reporting on page 211 of Chapter 8).

Figure 2.25

This teacher included a list of all of the children's names glued on the inside front cover of the appointment book in the Doctor's Office Center. What a great idea!

- **Conduct mini-lessons.** Daily mini-lessons must occur based on children's needs. The Gradual Release of Responsibility Model provides the best support. Modeled writing (*I do it*), shared writing (*We do it*) while you think aloud, guided writing (*We do it* in a small group), and then independent writing (You do it) are the most important approaches to scaffold the craft of writing. Mini-lessons are short and focused. They can occur anytime during the day, but most occur during writing workshop. (For more information on writing workshop, see Chapter 5. Additional mini-lessons to support fiction and nonfiction writing are provided in Chapter 6. Mini-lessons to support writing poetry and songs are included in Chapter 7.) As you assess children's writing, determine appropriate mini-lessons (see Chapter 3: Assessing Writing in Preschool and Kindergarten).

- **Create a rich oral language program.** An oral language program that includes mini-lessons to teach vocabulary and builds on the children's own background knowledge is the foundation of effective writing instruction in kindergarten. Richard Allington's research (2006) indicates that classrooms are too often interrogational rather than conversational. In other words, teachers ask children many questions but infrequently involve them in actual conversations. Time must be spent encouraging children to incubate their ideas through drawing, role-playing, and talking before writing.

Gradual Release of Responsibility

I do it.
We do it.
We do it
(small group).
You do it.

Check It Out!

Try these read-alouds to support list making:

Don't Forget the Bacon by Pat Hutchins (New York: HarperCollins, 1989).

Frog and Toad Together by Arnold Lobel (New York: HarperCollins, 1979).

Scaredy Squirrel by Mélanie Watt (Toronto, ON: Kids Can Press, Ltd., 2008).

Wallace's Lists by Barbara Bottner and Gerald Kruglik (New York: HarperCollins, 2004).

Figure 2.26
Incubating ideas through sharing each other's work.

- **Use read-alouds and shared reading daily.** Read-alouds and shared reading can and should support writing. The effectiveness of their use, however, depends on what texts are chosen and how you connect the reading to the writing. Reading to and with children stimulates their language and concept development. It also builds their familiarity with and understanding of printed texts.

There is a close relationship between the kinds of texts children experience in read-alouds and shared reading and what they choose to write and are able to write (Duke and Bennett-Armistead 2003). For example, lists are one of the easiest and most authentic forms of writing and there are great read-alouds to support list making. (see List Making in Chapter 6, page 162 [see also Reproducible 2.4: Writing Lists, on the CD]).

 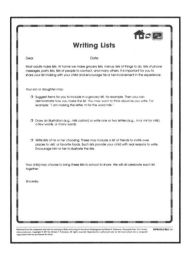

Ralph Fletcher and JoAnn Portalupi (1998) among others have stated that literature may be the most important influence of all for writing development. However, they also explain that simply enjoying good literature will not enable most children to become effective writers. It is through mini-lessons (craft lessons), reading and rereading, talk, and writing that children learn what effective authors do when they compose.

Figure 2.27
Both The *Name Jar* by Choi and *Chrysanthemum* by Henkes promote critical literacy prompting deep thinking and discussion about social issues.

Using mentor texts and mini-lessons help kindergarteners to understand
- that there are different genres of writing
- what the characteristics of these genres are
- when and how to use these genres

It is advisable to read aloud a number of texts by the same author so that the children become familiar with the author's style. Frequently, young writers will try to replicate the style in their own writing. Try to pick mentor texts where the author is also the illustrator, such as books by Patricia Polacco and Kevin Henkes. The children connect well to these types of texts because when they write they are also both author and illustrator.

Figure 2.28

Both *The Name Jar* by Choi and *Chrysanthemum* by Henkes encourage the children to make text-text connections.

Very often the urge to write comes from a story shared with a group of children, chosen by the teacher or read by a child who has authored a text (Clay 1991).

Mentor texts may also be written by young children themselves. Do not underestimate the importance of peers sharing their writing, especially books they have written. By celebrating the writing of their classmates on a daily basis, children are encouraged to believe that they too can achieve success in their writing.

- **Celebrate children's writing.** Daily writing, celebrations, and sharing of individual children's writing and feedback are crucial. Publish children's writing. (See Chapter 5 for many different ways to celebrate writing.)

Figure 2.29

- **Establish a purpose and audience for writing and encourage topic choice.** Children are more successful and motivated when they see a purpose for writing and are given a choice of what to write. Your task is to recognize opportunities for authentic writing and to help the children take advantage of these opportunities. Functional experiences serve a real purpose for writing (for example, making a list, writing a note, writing a letter that requires a reply, and so on). Encourage the children to ask themselves, "What is my purpose?" and "Who is my audience?" (i.e., "Who am I writing this to?"). (See Writing Nonfiction beginning on page 149 of Chapter 6 and Writing Messages beginning on page 213 of Chapter 9.)

Purpose + Audience = Form (Ontario Education 2005, 1.20).

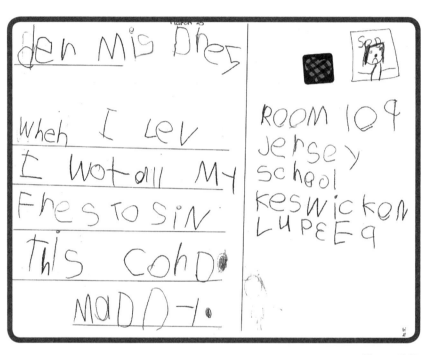

Figure 2.30

Maddy was sad about having to move away. She wrote her teacher this note: *When I leave I want all of my friends to sign this card. Maddy.* What a powerful reason to write!!

- **Use everyday activities to motivate.** Everyday activities in the child's life are another source of inspiration and stories, (including nursery rhymes and poems) that are dramatized, sometimes make children eager to write (Clay 1991). The power of an experience, a concrete object, a discussion, a picture, or a drawing that is used as a lead-in to writing should not be underestimated (Strickland and Morrow 2000). Encourage children to label their drawings. Once children are comfortable constructing spelling for individual words, they typically will begin to apply their newfound knowledge to (longer) written texts (Neuman and Roskos 1998).

Children who realize the functional relevance of written language are more likely to be motivated to explore its use for their own purposes. Alan Farstrup and S. Jay Samuels (2002) discuss such purposes as writing notes and letters, and making and using lists.

Figure 2.31
Acting out *Little Miss Muffet* . . . before writing.

- **Include a lot of nonfiction writing opportunities.** "Contrary to the popular assumption that young children's first writing is narrative, educators have found that kindergarteners and first graders write many non-narrative compositions in which they provide information about familiar topics, such as 'Signs of Fall,' or write directions for familiar activities, such as 'How to Feed Your Pet'" (Tompkins 2000, 251). There is ample evidence that children are quite comfortable with expository or informational writing even before they enter kindergarten (Neuman and Roskos 1998). Nonfiction writing is the most functional and commonly used form of writing. Projects engage children in using reading and writing for multiple purposes while they are learning about topics meaningful to them (IRA and NAEYC 1998). See the Project Approach page 180.

Figure 2.32

- **Encourage invented spelling.** Invented spelling, a form of kid writing, is an important step for emerging and early writers. (See Spelling pages 35–43 and 75–78.)
- **Create a literacy-rich classroom.** A literacy-rich physical environment is also important. For example, highly visible print labels on objects, signs, and bulletin boards in classrooms demonstrate the practical uses of written language (IRA and NAEYC 1998). Charts can be used to record classroom helpers. Other charts may show a picture of each child labeled with his or her name. Children may also be encouraged to sign their names on a chart (or an interactive whiteboard) under the headings *yes* or *no* to indicate their response to a written question. For example, "Do you think a bear sleeps all winter?"

Figure 2.33

Songs, poems, and word walls are also important. Environmental print must be used or it will go unnoticed (see Using Environmental Print on page 157 of Chapter 6).

Children are encouraged to read it, copy it, and to use the word labels in their writing (Neuman and Roskos 1998). The ideal is to have many, many Little Books, Big Books, newspapers, and magazines for the children to examine alone and with a partner. Give them time to just "read." Also include and highlight the children's published books in your classroom collection. Ensure each child is given a classroom book bag or book box in which to store familiar text that he or she can "read" and enjoy over and over again.

Studies suggest that temporary invented spelling may contribute to beginning reading. Every child is entitled to writing experiences that allow the flexibility to use non-conventional forms of writing at first (invented or phonic spelling) and then, over time, to move to conventional forms (IRA and NAEYC 1998).

One day an administrator suggested to me that there was little need for many books in kindergarten classrooms since after all, he said, "These kids can't read yet." How little this individual knew about children and literacy development!

The following reproducibles referenced in Chapter 2 are available on the *Learning to Write and Loving It!* CD:

Reproducible 2.1: Assessing Writing Checklist

Reproducible 2.2: High-Frequency or Pop-Up Words (End of Grade 1)

Reproducible 2.3: Kindergarten or *Kid* Writing: Kid Writing

Reproducible 2.4: Writing Lists

Reproducible 2.5: Picture Books in Many Languages

Reproducible 2.6: Spelling in Preschool and Kindergarten

Figure 2.34

Books especially appeal to young children when they are displayed on "rain gutters" (Jim Trelease, "The Rain Gutter Literacy Revolution," http://www.trelease-on-reading.com).

- **Promote the home–school connection.** Writing development is also dependent on the children's background knowledge and understanding, as well as on the support they receive at home. Parents/caregivers need to understand how writing at home can occur in authentic situations (for example, a grocery list, a note to grandma), can take very little time, and can be fun. Parents/caregivers are often asked to read with their children, but they are rarely asked to write with them. Both writing (for real purposes) and talk (conversation) should be regular "homework." Literacy-on-the-run writing activities such as helping to write an item on the grocery list or labeling something in the home takes just a minute or two to complete. Such writing will not occur, however, unless the parent/caregiver seizes the moment and encourages the child to write.

A number of reproducible letters to facilitate this home–school connection and support children's writing are included on the *Learning to Write and Loving It!* CD. The letters are jargon-free and content-rich, and include many easy-to-implement activities. The kinds of activities that are included are typical of those literacy-on-the-run activities Dr. Durkin found parents/caregivers did to help early readers learn to read and write before coming to kindergarten.

Chapter 3

Assessing Writing in Preschool and Kindergarten

Assessment (assessment *of* learning) is often used to show what the child has learned or can do. However, the purpose of assessment should also be used to help drive instruction (assessment *for* learning). Before assessing, you must know what is developmentally appropriate to expect. The assessment tools featured in this chapter are based on the four major goals for kindergarten writing and the specific writing skills and understandings expected by the end of kindergarten (see Chapter 2, page 33).

Assessment results will help you determine how much time should be spent on each instructional approach and which mini-lessons should be highlighted during writing workshop (see Chapter 5). A great deal can be learned by assessing children's skill level and degree of involvement during shared, interactive, guided, and independent writing (see Chapter 4, page 81, for an explanation of these instructional approaches), through writing conferences, and by examining writing samples. These are authentic forms of assessment. The children should also be self-assessing their writing (see Self-Assessment: Me as a Writer on page 79, as well as Reproducible 3.8: Look at Me. I Am a Writer! Self-Assessment; Reproducible 3.4: I Can Write and Draw; Reproducible 3.3: How Did I Write Today? A One-on-One Conference; Reproducible 3.5: *I Like* . . .: Interest Inventory; and Reproducible 3.6: Things That Interest Me: Interest Survey, on the CD. Parents/caregivers and administrators also become part of the process through classroom visits, conferences, portfolios, and other forms of documentation.

Assessing Writing Through Shared, Interactive, Guided, and Independent Writing

Begin by monitoring each child's level of participation in shared, interactive, guided, and independent writing.

- Does the child readily participate? How does the child participate?
- Are ideas volunteered to be scribed by you?
- What is the level of oral language/vocabulary used (in other words, what is the child's facility with oral language and how familiar is he or she with topic-specific vocabulary)?
- Is the child willing to take risks by sharing the pen in front of the class? (For an explanation of *sharing the pen*, see Chapter 4, page 84.)
- What does the child's interactive writing level reveal about alphabet letter knowledge, phonics, phonological awareness, and fine motor development?
- During independent writing time, how long does it take the child to get started?

WINDOW ON THE CLASSROOM

A Grade 1 teacher asked the children to take out their journals and pencils and to write. After 5 minutes, one little boy had not complied. The teacher asked, "Where is your journal?" He responded, "In my desk." She then asked, "Where is your pencil?" He responded, "In my pencil box." The teacher queried, "What is it doing there?" The child replied, "It's snoozing!"

- Does the child easily come up with writing topics?
- How long does the child persevere with writing?

Unfortunately, there is limited time in most preschool and kindergarten classrooms to work one on one with each child. But through shared, interactive, guided, and independent writing, done with the whole class or with a small group, a great deal of diagnostic information can be learned about the whole child and his or her literacy skills. This is authentic assessment done on the run!

Assessing Writing Through Writing Conferences

Writing conferences allow you to assess children's interests and writing ability and to scaffold learning. They also allow the children to self-assess and then edit or revise their writing (see Reproducible 3.8: Look at Me. I Am a Writer! Self-Assessment; Reproducible 3.3: How Did I Write Today?

A One-on-One Conference; Reproducible 3.5: *I Like . . .*: Interest Inventory; and Reproducible 3.6: Things that Interest Me: Interest Survey, on the CD).

For more information on assessing writing through writing conferences, see page 118 of Chapter 5.

Assessing Writing Through Writing Samples

The most authentic and revealing assessment tool or documentation tool is simply a writing sample. By assessing writing samples, you can determine what to teach to scaffold reading, writing, and oral language. Look for

- the child's ability to communicate a message through written text with or without illustrations (ideas)
- illustrations that support the print (ideas). Look for what details appear in the illustrations and how many there are.
- organization that makes sense (organization)
- invented spelling, which reveals much about the child's phonological/phonemic awareness and alphabet and phonics knowledge (conventions)
- an understanding of print concepts; for example, where on the page does the writing start? In what direction does the writing go? (conventions)
- the child's ability to write his or her name, the names of others, high-frequency words, and word-family words (conventions)
- the child's skill and will to copy or otherwise make use of environmental print (ideas and conventions)
- the ability to draw pictures and form letters, which help to indicate the level of fine motor coordination (conventions)
- word choice and sentence structure, which reveal oral language development (word choice)
- the child's voice coming through in the message (voice)

For more information on ideas, organization, conventions, word choice, and voice, see The Traits Defined in Preschool and Kindergarten on page 71.

It is also *very* important to assess how much the child writes and what she or he chooses to write. Samples should be dated and kept in a portfolio to track the writing forms and genres the child has undertaken and to monitor progress over time. Reproducible 2.1: Assessing Kindergarten Writing Checklist is another excellent tool for monitoring each child's writing skills and understandings, and will also provide a profile of writing development over time. (For more information on portfolios, see page 68.)

Some teachers put a small *i* at the bottom of the child's page of writing to indicate that the child wrote the text independently. A small *wh* indicates that the child wrote the text with help from an adult or peer.

Marie Clay among others recommends comparing writing samples on a daily basis to assess not only what the children are learning but also the effectiveness of the writing instruction. Dated writing samples help to guide instruction, revealing areas where more support is needed. They also verify each child's literacy progress (Schulze 2006).

Using Portfolios

Portfolios establish a documentation process for collecting, selecting, reflecting on, storing, and sharing work samples. They help you to monitor each child's literacy development over time and to link assessment to instruction. They also help you to engage parents/caregivers in their child's progress, and especially help the children themselves to set goals, make choices, reflect on their work, and celebrate literacy learning. Finally, portfolios provide an excellent way to demonstrate to families, administrators, and others how play and literacy learning support each other. (see Reproducible 3.1: Your Child's Portfolio; Reproducible 3.2: Preschool and Kindergarten Portfolios: Parent Response; and Reproducible 3.7: My Portfolio—Self Reflection: Portfolios, on the CD).

Create a portfolio for each child at the beginning of the year. You might use file folders, large envelopes, magazine holders, or boxes. Encourage the children to personalize the outside of their portfolios.

Figure 3.1

Pizza boxes make great portfolios.

Items that might be filed in the children's portfolios include

- writing samples
- reading logs
- reading responses (for example, journals)
- writer's notebook (see Writer's Notebook in Chapter 5, page 106)
- artwork (for example, drawings, collages)

- taped passages (for example, a recording of the child talking to you about his or her writing, sharing his or her writing with the class, reading his or her writing aloud, and so on)
- computer printouts
- shared writing such as songs, poems, and chart stories
- scribed/interactive writing
- DVDs

You, the child, and occasionally the parent/caregiver can choose items to file in the child's portfolio. Items are selected that the child likes, feels proud of, and can explain why, or does not like and can explain why.

At each reporting period, you and the children revisit the contents of the portfolios and select eight favorite and two nonfavorite items to keep in the portfolio. The children can then share one of their items with a partner, a small group, or the whole class and can explain why they chose it.

Portfolios might also be used during parent–teacher conferences during which the child takes a leadership role. Encourage the child to
- share and discuss some of the items in his or her portfolio
- reflect on the items
- have a parent/caregiver select an item to keep in the portfolio

At the end of the year, celebrate each child's literacy learning by comparing a spring item with a fall item. Sharing a few portfolio samples with the child's anticipated kindergarten or Grade 1 teacher also proves helpful.

Documentation as a Form of Record Keeping

Documentation, a term to describe a form of record keeping, has become well known in early childhood classrooms. "Documentation typically includes samples of a child's work at several different stages of completion; photographs showing work in progress; comments written by the teacher or other adults working with the children; transcriptions of children's discussions, comments, and explanations of intentions about the activity; and comments made by parents" (Katz and Chard 1996, 2).

The Reggio Emilia approach to learning and the project approach bring documentation to life. Frequently, teachers use documentation when using

Documentation helps to make learning visible and helps to drive future learning.

the project approach. Documentation really allows for communication with the children, parents/caregivers, administrators, and others about how and what the children are learning. It allows the children to relive the experience as they "reread" the documentation, frequently posted on the walls. It also often leads to other learning.

Documentation can appear in many forms, such as portfolios, class books, slide shows, and movies, but most often is seen on presentation. However, it is important to note that documentation should tell the whole story of *one* topic studied or *one* project or event.

Determining Each Child's Writing Category

At the beginning of the year, determine which category the child's writing typically reveals (see The Categories of Kindergarten Writing on page 29 of Chapter 2). This is a simple way to provide both you and parents/caregivers with an idea of where the child is on the developmental continuum. It is not uncommon for children to be at the scribbling level at the beginning of the year. Keep dated writing samples that demonstrate growth over time. It is important to share with parents/caregivers that their children may not neatly fit into one category but may be moving from one category to another depending on what they are writing and how much support they are given. However, there should be definite growth as the year progresses; for example, a child should not still be at the scribbling stage in January. It is very important that spelling approximations also improve as the year progresses.

Beyond the broad categories, it is also important to note the specifics. Can the child write her or his name, use a pattern to create similar text, and write a sentence or even several sentences on a topic? Does the child write for different purposes, such as to make lists, labels, notes, or books? (See Reproducible 2.1: Assessing Kindergarten Writing Checklist, on the CD.)

Another way to look at a child's writing is through using trait-based scoring scales. The six traits are the six qualities or characteristics that define good writing. Many teachers across all levels, kindergarten to high school, have embraced the traits as a way to both assess and teach writing. The traits provide a common language for teachers, the children, and parents/caregivers, and a consistent approach to assess and teach writing from classroom to classroom and grade to grade. They provide diagnostic information for writing just as a running record does for reading. For example, a child might be strong in ideas but weak in conventions or vice versa.

THE TRAITS DEFINED IN PRESCHOOL AND KINDERGARTEN

Ideas: A clear message; the content of the piece; the main theme or idea, together with the details that develop that theme. One can see (picture), hear, smell, touch, or taste what is being described. Through rich details, both written and/or drawn, the reader can easily deduce the general idea.

Organization: The structure of the piece; the logical ordering of the piece. Text and pictures support one another. Sentences relate to each other and to a common theme.

Voice: The heart and soul of the individual writer. Voice is what captures the reader. It makes the reader "feel." Voice is supported by both words and drawings.

Word Choice: Million-dollar or yummy words move the reader. The words and drawings paint the picture.

Sentence Fluency: Letters and words form readable phrases and sentences. The piece is easy to read aloud.

Conventions/Presentation: Concepts of print, spelling (invented spelling and *for-sure words*), *capitals, and punctuation; readable text; pleasing presentation*

Trait-Based Scoring Scales: Early Beginning Writers (Often Preschool to Early Grade 1)

Use trait-based scoring scales with writers who write, whether scribbles, picture writing, labeled pictures, letter and number shapes, letter strings, or single "sentence(s)."

	Exploring	*Developing*	*Accomplished*
Ideas	• Marks on paper • Meaning "lives" with writer as he or she writes	• Letter/number shapes • Pictures • "Take a guess" • Reader creates meaning through inference/guessing • Minimal detail	• Recognizable letters/ numbers • Recognizable pictures • Reader can easily infer general idea • Pictures often carry more meaning than text • Detail in picture: face, fingers, toes, movement, etc. • Writer can "read" text back and elaborate
Organization	• Random use of space	• Pattern-centered, left-to-right, etc. • Beginning of ordering of text and pictures	• Balanced look • Definite left-to-right "writing" or pictures thoughtfully centered or placed • Events in order • Coordination of text and pictures • May write "the end"
Voice	• Bold lines • Use of color • Voice expressed through dictation	• Pictures show mood/feeling • Exclamation points or periods • BIG LETTERS • Multicolor pictures	• Recognizable as "this child's piece" • Unique flavor, style • Expressive pictures • Expression of feeling in text

Word Choice	• Scribbles • No real letter/number shapes yet	• Recognizable letter/number shapes • Borrowing from environmental print • Labels • Letter strings—may be difficult to read even with writer's help	• Easy-to-read letter/number shapes • Some recognizable letter-string words • Variety of words
Sentence Fluency	• No letter/word strings yet • Dictates sentences to go with writing	• Letter strings suggest beginning sentences: ilpdg. • Not translatable without help • Dictates multiple sentences	• Letter strings form readable sentences: I 1k t p 1w m d (*I like to play with my dog*) • Dictates a whole story, personal recount, or informational piece
Conventions	• No recognizable conventions yet • Can point to conventions in environment	• Places punctuation randomly in text • Scribbles imitate look and shape of text • Writes readable name on paper, which may or may not be spelled correctly • Writes one or two readable words (often using invented spelling)	• Improving use of conventions of print • Includes a title • Writes name on work and spells it correctly • Writes several or many readable words • Use of *I* (capitalized) • Periods placed correctly • Other closing punctuation attempted

Source: Adapted from Vicki Spandel, *Creating Writers through 6-Trait Writing Assessment and Instruction*, 3rd ed. (New York: Addison-Wesley Longman Inc., 2001), 353–54.

Using the six traits even in kindergarten makes good sense. Through many read-alouds and mini-lessons, children come to develop a beginning understanding of the traits. It is not uncommon to hear very young children comment on "great word choice," "yummy words," or "million-dollar words." They also come to understand the concept of ideas and how important details are. This is easily demonstrated in their illustrations. Their writing—text and especially illustrations—often exhibit voice!

Ideas: This early writer captures four complete thoughts. The meaning is recognizable. It provides important details (color, name).

Organization: The child has written four sentences across the page. It wraps around several lines. The child has obviously written left to right and started at the top of the page. The ideas follow logically ending with *I am so excited!*

Voice: There is voice in the piece. The child is writing about something important to her. You can sense the excitement.

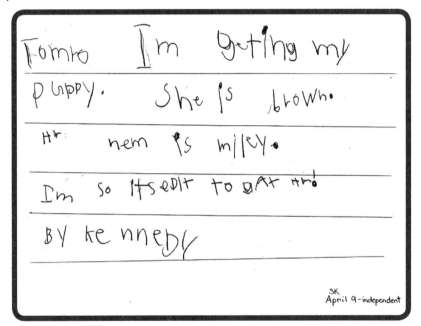

Figure 3.2

Tomorrow I'm getting my puppy. She is brown.
Her name is Milly. I'm so excited to get her.

This kindergarten writer falls into the Accomplished category.
This writing occurred in May. It is something to celebrate!

Word Choice: The child uses recognizable words correctly. They are Tier One words—basic words that are commonly used by most kindergarten children. The words are put together to form four sentences that make sense.

Sentence Fluency: There are four simple sentences. There is some variation in sentence beginnings making the writing flow.

Conventions: The child is using standard letters to write. There is word spacing. There is an appropriate mix of upper- and lower-case letters. There is accurate final punctuation. The spelling is strong. Invented spelling indicates strong sound–symbol correspondence as in the word *itsedit* (excited).

Determining Each Child's Spelling Stage

Begin by determining which stage of spelling the child's writing reveals, and then determine the strategies and approaches that will best scaffold the learning. Richard Gentry (1993) created a very easy to use developmental spelling test—also known as the Monster Test—to determine each child's spelling stage (see below). The test is designed for 5-, 6-, or 7-year-olds and helps to reveal the spelling strategies that the children are already using. Gentry also provided many examples of activities to support each spelling stage. You might, for example, see *TR* to represent the word *tower* and know that this is an example of semiphonetic spelling, whereas *TOWR* is an example of phonetic spelling. However, writing samples from the same child may at any point in time vary greatly.

The advantages of using the Developmental Spelling Test are that it is controlled, quick to administer (it consists of only ten words), easy to analyze, and generally provides the same results as painstaking analysis of numerous invented spellings taken from a child's writing (Gentry 1993). Gentry believes that by the end of kindergarten most children should at least be at the semiphonetic stage, but many will be at the phonetic stage or beyond. It is advisable to give the test to the whole class at least three times throughout the year. Spelling approximations should improve and more high-frequency words (*for-sure words*) should be written correctly as the year progresses.

The Developmental Spelling Test: Step by Step

1. Explain to the children that you are going to ask them to write some words. You may want to have them write in a numbered list to ensure you can match their written words to the words dictated. Although the words may be daunting to kindergarten children, encourage them to make an attempt, to "give it a go." Explain that you know the words are big words for kindergarteners, but you think that they can write some of each word anyway. Say, "Show me how you can write these words in kid writing." Make it gamelike. You may want to try one or two practice items together as an interactive writing (see Chapter 4, page 84). Celebrate approximations; for example, *music* may be spelled *mk* or *muzc* and played may be spelled *p*, *pd*, or *pad*.

2. Dictate each word. Provide a sentence incorporating the word. Repeat the word.

Words	Sample Sentences*
monster	There is a picture of a *monster* in my book.
united	The children *united* to cheer for their team.
dress	The girl wore a new *dress*.
bottom	A big fish lives at the *bottom* of the lake.
hiked	She *hiked* to the top of the mountain.
human	A dog is not a *human*.
eagle	An *eagle* is a powerful bird.
closed	The little boy *closed* the door.
bumped	She *bumped* her knee on the desk.
type	What *type* of fruit do you like?

Note: Use sentences that you feel are most appropriate for the children in your classroom.

"Children's misspellings are what provide snapshots of their minds to reveal their developmental level." (Gentry 1993, 44)

3. Analyze the completed tests to determine each child's spelling stage using the chart and examples that follow to help you. Also refer to The Five Stages of Spelling Development on page 41 of Chapter 2. The stage where most of the child's spellings fall is the child's probable developmental level. This will be the level at which the child will likely write when writing independently.

Words		Precommunicative	Semiphonetic	Phonetic	Transitional	Conventional
1.	*monster*	Random letters	MTR	MOSTR	MONSTUR	monster
2.	*united*	Random letters	U	UNITD	YOUNIGHTED	united
3.	*dress*	Random letters	JRS	JRAS	DRES	dress
4.	*bottom*	Random letters	BT	BODM	BOTTUM	bottom
5.	*hiked*	Random letters	H	HIKT	HICKED	hiked
6.	*human*	Random letters	UM	HUMN	HUMUN	human
7.	*eagle*	Random letters	EL	EGL	EGUL	eagle
8.	*closed*	Random letters	KD	KLOSD	CLOSSED	closed
9.	*bumped*	Random letters	B	BOPT	BUMPPED	bumped
10.	*type*	Random letters	TP	TIP	TIPE	type

Experienced teachers know that many young children who are at lower developmental levels often memorize how to spell simple words like *cat*. This is good. However, by having them attempt more difficult words, you gain an understanding of children's spelling skills. The same is true in reading. Taking running records of children reading texts that provide some challenge gives you diagnostic information about their reading skills and what to teach next.

4. Once you have determined the spelling stage, identify which teaching strategies would be most effective (see Strategies and Activities that follow).

Source: Adapted from Richard Gentry and Jean Wallace Gillet, *Teaching Kids to Spell* (Portsmouth, NH: Heinemann, 1993), 41–48.

COMMON STAGES OF SPELLING DEVELOPMENT IN PRESCHOOL AND KINDERGARTEN

The key to developing proficient spellers is to ensure children write often every day about things that are real and important to them. Emphasis should be placed on the message, not on the correctness of the language or the spelling (Gentry and Gillet 1993).

Stage 1: Precommunicative

Only the child may be able to read his or her writing. The child uses scribbles, numbers, mock letters, and real letters to write words, but the letters are strung together randomly. The same letter is often repeated over and over. The letters do not correspond to the sounds.

Strategies and Activities to Support Precommunicative Spellers

Children at this stage need many engaging activities that develop letter–sound correspondence and phonological awareness, specifically identifying the concept of a word, beginning sounds and phonemic segmentation (for example, segmenting the word *cat into c-a-t and c-at*), and clapping syllables.

Stage 2: Semiphonetic

Sometimes the writing is readable by the child and/or the teacher. The writing shows some letters representing sounds in words. Spellings are often abbreviated and reflect initial and/or final sounds (for example *NS* for *nice*). These spellers may also use the literal name of a letter to represent a word (for example, *u* for *you* or *r* for *are*).

Strategies and Activities to Support Semiphonetic Spellers

Children at this stage need many engaging activities to develop more letter–sound correspondence, phonological awareness, word families, and rhyming words.

Kid Pix and KidDesk are two graphics and writing software programs that work well at the semiphonetic stage.

Once children are using phonetic spellings, "talking word processors" such as ClarisWorks for Kids allow the children to hear the words they have written.

Individual alphabet strips may prove useful.

Stage 3: Phonetic

Frequently, the writing is readable by the child, the teacher, and some of the child's peers. All the phonemes in a word are represented, although not necessarily conventionally (for example, *LAN* for *lane* and *STOPT* for *stopped*).

Strategies and Activities to Support Phonetic Spellers

Children at this stage need many engaging activities that extend letter–sound correspondence, word families, making words, rhyming words, word-wall activities, and activities to develop visual memory.

Alternative Word-Writing Assessment: Step by Step

Another word-writing assessment involves giving children 10 minutes to write all of the words they know.

1. Begin by modeling the activity. Think aloud as you write your own name, the name of a family member, and the name of a friend. Also remind the children, "If you can write *at,* you can write *cat, mat, sat,* and so on."

2. Prompt the children to write their own names, names of family members, color words, and words such as *yes* and *no.*

3. Score the text using one of the following methods:
   - Calculate how many words were written, including those with invented spelling. The invented spelling might be analyzed for the writing strategies the child used to spell the words (for example, initial consonant sound, word family, spelling patterns, high-frequency word, and so on).
   - Simply identify how many real words the child can write in a 10-minute time frame, whether or not the child has copied them or can read them. The results can then be compared with subsequent tests. Look for improvements in the quality (letter–sound correspondence or at least better approximations in invented spelling, inclusion of *for-sure words*, and the quantity of words written).

Source: Adapted from Robinson (as cited in Schulze 2006 and Clay 1993a).

Writing samples and word tests are not enough, however. Additional assessments that reveal a great deal about writing include assessments of oral language and reading.

Self-Assessment: Me as a Writer

Self-assessment is important in kindergarten. Having the children assess their own literacy learning reveals their perceptions of their writing skill level as well as their attitudes toward writing (see Reproducible 3.4: I Can Write and Draw and Reproducible 3.3: How Did I Write Today? A One-on-One Conference, on the CD). For most young children, this self-assessment would have to be done with the support of an adult or an older buddy. Additionally, children should be prompted during writing conferences to self-assess their interests as well as their beliefs about and attitudes toward themselves as writers. (See Reproducible 3.5: *I Like . . .:* Interest Inventory and Reproducible 3.6: Things That Interest Me: Interest Survey, on the CD.)

For more information on self-assessment during writing conferences, see Writing Conference, Step by Step, on page 120 of Chapter 5.

The following reproducibles referenced in Chapter 3 are available on the *Learning to Write and Loving It!* CD:

Reproducible 2.1: Assessing Kindergarten Writing Checklist

Reproducible 3.1: Your Child's Portfolio

Reproducible 3.2: Preschool and Kindergarten Portfolios: Parent Response

Reproducible 3.3: How Did I Write Today? A One-on-One Conference

Reproducible 3.4: I Can Write and Draw.

Reproducible 3.5: *I Like . . .:* Interest Inventory

Reproducible 3.6: Things That Interest Me: Interest Survey

Reproducible 3.7: My Portfolio—Self-Reflection: Portfolios

Reproducible 3.8: Look at Me. I Am a Writer! Self-Assessment

Chapter 4

Effective Instructional Approaches

Modeled and shared writing, interactive writing, guided writing, and independent writing are key instructional approaches used to scaffold learning. These approaches allow for a range of assistance from extensive support (modeled and shared writing) to limited support (independent writing). Although it is difficult for teachers to "get it all in," especially in a half-day program, integration definitely does help. Hand in hand with all of the writing approaches go all of the approaches to reading, word work, and phonics. For example, a good story or nonfiction read-aloud helps children to understand different purposes for writing, the different writing genres (see Chapter 6), and the traits of writing (see The Traits Defined in Preschool and Kindergarten on page 71 of Chapter 3). Oral language activities that incorporate lots of rhyme, rhythm, and song while supporting the development of phonological and phonemic awareness also support writing development. Many writing experiences occur in joyful, playful situations at centers.

Modeled and Shared Writing (Writing *for* and *With* Children)

Figure 4.1

Writing instructional approaches support the Gradual Release of Responsibility Model of teaching.

Modeled Writing

(I do it.)

Shared, Interactive, and Guided Writing

(We do it.)

Independent Writing

(You do it.)

I think...

Thinking aloud is a very important part of modeled and shared writing. It helps the children to understand what really goes on when one writes. However, there is a danger that if an inordinate number of think-alouds occur, the children may lose interest and become less engaged in the activity. They may also lose the gist of what is being composed.

Modeled writing is an activity during which you model and think aloud (write aloud) while composing in front of the children. By thinking aloud, you are making the writing process obvious. Model how to pick a topic to write about or where to begin writing on the page. As you write, talk about what you are doing and why you are doing it. This is an important key to kindergarten writing success. Modeled writing is frequently but not always a part of shared writing.

Shared writing is a cooperative activity whereby you and either the whole class or a small group of children compose together. This interactive approach to the writing process allows the children to discuss and jointly decide on topics, compose the text, and then revise and edit the written piece together as appropriate. During shared writing, you assume the role of scribe, modeling the writing process and pointing out conventions of print while writing.

Purposes of Modeled and Shared Writing

Modeled and shared writing in the preschool and kindergarten classroom allows you to

- make the writing process obvious
- show the children that writing is print written down and that it conveys ideas, facts, feelings, or opinions
- motivate the children to write together and independently
- increase awareness of the conventions of writing (for example, phonics, punctuation, use of capitals, spacing)
- support alphabet letter knowledge, phonics, and phonological awareness
- support vocabulary and oral language development
- discuss the purposes and types of writing styles
- encourage the children to participate in and enjoy writing experiences
- provide the classroom with shared writing products, such as class-generated chart stories and Big Books, which can be reread by the children
- provide children with the opportunity to manipulate the shared writing text by contributing to the writing process
- assess both writing skill and will
- assess oral language and vocabulary

Modeled and Shared Writing: Step by Step

For both modeled and shared writing you need to first decide on the purpose or focus of the writing experience (for example, to demonstrate a particular form or convention of writing). Next, gather the children together as in shared reading so that all of them can see you and the text that is being written. In modeled writing, the children observe and listen as you think aloud the writing process. The steps that follow outline the process of shared writing in which the children are active participants.

1. Involve the children in prewriting activities, such as selecting a topic and generating ideas.

2. Act as a scribe to record the children's thoughts.

3. Guide the composing process by questioning the children and encouraging them to clarify and elaborate on what is being written.

4. Revise and edit the written piece together as necessary and as appropriate to the children's writing development. As you revise and edit, continually go back and reread with the children.

5. Provide the children with a copy of the final shared writing text, to be kept at home as a shared reading book (see Reproducible 4.1: Reading Our Writing, on the CD).

6. Consider publishing the final text in a variety of ways. For example:
   o Create a Big Book, illustrated by the children, of classroom or school rules, daily news, or captioned pictures.
   o Make individual copies with text alone for the children to illustrate.
   o Display a wall chart of, for example, classroom rules and expectations.
   o Mail a letter.
   o Send a newsletter home to parents/caregivers.
   o Display a wall story (see Wall Stories on page 140 of Chapter 6).

Think Aloud

Making Big Books from the shared writings and even creating individual copies for the children to illustrate makes the classroom library (and even the school library) so much richer! "(T)exts that we write in a classroom are potentially texts for you and me and our peers to read to one another. That's a wonderful kind of expectation to promote in classrooms: What we write is written to be read . . . by a real person other than a teacher." It is not simply an assignment to do ("Thinking about the Reading/Writing Connection" 2002, 9).

PROMPTS FOR A SHARED WRITING ACTIVITY

1. Tell me what you are going to write about.
2. What do we need to write?
3. What should the title be?
4. Where do I put the title?
5. Who should we write to?
6. How should we begin our letter/story?
7. Where do you think we should put that?
8. How should we add that in?
9. What happened then?
10. What do you think?
11. Does that fit?
12. What else do you want to say about . . . ?
13. Why did I use an uppercase letter on this word?
14. What is this called (for example, point to closing punctuation such as an exclamation mark or a question mark)?
15. Why did I leave a space?
16. How about if we say . . . ?
17. Tell me what you notice about this word.
18. Would you like to change . . . ?

Interactive Writing (*Sharing the Pen* With Children)

Interactive writing, also known as *sharing the pen,* involves a group of children physically contributing to a shared writing experience. The children participate with you in the act of writing. While the children work with you on meaningful text, they attend to the details of letters, sounds, words, punctuation, and illustrating the piece.

Purposes of Interactive Writing

Interactive writing in the preschool and kindergarten classroom allows you to
- compose a text together with the children
- draw attention to the formation and sounds of letters and words (concepts about print)

- model and demonstrate the writing process
- include the children in contributing to the actual writing as appropriate
- create texts that can be used for shared reading (connect reading and writing)
- assess both writing skill and will
- assess oral language and vocabulary

Figure 4.2

Interactive Writing: Step by Step

1. Gather the children together so that they can clearly see and easily access the writing surface to contribute to the writing process.

2. Decide with the children what the purpose and type of writing will be (for example, list, letter, story, directions).

3. Point out how words are formed by saying the words slowly and sounding out the letter sounds.

4. Ask the children to think about how some high-frequency and *for-sure words* are spelled.

5. Include the names of individual children to draw attention to their writing and allow many children to contribute. For example, if

Typically, interactive writing involves a number of children sharing the pen with you. However, if more than a few turns are taken, the rest of the group may become bored and not remain engaged. An alternative approach would be for each child to write in a notebook or on a small whiteboard or chalkboard, such as in guided writing (see page 86). The children then compare what they have written to what the children who have been called up have written. This keeps everyone writing, thinking, and participating.

children add a drawing or write a phrase or sentence, encourage them to write their name after their contribution. They are so proud of their special contribution! They also especially love to revisit their part when reading around the room.

6. Highlight the use of punctuation.

7. Have individual children use a writing tool (for example, a marker of a different color) to write a letter or word or to add punctuation.

8. Draw attention to spaces between words and correct letter formation.

9. Encourage the children to help illustrate the text.

10. Reread the text with the children to review it and to decide what to write next.

Guided Writing (Writing With Children)

Guided writing is similar to guided reading. Children with a common need are brought together in a small group for a mini-lesson and are supported as needed. The mini-lesson may occur during modeled, shared, or interactive writing. The children then practice the strategy or strategies in their own writing either in the group setting or independently while you or another adult provide support through monitoring and feedback.

Purpose of Guided Writing

Guided writing allows you to
- provide support to the children, typically in a small-group setting, to enable them to apply the strategies demonstrated in modeled, shared, and interactive writing
- assess both writing skill and will
- assess oral language and vocabulary

See Modeled and Shared Writing (Writing *for* and *With* Children), beginning on page 82, for specific strategies. Guided writing provides the step between modeled, shared, interactive, and independent writing.

Guided Writing: Step by Step

1. Bring a group of children with a common need together in a small group for a mini-lesson during modeled, shared or interactive writing.

2. The children then practice the strategy, by writing independently or with others in the group setting. An adult remains with the group for a few minutes to monitor and provide feedback and scaffolding.

Independent Writing (Writing *by* Children)

Independent writing provides opportunities for the children to communicate by writing. Young children need many of these daily opportunities right from day one of preschool and kindergarten. But writing alone is not the answer. They also need mini-lessons and many opportunities to talk. Their "writing" may consist of pictures only, scribble, individual letters, strings of letters, words, phrases, or sentences. Invented spelling is important to both develop and assess phonological awareness, knowledge of sound–symbol correspondence, concepts about print, and motivation to write. (For more information on invented spelling, see page 36 of Chapter 2.) You may also help the children by scribing where appropriate (see Dictation: The Pros and Cons of Scribing on page 55 of Chapter 2).

Figure 4.3

Purposes of Independent Writing

Independent writing in the preschool and kindergarten classroom allows you to
- build an understanding that writing is a powerful way to communicate
- build an interest in writing
- stimulate writing as an enjoyable and meaningful activity
- encourage risk taking in writing
- develop writing skill and will
- assess a child's self-initiated interest in writing
- assess phonological awareness, concepts about print, and sound–symbol correspondence

Independent Writing:
Suggested Teaching Strategies
- Equip the Writing Center appropriately and distribute writing materials at other centers.

- Give the children free access to journals, whiteboards, books, magazines, newspapers, picture files, and so on to facilitate independent writing during activity time.
- Set up a mailbox system so that the children can send written notes to one another, to a "magic creature" (see page 222 of Chapter 9), or you via individual mailboxes or cubbies in the classroom.
- Provide each child with a writer's notebook and model how to use it (see Skill and Strategy Mini-Lessons 5.4: Keeping a Writer's Notebook on page 107 of Chapter 5).
- Share notes, messages, or signs that have been written independently by some children to encourage similar writing behaviors among other children.
- Encourage the children to write notes, messages, labels, or directions to be posted around the classroom or school.
- Establish a sign-in/sign-up procedure that encourages the children to write their names for a variety of purposes (for example, to mark their attendance, to indicate their preference on a graph, to volunteer for a classroom chore, to indicate their membership in a small group, and so on).

Figure 4.4

SIGN IN, SIGN UP, SIGN ON!

Providing the children with many opportunities to sign their names for real reasons is important. You can use these opportunities to assess word spacing, directionality, letter choice, letter formation, and letter–sound correspondence.

Here are some other sample sign-in/sign-up opportunities:

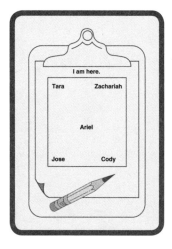
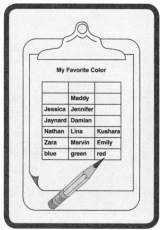

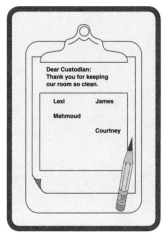
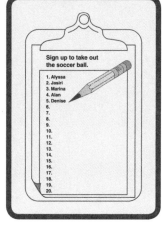
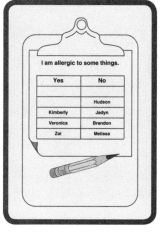

Figure 4.5

- Hold writing conferences to
  - encourage the children to write and to share their writing
  - help those who are hesitant to write to incubate ideas by drawing a picture, creating a story board, talking to a friend, or acting out the idea
  - offer a verbal or written comment about the children's writing
  - prompt the children to refer to words around the room (for example, on the word wall)

Reproducible 4.1: Reading Our Writing, referenced in Chapter 4, is available on the *Learning to Write and Loving It!* CD.

o encourage the children to sound out words by rubber-banding or stretching the sounds and by writing down the letters to match the spoken sounds

o help the children select a piece of writing for editing and/or revising, perhaps to be used in their portfolios

o ask questions as in a shared writing activity (see page 84)

For more information on conferencing, see Writing Workshop Stage 3: Writing Conferences, beginning on page 118 of Chapter 5.

Chapter 5

Writing Workshop

The benefits of writing workshop (or writer's workshop) to each child's writing and reading development cannot be overstated. Arlene Schulze (2006) cites research by Marie Clay and others showing that when writing and reading workshops are an integral part of a quality kindergarten literacy program, reading achievement improves. Furthermore, children who are struggling will learn to write through writing workshop. This is particularly significant because writing is a precursor to reading. Research also indicates that writing workshop should occur daily. There are days when classroom routines are disrupted; however, writing workshop must not be postponed, even for a day. Shortened perhaps, but not postponed.

Planning for Writing Workshop

"[F]irst and foremost, the writing workshop is about making a time every day for children to get this experience with writing that we so value, much as we plan for children to have meaningful encounters with books each day" (Ray and Cleaveland 2004, 25). But it is not just about having the children write. Children also need teaching to support their writing. So, before the children write for an extended period, a mini-lesson occurs. While the children are writing, support individuals and small groups typically through writing conferences. The fourth stage of writing workshop—author share (or author's chair)—provides further opportunities for teaching and celebrating writing. Young children thrive on routines and benefit when the workshop occurs at the same time every day.

Writing workshop is broken down into four stages: mini-lessons, writing, conferencing, and author share. Literacy experts agree that writing workshop must

- occur daily
- provide the children with a block of time to write
- include scaffolding through mini-lessons, conferencing, and author share

Although educators seem to agree that children need a stretch of time to write daily, there is little agreement as to exactly how much time should be spent on writing workshop and how the four stages should be implemented (see Suggested Daily Writing Workshop Frameworks, below). There is another important factor to consider when planning

Don Graves (1994) explains that if a writing workshop cannot be scheduled at least 4 days a week for 35 to 45 minutes each time, it should not occur at all because writers need to be in a constant state of composition to learn and grow as writers.

"Why do we believe that a daily hour-long writing workshop is essential for our teaching of writing to young children? The answer to this question really comes down to a belief that two things are essential for children's development as writers: experience and teaching. A writing workshop creates a space for both to happen naturally, side by side." (Ray and Cleaveland 2004, 23–24)

writing workshop: full-day versus half-day kindergarten programs. The reality is that in a full-day program, it is much easier to "get it all in." However, even in a half-day program, writing is so important that it needs to be given priority. Integration of literacy across subject areas makes this possible.

Suggested Daily Writing Workshop Frameworks			
Length of Workshop	Whole-Class Mini-Lesson	Writing Time	Author Share
55–75 minutes (Ray and Cleaveland 2004)	10–15 minutes	35–50 minutes	10 minutes
35–60 minutes (Schulze 2006)	10–15 minutes	10–30 minutes	15 minutes
22–52 minutes (Freeman 1998)	2–20 minutes	15–20 minutes	5–12 minutes

Regie Routman defines writing workshop "as a time in which everything that writers do to create a meaningful piece of writing for a reader takes place. . . . There are no rigid procedures or one set of best practices" (2005, 174).

WRITING WORKSHOP DEFINED

- Sustained, daily writing across the curriculum of mostly self-chosen topics
- Writing for purposes and audiences that the writer values and understands
- Playing around with language and learning how to craft writing
- Conferring with the children to respond to their writing, celebrating what they have done well, and teaching the next steps for moving the writing forward
- Teaching the children what they need to know to write fluently and accurately
- Doing what writers do to make a piece engaging for the reader
- Publishing for real audiences

(Routman 2005, 174)

Of course it is not just about how much time one spends on writing workshop. Success is also measured by the quality of the mini-lessons taught, how engaged the children are in their writing, the quality of the conferencing, and the level of class engagement during author share. (For specific strategies, see the four stages of writing workshop that follow.)

Writing Workshop Stage I: Mini-Lessons

A mini-lesson (typically whole-class or small-group) is defined by Lucy Calkins as "a forum for making a suggestion to the whole class, raising a concern, exploring an issue, modeling a technique, reinforcing a strategy (that the class has demonstrated a need of in their writing)" (1994, 193). Mini-lessons are based on your observations and assessment while the children write and after examining the quality of their writing. Generally, teachers anticipate that most children will apply the strategy or technique in their own writing the same day. The goal is for the children to demonstrate the strategy in future pieces of writing. It is possible and likely that not all children in the class need practice in the same area. However, most kindergarteners are happy to "give it a go" and show you that they can apply the writing technique or strategy, since the activity will be engaging.

One of the best ways to learn to write well is to listen to or read well-written texts.

Figure 5.1

The most common and effective ways to present mini-lessons include the following:

- Demonstrate a strategy or skill using modeled writing and think-alouds.
- Highlight a strategy or skill using good literature.
- Highlight a strategy or skill using a child's writing sample from your class, another class, or a past class after asking the child's permission to share.
- Provide a quick demonstration, and then have the children "give it a go" right there.
- Have a conversation with the class about some aspect of writing workshop—something that is not working or perhaps something to celebrate. For example, you might discuss what the rest of the class might do to solve problems while you are conferencing with another child. This conversation would occur after you have caught a child in the act of effectively problem solving. (See Procedural Mini-Lessons 5.1: Solving Problems Without the Teacher, page 96.)
- Use a combination of approaches. For example, if you plan to focus attention on word choice, consider reading a paragraph that demonstrates excellent word choice (for example, a paragraph from *Chrysanthemum* by Kevin Henkes). Point out what makes the words "yummy words," and talk about why the author might have chosen them over tired words such as *said*. Next, choose another word from the book and brainstorm other million-dollar words (or yummy words) to use instead. Create the word list as a shared writing, and then remind the children to focus on word choice or using yummy words in the writing they do that day.

Figure 5.2

Although there are a variety of ways to categorize writing mini-lessons, the simplest is to divide them into two categories: procedural and skill and strategy. *Procedural mini-lessons* focus on classroom management issues and routines. These should occur all year long but more so in the first few months of the year.

Examples of procedural mini-lessons include
- what dismissal from the mini-lesson looks like to avoid chaos
- where the supplies are kept and when and how to get them for writing
- how to get work date-stamped
- what the children might do to avoid interrupting you during conferences (see Procedural Mini-Lessons 5.1: Solving Problems Without the Teacher, page 96)

Figure 5.3
Consider wearing a hat or scarf or using a portable stop sign to indicate you are not to be interrupted when you are conferencing.

- what it means to be finished. Teach the children that writers are never finished . . . even if it means starting a new piece of writing. There is always more to write.
- how to respond to a timer if one is used. Katie Wood Ray and Lisa Cleaveland (2004) set a timer during writing time. This serves two purposes. The first is to help the children understand that when the timer is on they are to be writing and only writing. (The first day set it for just a minute so all children will be successful.) The second reason for the timer is to teach the children that once it goes off they have 5 minutes and only 5 minutes to clean up and get to the carpet for author share. This teaches the children that time is valuable. Every minute counts . . . especially in early childhood classrooms!

Figure 5.4

PROCEDURAL MINI-LESSONS 5.1
Solving Problems Without the Teacher

In her book *Teaching the Youngest Writers: A Practical Guide* (1998), Marcia Freeman suggests using a Help Strip to foster peer teaching. This approach teaches young children how to get help without interrupting you during writing conference time. The Help Strip is simply a large sheet of brown paper taped to the wall, a desk, or the floor. An interactive whiteboard could also be used. Children take turns as designated helpers.

1. Beginning the second week of school, model many times how to obtain and give help using the Help Strip. Explain to the children that if they are having trouble drawing a picture or making an illustration, they should go to the illustrator helper who will draw the picture on the Help Strip for the child to trace over and then copy. The same process is used for writing a letter or a word.

2. After the children are familiar with the Help Strip process, assign three helpers per day: a letter helper, a word helper, and a drawing helper. When choosing helpers, Freeman suggests starting "with children who have some command of the sound-to-symbol relationship, can make some of their letters, can write or find words around the room, or who can draw. . . . When children know they will have a turn at being a designated helper, they take it seriously and try to help" (p. 23).

3. Develop a system for identifying who the helpers are each day. For example, the helpers might wear a name tag or display signs on their desks.

Figure 5.5

Skill and strategy mini-lessons help the children to learn strategies that they can then apply as skills. There are the skills of conventions, but there are many other skills that children should be taught as well (see the list that follows).

KEY SKILL AND STRATEGY WRITING MINI-LESSONS

- What writers need to be writers (see Mini-Lessons 5.3 on page 103)

- Solving a problem when writing independently (see page 96)

- Letter formation (see Mini-Lessons 5.2 on page 101)

- Placing one's name on the written piece to signify authorship

- Where to start writing on the page

- Directionality

- Word spaces; how many words in the sentence; play be a sentence (see Figure 5.7)

- Letter spaces

- Writing words by rubber-banding or stretching the sounds

Figure 5.6

The last word card must include the closing punctuation after *ball*.

- More consistent use of lowercase letters

- Wraparound or return sweep (when the end of one line is reached, you return to the far left side of the page and continue writing on the next line)

- Where authors get writing ideas (see page 112)

- Using book bags or book boxes to get ideas

- How to pick a writing topic

Figure 5.7

We can all play Build a Sentence.

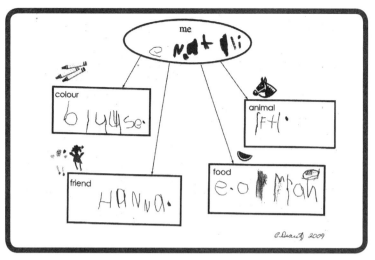

Figure 5.8

Sometimes graphic organizers help the children
to incubate ideas.

- Different kinds of writing, their characteristics, and when they are used (for example, lists, labels, letters, notes, and so on)

- Million-dollar words (yummy words)

- Finding the traits (ideas, organization, voice, word choice, sentence fluency, and conventions) in read-alouds, shared readings, and texts written by peers

- What makes an interesting conclusion and why it is important to write one

- Composing a title (when and how)

- What a table of contents is, what it is used for, and how to create one

- What a survey is, why it is used, and how to conduct one (see Chapter 6)

- How to use the word wall and other environmental print to support writing (see Chapter 6)

- How to incubate ideas before writing (see page 57)

- Organizing and adding details

- Using periods, question marks, and exclamation marks

- Using an uppercase letter for the pronoun *I*, at the beginning of proper names, and at the beginning of a sentence

- Sharing writing (see page 126)

- Responding to a peer during author share (see page 126)

- Using labels and diagrams

- Spelling a few high-frequency words correctly

- Editing and revising

- Learning what to do when the writing is done

Learning to Draw and Mini-Lessons

Drawing is an important part of writing especially for emerging and early writers. Drawing helps the writer to think, to express him/herself, to improve writing. Many children who struggle with forming of letters and words can in fact express themselves very well through drawing and sketching. Others who can print letters very well struggle with drawing. Most children come to school already drawing. However, many teachers do not scaffold this important skill. I am included in this group of teachers. I taught the children how to form letters and words and how to use punctuation. I also encouraged them to draw throughout the day, to use drawing or sketching to incubate their ideas before writing… but I did not show them how to draw. I knew that there was something missing but I did not teach drawing simply because I did not know how to draw myself.

In order to scaffold drawing it is important to:
- Encourage drawing with writing, at centers, across the day and across the curriculum
- Celebrate their drawings
- Find out more about teaching simple drawing yourself. See the Check it Out!.
- Teach drawing or sketching during writing workshop. Think aloud often. Make the implicit explicit.
- Encourage drawing to incubate ideas before they "write."
- Select read alouds and shared readings that exhibit interesting art that might excite the children. Use these as mentor texts to support the children's drawing.
- Establish a drawing center. Include a great variety of pencils, sketch books for each child, markers, interesting items that you and the children bring that they might like to sketch, a magnifying glass, read alouds with interesting art, photos and books on drawing such as Ed Emberley's how-to-draw books. Show the children how to "look" at the items.. how to note the details. Model, Model, Model.

Check It Out!

For many practical ideas on how to teach drawing see *Talking, Drawing and Writing, Lessons for Our Youngest Writers* by Martha Horn and Mary Ellen Giacobbe, 2007. Also enjoy Ed Emberley's *Drawing Book of Animals, Drawing Book of Trucks and Trains, Drawing Book of Faces* and the *Fingerprint Drawing Book,* among others.

MINI-LESSONS 5.2

Skill and Strategy: Letter Formation

The work of Marie Clay (1991) presents research done on the teaching of letter formation. The following steps are recommended:

1. Write the letter in front of the child or children. Think aloud as you describe each stroke. You may choose to use familiar terms such as *sticks, circles,* and *curves,* and directional words such as *up, down, over, across, slant, forward, backward.* (For example, "Watch me make a *b.* I start at the top and go straight down to make a stick. Next, I make a circle at the bottom of the stick."

2. Show the children how to examine the letter for specific characteristics. You might begin with three categories of letters: Tall letters (for example, *b, h, l, t*), short letters (for example, *a, e, n, r*), and letters that hang down (for example, *g, j, p, y*).

3. Next, break down the categories further by encouraging the children to examine each letter for distinguishing features. For example, a tall letter with a cross near the top (*t, f*), a letter with a circle on the bottom (*b, d*), a letter with a circle at the top (*p, q*), a letter with a dot above (*i, j*), a circle letter (*o*), a letter that looks like a snake (*s*), a letter that looks like a *c* but has a line in it (*e*), a letter that looks like two *n*'s together (*m*), a t bent over (*f*). When children come up with their own specific letter characteristics and are encouraged to think aloud as they form each letter, they are more likely to remember the letter and how to write it.

Teaching children how to analyze letters for distinguishing characteristics and ensuring their engagement in many meaningful writing experiences are the keys to learning to write readable letters.

UPPER- AND LOWERCASE LETTERS

Teach upper- and lowercase letter pairs separately. This is especially important for children who start kindergarten with minimal letter knowledge. Introducing two letters with the same name and different shapes can be very confusing. Preschool children often find uppercase letters easier to discriminate, as they are more visually distinct from one another than are lowercase letters (for example, *A B C D* as opposed to *a b c d*). Also, because uppercase letters are more often found in environmental print, such as on signs, very young children tend to be more familiar with them. Starting with uppercase letters rather than lowercase letters will provide more immediate success.

Check It Out!

Online lessons to support learning color and shape words, letters, numbers, and letter formation are available at The Literacy Center Education Network (www.literacycenter.net). The activities are available in English, Spanish, German, and French.

4. You can prompt letter formation by describing each stroke as it is made. Some children will benefit from replicating your steps; however, children will more likely remember the letters and how to make them if they are each allowed to follow a sequence of letter formation that works best for them. Additionally, it is important to remember that left-handed children may find alternative steps in letter formation work better for them.

5. For a child having a great deal of difficulty forming letters, try guiding her or his hand while writing in the air or tracing magnetic letters. Feeling letters made of felt or sandpaper often helps. Use familiar terminology to describe the sequence of motions (for example, "To make a *b*, start at the top, feel the stick by going down, and then feel a circle at the bottom").

Figure 5.9

STEP UP AND WRITE ON

Lea M. McGee and Lesley Mandel Morrow (2005) suggest two shared-writing activities to support letter recognition and formation.

Step Up: The children are called up to a shared writing chart and asked to circle a letter they know, a specific letter, or two letters that are alike. The strength of the latter task is that the children are required to look for distinguishing features or characteristics that are common but not necessarily identical (for example, *i* and *j* or *c* and *e)*. The children must then use metacognition (thinking about their own thinking) to explain how the letters are similar.

Write On: The children find a letter on the shared writing chart, name it, and write it somewhere on the chart. More advanced writers might be encouraged to write a word that starts with the letter or has the letter somewhere in the word.

Check It Out!

For more information on what writers need to be writers, see *Creating Young Writers: Using the Six Traits to Enrich Writing Process in Primary Classrooms* by Vicki Spandel (Boston: Allyn & Bacon, 2007) and *Write Traits Kindergarten: Bringing the Traits to Kinderwriters* by Vicki Spandel and Jeff Hicks (Wilmington, MA: Great Source Education Group, 2008).

MINI-LESSONS 5.3

Skill and Strategy: What Writers Need to Be Writers

Vicki Spandel (2008) suggests starting the year with a lesson that helps the children understand what tools a writer needs: something to write on, something to write with, and ideas.

1. Make the concept of writing tools concrete for children by bringing a toolbox to class in which there are hand tools (for example, a hammer, a screwdriver, and a measuring tape).

2. Encourage the children to name the tools and to identify their possible uses. Emphasize the idea that when we create something, whether it involves building a table or making a cake, we use special tools.

Figure 5.10

3. **Make the connection between hand tools and writing tools. Using a shared writing format, brainstorm a list of writer's tools with the group.**

4. **Next, open a writer's toolbox (such as a shoebox) in which the children see the following writing tools. Discuss the purpose of each tool.**

   ○ paper

   ○ pencil, crayons, markers

   ○ a clock to represent that writing takes time

   ○ a small flashlight (or an incandescent light bulb) to represent that writers have to have ideas to share

   ○ a picture of people to represent an audience of readers

   ○ items to represent experiences or ideas, such as a photo, postcard, book, addressed envelope with a stamp, a cereal-box toy, and a ticket stub

   ○ a picture of a heart to represent feelings that are put into writing (sometimes writers write about happy times, and sometimes they write about sad times)

5. Model how a writer can use one of the items from the toolbox to spark a writing idea. For example, hold up the stamped envelope and think aloud, "This letter came from my friend Tony. I could write about Tony like this." Draw a stick figure on chart paper or on the chalkboard. Consider labeling the stick figure *Tony*; however, not labeling the picture will be encouraging to those children who are not yet writing alphabet letters. Because they too can draw, they will also see themselves as writers.

You might then hold up a ticket stub from an event such as a play or a hockey game. Think aloud, "This ticket stub was for a hockey game that my brother played in. I have an idea. I can draw my brother's hockey jersey (shirt). He is number 5 so I will put a number 5 on it." Ask the children what a ticket stub makes them think of. What could they write about? Encourage the children to turn and talk.

Finally, you might hold up a picture of a favorite pet. Tell the class (thinking aloud) that you love the pet (mention the pet's name) very much. Sketch the pet and write under the sketch *I love you, (pet's name)*. You may also want to add a heart symbol.

Figure 5.11

6. Support children individually as they create their personal writer's toolboxes.

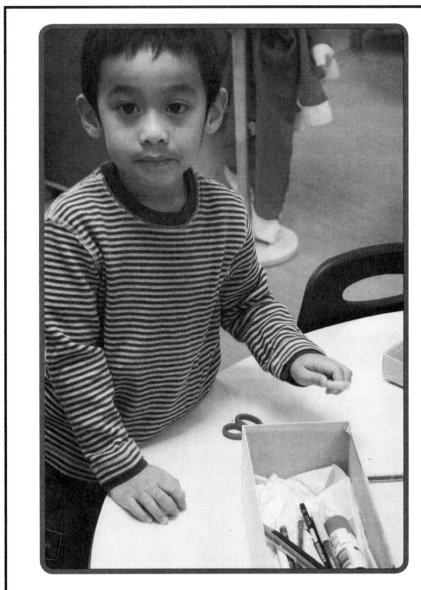

Figure 5.12

This is my writer's toolbox.

A Writer's Notebook

Published authors frequently keep a writer's notebook. A writer's notebook is neither a journal nor a diary. It is simply a notebook used to store ideas, memories, special words, drawings, mementos, souvenirs, photos, ticket stubs, stickers, stamps, and so on. Some kindergarten children have even included a special leaf from the playground; some of their pet's fur; a piece of their baby blanket; a list of special (yummy) words; a list of numbers, alphabet letters, or their friends' names; a picture of a toy taken from a newspaper ad; and lots of drawings. The whole purpose of a writer's notebook is to remember special ideas, times, people, or things to motivate writers to write! To encourage children to keep a writer's notebook and to scaffold their use of it, model using one from the beginning of the year.

Skill and Strategy: Keeping a Writer's Notebook

1. Point out to the children when you are writing in your writer's notebook and what exactly you are including. Let them catch you in the act! Explain why you regularly write in your notebook (for example, to provide you with writing ideas, things to remember, and motivation to write).

2. Show the children that some of your pages only have a word or two, while others have just a picture or a picture and a label. Write a page in your notebook in front of the children as a modeled writing activity.

3. If you have any writer's notebooks kept by children from past years, display and discuss some of the pages. Nothing motivates young writers to write more quickly than celebrating the writing of other children. "If he can do it, I can do it too!"

4. Read aloud the wonderful picture book *Lilly's Purple Plastic Purse* by Kevin Henkes. The story describes Lilly who brings her plastic purse to school for show-and-tell. She cannot wait to show her purse and interrupts the teacher's read-aloud in her excitement to show the purse.

5. Ask the children to speculate as to why the author used a purse and specifically a purple plastic purse in the story. (Explain that the author was sitting in an airport waiting for a plane when he looked over and saw a little girl holding a purple plastic purse that played music. He got out his writer's notebook and wrote *purple plastic purse*. If he had not written it down, he would likely have forgotten about the purple plastic purse. That is where he got the idea to write his book.)

6. As a shared writing, make a list of possible items that might be recorded in a writer's notebook.

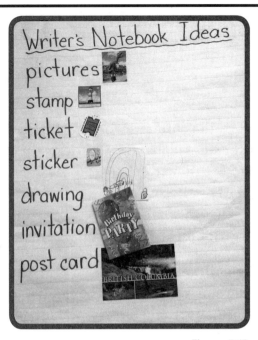

Figure 5.13

7. Tell the children that in a day or two day they will receive their own writer's notebook. Send a letter home to parents/caregivers describing the purpose of a writer's notebook and asking them to encourage the children to bring items to school to include in the notebook. (See Reproducible 5.1: Keeping a Writer's Notebook, on the CD.)

8. Before distributing the notebooks, invite volunteers to share with the class some of the items that they brought from home.

9. Start by sharing with the children what you did last night (for example, you may have tried a new food or recipe at dinner, took your dog for a walk, or bought a get-well card for a friend). Sketch the memory and label it. Modeling this approach will encourage the children who did not

bring anything from home to still make use of their writer's notebook. They need to learn that experiences and ideas are even more valuable than objects!

10. Distribute the notebooks and give the children an opportunity to write and/or glue into their notebooks the items they brought from home.

11. Next, have the children turn to a partner to talk about what they did last night or even yesterday.

12. Direct the children to sketch and label their experience in their writer's notebook.

13. Additionally, the children might create a list of favorite people, favorite activities, and what makes them happy or sad. Remind them that they are making lists.

Writing Workshop Stage 2: Children Engaged in Writing

Children need to understand that they must write during writing time. It is sacred time, but it need not be quiet time. There are many reasons for the children to be talking with peers, volunteers, buddies, or paraprofessionals. They may be discussing writing ideas, sharing their drawings, helping one another actually write a word, rubber-banding or stretching sounds when trying to spell a word and write it (for example, *t-o-p*), or sharing their completed or partly completed products. Incubating ideas by drawing and talking about them is an important prewriting planning tool. Young children also talk to themselves as they think about what they are going to write and as they draw, write, edit, and revise. Encourage the children to go back and reread or rehearse what they have written before going on. Emerging and early writers typically sub-vocalize.

Check It Out!

Talking, Drawing and Writing Lessons for Our Youngest Writers by Martha Horn and Mary Ellen Giacobbe (2007) is a great resource to help teachers more effectively scaffold drawing, talk, and, in the process, writing.

Figure 5.14
Notice the sharing or incubating of ideas by the children at the back table. This is so important!

It is important to encourage the children to use some of the strategies, skills, or routines taught in the mini-lessons. It is also helpful to walk around the classroom at this time or sit at a table with a group to assess and support the children through guided writing. Alternatively, you might conference with an individual or a small group.

The Importance of Sustained Writing

The research is clear: the more children write the better, and young children need to write a great deal. Quantity does matter! The biggest frustration many preschool and kindergarten teachers face is that they cannot get some children to write for an extended period of time. In addition, there is no agreement among the experts as to how long this time should be. Katie Wood Ray and Lisa Cleaveland (2004) recommend 35 to 50 minutes of daily writing time during writing workshop, Arlene Schulze (2006) recommends 10 to 30 minutes, and Marcia Freeman (1998) recommends 15 to 20 minutes (see page 92).

Strategies for Implementing Sustained Writing

Realistically, the amount of time you can get young children to stick with writing depends on many factors, including
- the nature of the writing tasks (How motivating are they? Is there managed choice?
- the difficulty level of the task (If it is too easy, the child will be bored. If it is too difficult, the child will be frustrated.)
- classroom management and routines
- the nature of the class (for example, behaviors)
- the time of year (some experienced teachers find that the weather and even the phase of the moon can affect a child's behavior and motivation to write)

Research shows that children will write a great deal more and for extended periods of time if you
- show them how (modeled writing)
- write with them (shared, interactive, and guided writing)
- give them choice (managed choice)
- introduce the writing stage by spending just a minute or two on the first day so that all children will be successful. This helps to build writing stamina.
- celebrate writing daily
- stock the classroom with books (including peer-authored books), magazines, pictures, and different types of writing tools and materials

Managed choice is a term coined by Richard Allington. Children have choice, but often it is not unlimited.

To help stimulate and support writing, Katie Wood Ray and Lisa Cleaveland (2004) recommend providing children with access to different types of paper, pens, scented markers, thin markers, colored paper clips, clipboards, scissors and glue, and sticky notes.

- provide environmental print and foster the children's use of environmental print through activities. Examples of environmental print include alphabet charts, calendars, signs, labels, word walls, poem charts, song charts, wall stories (see page 140), and word-family houses.

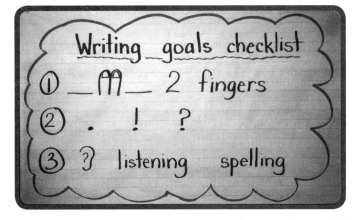

Figure 5.15

- read aloud daily, ensuring you provide a balance of fiction, nonfiction, and poetry using mentor texts. Teach mini-lessons using these texts.
- involve writing across the day, including at centers
- make writing project-based (for example, have the children create their own books) and functional (for example, have them write letters and lists) whenever possible
- support writing in different genres (see Chapters 6 and 7)
- provide feedback through conferencing (see Writing Workshop Stage 3: Writing Conferences, beginning on page 118)
- schedule writing workshop daily
- establish and maintain effective classroom routines that are implemented daily
- encourage children to read and share books, especially those they have made
- promote conversation in the class (the sharing of ideas)
- create a classroom mascot or mascots to which the children can address their writing (see the section on writing to magic creatures on page 222 of Chapter 9)

Alphabet strips on classroom tables or desks are very important!

One technique Katie Wood Ray and Lisa Cleaveland (2004) find successful in getting children to write for sustained periods of time is to fold up paper and staple it together so that it looks like a book. Stapling it together and calling it a book makes a big difference in what children produce. Children know that picture books have text and pictures on each page, so they are motivated to fill all of the stapled pages to make a book.

Figure 5.16

- emphasize the importance of writing as often as possible and never skip writing workshop
- encourage writing at home (see Reproducible 5.1: Keeping a Writer's Notebook, on the CD, as well as the home–school links reproducibles referenced in Chapters 2, 3, 4, 6, 7, and 9)

Helping Young Children Find Writing Ideas

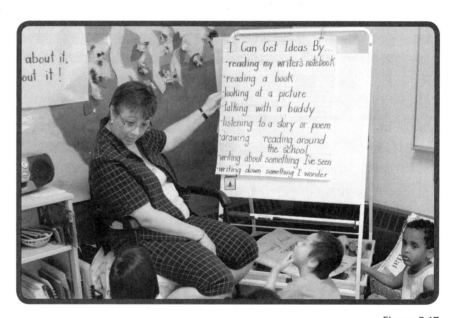

Figure 5.17

Helping children to create their own books just makes sense. Books are a big part of their lives. They hear books read to them every day. Using fiction, nonfiction, poetry, and especially pattern books as mentor texts help to make the process of writing books very engaging. Begin by creating some shared-writing class pattern books. The children soon develop the goal to become a writer just like Eric Carle!

Often, especially at the beginning of preschool and kindergarten, the writing is intentionally scaffolded by teachers. Writing models, patterns, or sentence stems like *I can . . .* are provided to prompt children with writing. The children can easily begin writing because of the prompt. They may follow the pattern with *I can run. I can jump. I can see . . . .* However, the result is minimal writing and only for that one day. The writing is not motivating and does not extend to other days. Katie Wood Ray and Lisa Cleaveland (2004) do not believe in the need for prompts, story starters, or sentence stems, even for the youngest writers. They feel that when children are creating their own books and are engaged in other authentic forms of writing, they will remain interested and write more.

"Sometimes, teachers are reluctant to trust that children will discover their own topics. . . . Letting children arrive at their own topics requires patience on the part of the teachers" (Feldgus and Cardonick 1999, 97).

While allowing children to arrive at their own topics does require patience, it also requires a great deal of teacher support. Children often get their writing topics from mini-lessons during writing workshop. Often they experience read-alouds or shared readings followed by modeled, shared, or guided writing. Finally, each child "gives it a go."

Using patterns from great children's literature can motivate young children to write. For example, after reading *Rosie's Walk* by Pat Hutchins, you could begin with a shared writing (see Elizabeth's Crawl, below) and then have the children use the pattern to create their own text. The poem "Bugs!" by Margaret Wise Brown begins and ends with the line *I like bugs*. It is well loved by the children. (See Figures 5.18 and 5.19 for some examples of shared writing innovations.)

Check It Out!

See the lesson "Creating a Class Pattern Book with Popular Culture Characters" at ReadWriteThink (www .readwritethink.org).

Check It Out!

A superb website is the Early Literacy Telecollaborative Project (www.earlyliterature .ecsd.net). Here you will find lists of quality Predictable books to use as mentor texts for writing.

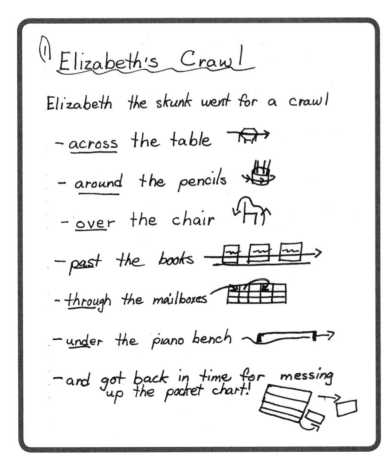

Figure 5.18

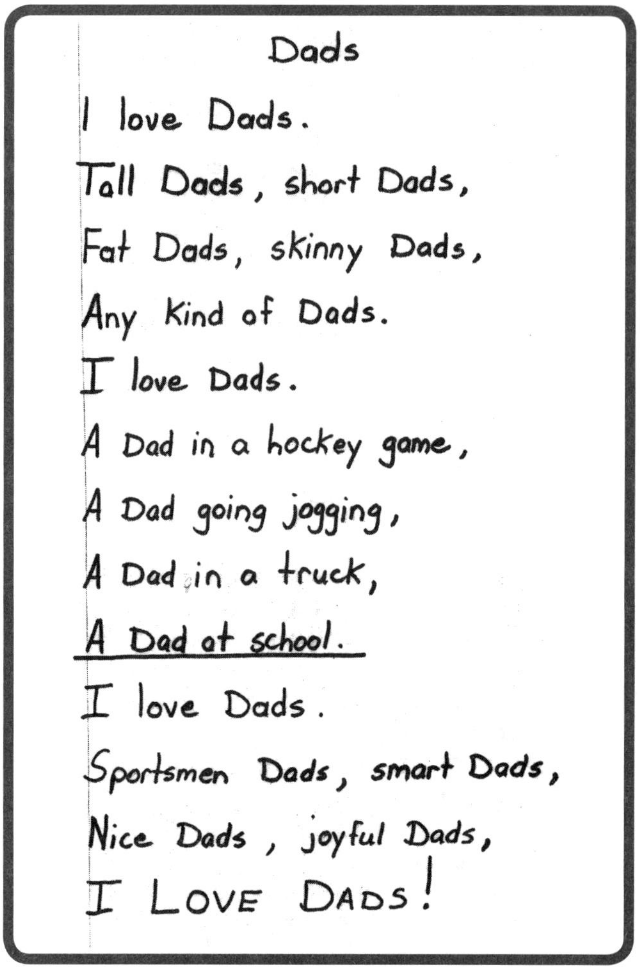

Dads

I love Dads.

Tall Dads, short Dads,

Fat Dads, skinny Dads,

Any kind of Dads.

I love Dads.

A Dad in a hockey game,

A Dad going jogging,

A Dad in a truck,

A Dad at school.

I love Dads.

Sportsmen Dads, smart Dads,

Nice Dads, joyful Dads,

I LOVE DADS!

Figure 5.19

Ultimately, children should be encouraged to pick any writing topic they wish. When they are given this option, their writing is richer and has more voice. They have a desire to write and a purpose in mind. Remind the children that if they can think about it, they can talk about it, and if they can talk about it, they can write about it.

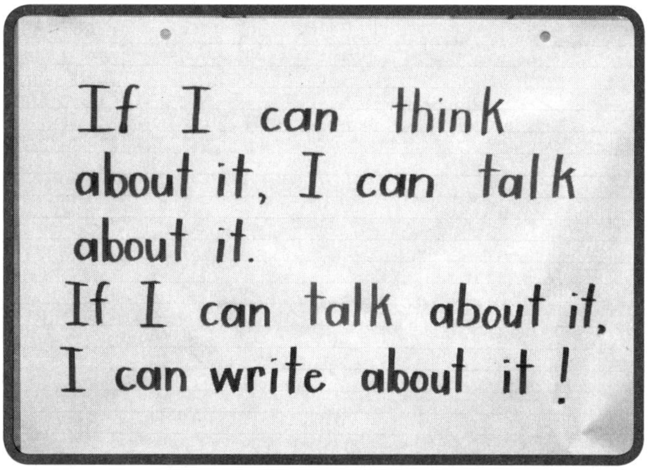

If I can think about it, I can talk about it.
If I can talk about it, I can write about it!

Figure 5.20

Skill and Strategy: For Those Who Need Help Getting Started

Some children may initially need a structure to get started.

1. Hold up a book that you have read to the children. Remind the children that the person who wrote the book is the author and the person who drew the pictures is the illustrator. See if they can come up with the terms themselves.

2. Explain to the children that they are all authors and illustrators, too!

3. Create a modeled writing chart titled "I Can Write" (see Figure 5.21).

4. As you create, think aloud. For example,

   ○ First, I write my name up here in this corner. I always start writing up here on this side of the page.

   ○ Now I will think of an idea to write about. I will look in my writer's notebook. Oh, here is a picture of my dog Miko. I could talk to a friend about Miko to get writing ideas.

   ○ Next, let me see, what should I write? I could write about how she loves to eat cheese or about the time she got lost on her way home. What do you think I should write about?

   ○ Now I will draw a picture of Miko to help me write.

   ○ I could write like this . . . (add some scribble writing to the chart)

     Or like this . . . (write some mock letters)

     Or like this . . . (write M DG GT LT ON HR WA HOM)

     Or like this . . . (write My dog got lost on her way home.)

   ○ Think aloud as you draw. Teaching young children how to draw or sketch is important. See Learning to Draw and Mini-lessons on page 100.

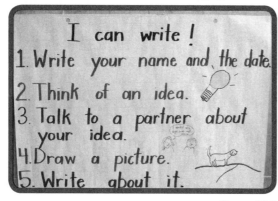

Figure 5.21

As you do each kind of writing, explain to the children that some writers begin to write like the examples you have written (point to the scribbles, mock letters, and letter–sound attempts), but when they get to be much older, they will write like an adult (point to *My dog got lost on her way home.*).

5. After creating the I Can Write chart, direct the children to look in their writer's notebooks or their writer's toolboxes for ideas to write about.

6. Next, brainstorm their ideas as a shared-writing list.

Figure 5.22

7. Have the children share their writing idea with a friend.

Figure 5.23

8. Have each child draw a picture and write.

Source: Adapted from Schulze 2006, 161.

Other sources of writing ideas can come from keeping a writer's notebook (see Skill and Strategy Mini-Lessons 5.4: Keeping a Writer's Notebook on page 107), talking with peers, participating in author share (see page 126), drawing, writing an informational piece about a familiar topic (see Writing *All About . . . Books:* You're an Expert! on page 172 of Chapter 6), and looking at photos. The children also enjoy writing notes, letters, memos, and messages (including invitations). With these forms of writing, children have an authentic reason to write, a real audience, and the potential for a response (see Writing Notes, Memos, Cards, Invitations, Tickets, and Letters on page 219 of Chapter 9).

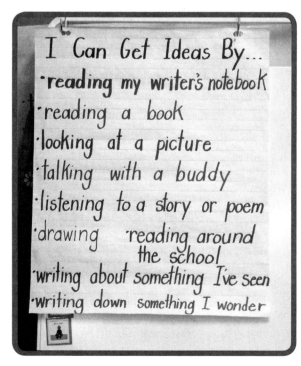

I Can Get Ideas By...
• reading my writer's notebook
• reading a book
• looking at a picture
• talking with a buddy
• listening to a story or poem
• drawing   • reading around the school
• writing about something I've seen
• writing down something I wonder

Figure 5.24

Classroom centers also promote writing.

Writing Workshop Stage 3: Writing Conferences

Research shows that conferencing with children helps them to become better writers. But many teachers have questions. For example,

- What exactly is a writing conference?
- Should I be assessing or teaching or both during conferencing? What are the best ways to scaffold learning?
- What should a writing conference look like in early childhood classrooms?
- How long should the conference last?
- How can I conference without being constantly interrupted?
- Which is most effective: individual, small-group, or large-group conferencing?
- What kinds of writing conferences are there?

The purpose of this section is to offer answers to these questions based on what the best and most reputable research indicates. The bottom line is that although we know a great deal more now about conferencing with young children than was known 30 years ago, there is still no one right way to do it! Use the research as a guide, but do what works for you.

What Is a Writing Conference?

According to Regie Routman (2005) conferences may celebrate, validate, encourage, nudge, teach, assess, and/or set goals.

A writing conference is any discussion that focuses on a child's writing. It can occur at any time: "on the run" as you move from child to child or in a public forum with a small or large group of children listening in. A writing conference can be initiated by you or by the individual writer.

The two main reasons for writing conferences are to scaffold learning (through assessing and teaching) and to celebrate each individual's writing. Nothing encourages writing more in preschool and kindergarten than celebrating children's work. Scaffolding and celebration will result in developing in children both the skill and will to write.

Setting the Stage for Conferences

For conferences to be successful, especially with very young children, certain non-negotiables must be in place. These include classroom procedures and routines and your ability to anticipate possible problems. Children must learn to solve their own problems or to get help from their peers (see Procedural Mini-Lessons 5.1: Solving Problems without the Teacher on page 96). The children must learn that during a conference you should only be interrupted if there is an emergency (for example, a classmate is ill or injured, or there is a fire). You might wear a conferencing hat or scarf indicating "Do Not Disturb," or create a Stop sign to display during conferencing. The bottom line is that for effective conferences to occur, even for 5 minutes, you cannot be interrupted. Some years it is obviously easier to conference than others, depending on the makeup of the class.

Other nonnegotiables include the following:
- Maintain a positive tone and a warm relationship with the child.
- Keep the conference brief (typically 5 minutes or less for a one-on-one conference).
- Sit side by side with the child (pull up a chair alongside the child or conference at a writing table or in front of the whole class).
- Have the child hold his or her paper (although sometimes the child may want you to hold it).
- Begin with a praise point—something the child has done well.
- Start the conversation with a question or prompt.
- Allow the child to do most of the talking.
- Respond mainly to the content of the piece.
- Extend the conversation by asking another question or making a comment, usually about the content.
- Encourage the child to self-assess. Prompt with, "What's one smart or clever thing you did today (or yesterday) as a writer?" Also prompt with, "What is one thing you could do better as a writer?" (Use Reproducible 3.8: Look at Me. I Am a Writer! Self-Assessment and Reproducible 3.4: I Can Write and Draw to support the self-assessment.)
- Teach one strategy that the child can apply right after the conference.
- Ensure that the child starts writing before the conference ends (if you get the child started, she or he will be more likely to apply the strategy taught).

Individual Versus Group Conferences

There is nothing like the special relationship that can develop from an individual conference. It is a special time you share with each child, and children love having the opportunity to have you all to themselves. With a half-day program, however, time is limited. An alternative to individual conferences is to conference with a small group composed of children with similar needs (see the section on guided writing on page 86 of Chapter 4).

Some experts feel that large-group, even whole-class conferences may be more effective than one-on-one or even small-group conferences. For example, Regie Routman, in her book *Writing Essentials: Raising Expectations and Results While Simplifying Teaching* (2005), provides common-sense reasons for whole-class conferences, often done during author share (see page 126). For example, whole-class conferences

Do not allow those lines of children needing help to occur near you while you are conferencing!

Do not overwhelm young children with more than one or two teaching points or writing strategies at a time.

- are productive and efficient and reduce behavior problems and interruptions
- enable you to teach certain strategies and skills to a larger group
- allow the children to learn from one another
- facilitate peer feedback or provide unsolicited feedback
- celebrate individual children in front of their peers, which elevates their status in the class
- encourage reluctant writers (when they see that their peers can do it, they believe that they too can do it)

Types of Conferences

Most experts, among them Lucy Calkins, Katie Wood Ray, and Regie Routman, agree that there are various types of conferences, including expectation conferences and content conferences. No matter what the conference, it is a good idea to include self-assessment. A key question to prompt self-assessment is, "What's one smart or clever thing you did today as a writer?"

Expectation Conferences

The purpose of expectation conferences is to "communicate to students precisely what is expected of them during writing time, and help them start doing those things" (Calkins, Hartman, and White 2005, 102). Although it is reasonable to assume young children need more of these conferences at the beginning of the year than during the middle or at the end, some children will need these conferences all year long!

Some examples of expectation conferences include the following:
- During writing time, the children should be writing (including drawing) and not wandering around the class. They also have to be taught that writing has to tell the reader something. Scribbling or simply creating shapes without a purpose is not acceptable.
- As the year unfolds, the children should be expected to use more and more letters and words, not just drawings. Use of environmental print should be encouraged.
- The children should also be encouraged to talk with others about their writing.
- Writing materials need to be shared!
- The children should solve their own problems with the help of peers while you are conferencing (see Procedural Mini-Lessons 5.1: Solving Problems Without the Teacher on page 96). Lucy Calkins, Amanda Hartman, and Zoë White (2005) explain to the children that they are all writing teachers!

Figure 5.25

- Help the children to understand that they are never done. When one piece of writing is finished, one of two things may happen: another one is started or a previous piece is revised.
- All completed writing should be stamped with the date and shared with someone.
- Lucy Calkins, in her DVD with the Teachers College reading and Writing Project Community, *Big Lessons from Small Writers* (2005), recommends using a two-pocketed writing folder for each child. One side of the folder has a green dot indicating unfinished or ongoing work. The other side has a red dot indicating finished work.
- The children need to speak with you, a small group, or a large group during conference time. They need to talk about what they are writing and what they are trying to do in their writing. They need to understand that you can only help them to be better writers if they share their thoughts.
- The children must learn that if they do not understand the questions being asked, then they should not be shy about asking for clarification. So many young children simply want to please the teacher. They may nod or agree in response to a teacher's question or prompt when in fact they do not understand. Being confused is not a bad thing, but not asking for clarification does not work. Children cannot become better writers if they do not understand!

When responding to "I'm done!" teach the children that writers often say, "When you're done, you have just begun."

Check It Out!

Watch these DVDs of skilled teachers conferencing with young children:

Big Lessons from Small Writers by Lucy Calkins (Portsmouth, NH: Heinemann, 2005).

Learning to Confer by Shelley Harwayne (Portsmouth, NH: Heinemann, 2004).

Writing Essentials by Regie Routman (Portsmouth, NH: Heinemann, 2005).

Also, read the text of numerous conferences on Lucy Calkins' CD *Conferring with Primary Writers* (Portsmouth, NH: Heinemann, 2005).

Content Conferences

The purpose of content conferences is to help the children select a topic, to zero in on what they want to say, and to write more effectively.

Some examples of content conferences include the following:

- Finding a topic and incubating ideas. There are three key steps:

    Step 1: Have the children talk about their topic and rehearse it by sharing aloud what they are going to write (incubate ideas). They may find it helpful to try to picture their topic in their heads.

    Step 2: Have them rehearse the writing by telling you what is going to go on each page.

    Step 3: Have them begin writing (get started) before the conference ends.

- **Narrowing the topic**. Many children never really focus in on or complete a piece of writing because their topic is too broad. It is important to ask the children what aspect of their topic they are trying to highlight, and then to help them limit their writing to that point. Many children go on and on with lists of events that happened during a personal recount. Writing lists in kindergarten is important, but some children are ready for the next step. Help them to understand that more interesting writing occurs when they pick one event to elaborate on by adding interesting details rather than when they write six pages about what they do each morning before school (a list).

- **Getting the writing down on paper.** Many mini-lessons may occur here:

    o Where to start writing on the page

    o Thinking about the beginning sound

    o Rubber-banding or stretching the sounds in a word

    o Making a picture of the word in one's head—is it a long or short word?

    o Using patterns or rimes to help with spelling (for example, "If I know how to spell *sit,* then I know how to spell *hit.*")

    o Using environmental print such as the word wall or a portable word wall

Sidebar

Incubating ideas through making a picture in one's head, talking, using graphic organizers (teacher modeling), and drawing are so important. (For specific mini-lessons and activities, see Skill and Strategy Mini-Lessons 5.3: What Writers Need to Be Writers on page 103, as well as Writing Fiction or Narrative in Kindergarten and Writing Nonfiction in Kindergarten in Chapter 6.)

Teach the children to create a writing snapshot or a small-moment story.

"Ask children to write their names in the upper-left corner of the page. This orients their eyes to the left and gives them nowhere else to go with their letters but to the right." (Bennett-Armistead, Duke, and Moses 2005, 147)

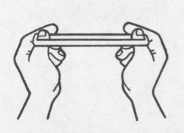

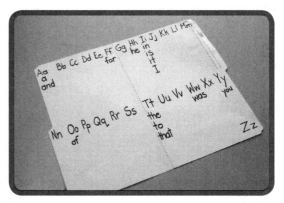

Figure 5.26

o   Using books, magazines, photos, and illustrations for ideas

o   Using a writer's notebook for ideas

o   Using punctuation

o   Making sure the print and the illustrations support one another

- **Extending the writing.** Teach the children to edit and revise by

o   adding an element (for example, a label, a word, a sentence, or details to their drawings). Explain that adding details to their drawing and/or printed text helps the reader to picture what is being said.

o   coloring a picture

o   improving spelling or adding a word(s)

o   improving word choice

o   adding punctuation

o   adding one's name to signify authorship

o   checking that what is written looks right and makes sense

I heard a woodpecker knocking on the wood.

Figure 5.27

Note all the details!

> "We can showcase children who finished a draft and then reread, adding more, and we can tell the class that those children are writing just like published authors. Some children will still whip through one piece after the next, but the truth is that no great harm results from this." (Calkins, Hartman, and White 2005, 25)

Writing Conference: Step by Step

Most writing experts agree that there are several steps to undertake in a writing conference. Lucy Calkins, Amanda Hartman, and Zoë White (2005) narrow it down to four steps: research, decide, teach, and link.

1. **Research:** This step involves observing a child who is actively engaged in writing and then conversing with him or her about the writing. This will enable you to better understand what the child is trying to write and assist you in deciding how best to support him or her. Just standing back and watching how long it takes for the child to get started and what strategies he or she uses to write and to solve problems is very helpful. Initial questions and prompts could include the following:

   o Tell me about your writing.

   o What is the picture or story about?

   o Describe your picture or your writing.

   o What are you going to do next?

   o How can I help?

   o What are you working on as a writer today?

   o What are you doing today as a writer?

   o I see that . . .

   o It looks to me like . . .

   o Let's fill out How Did I Write Today? A One-on-One Conference to see what you think about your writing. (See Reproducible 3.3: How Did I Write Today? A One-on-One Conference, on the CD)

   Provide praise, something that the child has done well. You might say something such as, "I saw you thinking about what you were going to write and then drawing your picture(s) before you added the words." Or, "I saw you copying a word off the word wall." Or, "Good for you! You used your writer's notebook to get an idea to write about."

2. **Decide:** This is probably the most difficult step of all—selecting just one teaching point or strategy to focus on with the child. Teachers often want to teach everything, but of course that is overwhelming to a child. Keep in mind you only have a few minutes for the whole conference. This is also a good place to encourage the child to self-assess. Prompt with, "What is one thing you could do better as a writer?" (See Chapter 3 for more information on assessing writing in preschool and kindergarten.)

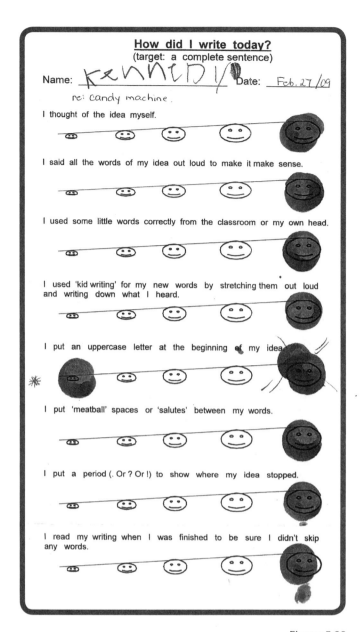

Figure 5.28

As Kennedy went over this sheet with her teacher, she realized that she needed an upper-case letter at the beginning of the sentence. Once the change was made, the teacher helped Kennedy to make the change to the self-assessment sheet.

3. **Teach:** Decide how best to teach the skill or strategy and then teach it. There are three main ways to teach during a conference: explain, demonstrate, or use guided practice. Some teachers use one or more of these strategies during a conference.

   o   Explain or simply tell. For example, if a child is looking for a word that often comes up in writing, such as the word *the,* tell the child to look on the word wall, under the letter *t.*

   o   Demonstrate, often by thinking aloud (*I do it*). This is a very powerful strategy. It involves not just telling the children, but showing them.

o Use guided practice to support the children as they write. Be their coach for a few minutes.

4. **Link:** Remind the child how important it is to keep doing this good work (smart or clever things) in future. A reminder does not guarantee that the child will follow through, but it will not hurt either!

Writing Workshop Stage 4: Author Share

According to Katie Wood Ray and Lisa Cleaveland (2004), author share (or author's chair) is not only a time for celebration but also a time for teaching. Share or have the children share something smart they tried in their writing. Prompt them with, "What's one smart or clever thing you did today as a writer?"

Allow them to share partly completed pieces as well; they may be looking for help as to where to go next.

Author Share: Step by Step

Author share should last, on average, between 10 and 15 minutes daily. Initially, some children may be shy and refuse to share, but as the year goes on and they see their friends' work being celebrated, they too will want to share.

1. Select three or four children to share. Generally, choose writers with whom you have conferenced who have done something clever in their writing that day. However, make sure that all children are provided with many opportunities to share.

2. Always ask the child's permission to share, but promote the idea of author share as being an opportunity to celebrate his or her writing. Providing the child with a toy microphone to use as a prop is often motivating!

3. On the first day, model what author share looks like by sharing something you have written. Before reading, always set the stage. Explain what the writing is about and where you got the idea.

4. Have an older buddy or an adult volunteer model a response to your model sharing. This helps the children to understand their role in author share. Have the volunteer model the *say something strategy* (Harste 1988), which encourages the children to say something about what they heard. Prompt the volunteer to go beyond such simple statements as "I like the writing" or "I like the picture" by adding details about what she or he specifically liked. Also have the volunteer model the *I remember* strategy (Harste 1988) to share something with the group that she or he remembered from the author share. *I remember* encourages the children to listen carefully to the author for something memorable.

5. Also encourage the children to ask questions of the author. Asking questions is important since some young children do not even

Author's chair promotes the use of a special chair in the classroom that only authors are allowed to sit on to share their work.

I think you used good colors in your picture.

I remember that you went for ice cream.

know what a question is. Children should always be encouraged to be kind and sensitive when responding to someone else's work. Sit beside the author to provide moral support, but behave as a member of the audience. This allows you to model responses and ask questions.

Figure 5.29

6. Do not allow the author to spend more than a second or two selecting a peer to respond to. Time is too valuable and should instead be used to share more examples of "smart or clever writing" from other children.

AUTHOR SHARE: WHAT TO HIGHLIGHT

During author share, always try to draw attention to something specific that can be determined by you and/or the child, such as

- something smart or clever the author did
- the source of the writing idea (since some children get stuck finding an idea to write about)
- the main idea of the piece

7. Since not everyone can be highlighted during each author share session, it is a good idea to spend 1 minute at the end of writing workshop encouraging each child to share his or her writing with a buddy. Having an audience of at least one makes the writing seem more purposeful for young children.

The following reproducibles referenced in Chapter 5 are available on the *Learning to Write and Loving It!* CD:

Reproducible 5.1: Keeping a Writer's Notebook

Reproducible 5.2: Wall Stories

Reproducible 3.3: How Did I Write Today? A One-on-One Conference?

Reproducible 3.4: I Can Write and Draw.

Reproducible 3.8: Look at Me. I Am a Writer! Self-Assessment

Why Does Writing Workshop Get Results?

Writing workshop is an important part of a comprehensive literacy program. It works because the four stages are crucial for scaffolding learning: teaching through mini-lessons based on children's needs, providing many opportunities for engaged writing on a daily basis, conferencing one-on-one or in groups (for the purposes of teaching and assessment), and celebrating writing. Writing workshop provides an effective and secure daily routine for you and the children to improve their writing. It supports the reading–writing connection. Ultimately it works because, as Katie Wood Ray and Lisa Cleaveland explain, "With lots of teaching surrounding them, we believe young children who have time to write every day can grow in all the important ways anyone who writes every day will grow. We believe, with lots of teaching, they can develop important understandings about what it means to write, useful strategies to guide them in the process of writing, a sense of form and genre and craft in their written texts, and a good beginning control of the conventions of written language" (2004, ix). It also works because with managed choice and lots of successful writing experiences, children develop both the will and the skill to write. They see themselves as writers!

Chapter 6

Writing in Fiction and Nonfiction Genres

Katie Wood Ray and Matt Glover (2008) describe *genres* as the various kinds of writing in the world that are written for different purposes and different audiences. Understanding the term *genre* and the different genres is important as it gives the writer a sense of why he or she is writing and for whom. Even very young children can begin to understand that there is a difference between a story (fiction) and nonfiction. They learn that some texts are functional, such as a list or a survey, and some are purely for enjoyment, such as a poem. They can also learn that they are able to write in several different genres using different formats within a larger genre. For example, a how-to book (procedural writing) and an *All About . . .* (informational) *Book* (see page 172) have very different formats from an alphabet book, and yet all are examples of nonfiction writing.

Figure 6.1

Often the terms *informational text* and *nonfiction* are used interchangeably. However, according to Nell Duke and Susan Bennett-Armistead (2003) informational text and nonfiction are not the same. Nonfiction includes any text that is factual, and informational text is a very important type of nonfiction. Informational text has a specific purpose: to convey information about the natural or social world. Therefore, procedural text such as how to make a gingerbread house is nonfiction writing, but it is not informational text.

To support young children in writing in different genres, you have to expose them to the genres over and over through read-alouds and shared readings. But their understanding does not simply come from listening to the text. Point out to the children, often through think-alouds, the different genres and their characteristics or features. What makes fiction fiction? What makes a poem a poem? Work with the children to write in the genre being taught.

Genre mini-lessons when reading to and writing with the children include
- what the genre is
- why we use it
- what the features of the genre are
- how the children might use it in their writing

I think...

As the year progresses, teach children to predict the genre based on the book cover, title and often author. This is a great pre-read-aloud activity.

Recounts are written to retell events or true experiences, with the purpose of either informing or entertaining—or both! (Buss and Karnowski 2002, 6).

The children then need to attempt these genres through guided and independent writing.

Writing in early childhood involves three main genres: fiction (narrative), nonfiction (including informational text), and poetry/songs. Examples of specific mini-lessons and activities to support all three areas are provided in this chapter as well as in Chapters 7, 8, and 9.

Writing Fiction or Narrative

Fiction or narrative writing tells a story. This form of writing includes a plot, characters, and a setting. Although there is a sequence—beginning, middle, and some form of resolution or ending—narrative writing involves more than describing a sequence of events. The research indicates that children first learn what a story is by listening to stories read aloud by others. By the time children enter kindergarten, most have already developed a concept of what a story is (Tompkins 2000). But kindergarteners rarely write a story. Instead, they frequently write a series of events—described as a personal recount—which they consider to be a story. A personal recount, such as the writing sample shown in Figure 6.2, is not narrative writing. It is nonfiction.

Children love to write about themselves. On their way to writing fiction, most children will write a great number of personal recounts. Teachers need to celebrate this form of nonfiction writing as it is a precursor to true story writing.

For more information on personal recounts, see Mini-Lessons to Support Organization in Writing Personal Recounts and Developing Storylines, beginning on page 150.

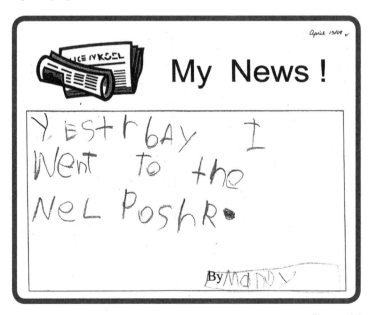

Figure 6.2

Yesterday I went to the nail polisher.
A personal recount is a form of nonfiction writing.
It is not a story.

Story comes to life through word choice, voice, ideas, organization, and sentence fluency (see The Traits Defined on page 71 of Chapter 3). In preschool and kindergarten, focus fiction mini-lessons on ideas (including details), organization, and word choice. Voice develops when the children care about the writing and are allowed to write about topics of their own choosing. Voice will also be evident in the children's drawings, letters or notes, and in pieces written from the perspective of a person, a place, or a thing.

Figure 6.3
The face says it all!

> Voice is the heart and soul of the individual writer. Voice is what captures the reader. It makes the reader "feel."

Writing fiction is very demanding. In fact, it is the most difficult genre to write. The main goal in preschool and kindergarten should be to help all children fall in love with story and develop an understanding of story structure. This is the initial scaffolding they need to prepare them to write story.

Mini-Lessons and Activities to Support Writing Fiction or Narrative

Children love to hear fiction read to them (Graves 1994). They love a good story and should hear many of them. These stories should include fairy tales and folk tales, legends, fantasies, and realistic stories. Support the children's understanding of story structures by using graphic organizers to help them retell a story (see Reproducible 6.10: Story Map 1; Reproducible 6.11: Story Map 2; and Reproducible 6.12: Story

Board, on the *Learning to Write and Loving It!* CD ROM); by getting the children to act out a story; and by using pictures, a flannel board, or puppets to retell a story. Shared writing can generate both fiction (see Wall Stories, page 140) and nonfiction (see Mini-Lessons and Activities to Support Writing Nonfiction, beginning on page 150).

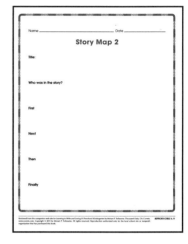

Helping children to create their own books or even a simple Reader's Theatre script for them to act out just makes sense. Also, encourage the children to retell a folk tale or a fairy tale and to create their own retelling as a book (see Figure 6.4).

Figure 6.4
This is a 5-year-old's fractured fairy tale. It went on for 16 pages.

Reading and creating wordless (and nearly wordless) picture books and traditional picture books (those with some text on most pages) are powerful ways to teach the concept of story.

Using Traditional and Wordless Picture Books to Teach Story Writing

Reading and discussing picture books helps to develop a love of story and helps the children to understand storyline or story structure. *Picture book* typically refers to any book that has more illustrations than text. The pictures and the text work together to support comprehension (for example, predict, determine main idea, detect sequence, note cause and effect, infer) and vocabulary development.

Wordless picture books (books without words or just an occasional word or phrase) are interpreted entirely through a sequence of illustrations. As children follow the pictures, they verbalize the action in their own words, a process that also builds vocabulary, comprehension, and story structure. In wordless picture books, the children really become the storytellers and are much freer to interpret the stories in their own way. Wordless picture books are excellent to use with all children, especially children who are just learning English and those struggling with decoding and/or comprehension. They support the development of both vocabulary and grammar through conversation. Using wordless picture books allows all children, no matter what their vocabulary or decoding skills, to read and discuss the same book.

Promoting the use of wordless picture books at home is a worthwhile endeavor. Parents/caregivers should be encouraged to help their children tell the story in their own language and/or in English. Families need support in understanding how best to use these books without words. (See Reproducible 6.4: Use Wordless Picture Books With Your Child, on the CD.)

It is important to note that there are two categories of wordless picture books: those that tell stories and those organized around a concept. Concept books focus on a specific topic, such as the alphabet, numbers, or colors. All picture books support children in developing visual literacy—their ability to read the pictures and illustrations.

Check It Out!

The National Center for Family Literacy (www .famlit.org) is a great online resource that will help you support parents/caregivers in the development of their child's literacy. See "Talking About Wordless Picture Books: A Tutor Strategy Supporting English Language Learners" (2006; available at www.famlit.org/ pdf/talking-about-wordless-picture-books.pdf).

Use picture books to develop visual literacy.

MINI-LESSONS 6.1

Using Traditional Picture Books to Teach Story Writing

1. **Do a picture walk of a book cover and make predictions.**

   o Begin by reading and discussing many traditional picture books over many days with a focus on what the pictures tell the reader. Each time, start by sharing the title and possibly the author's name. Have the children tell you all about the picture or illustration on the cover. Predict what the story will be about. If necessary, prompt children with

   o Who will be in the story?

   o Where do you think the story will take place?

   o Have you been to a place that looks like this?

   o What do you think will happen? Often the title gives you a hint (for example, *How a House Is Built* by Gail Gibbons).

   Write down some of the predictions as a shared writing.

   o Next, do a picture walk through the book. Have the children again predict the storyline from page to page. Specifically analyze the characters on each page: their facial expressions, their actions. Focus on what the details in the illustrations or pictures tell about the story. Help the children to see how the details bring the story to life.

2. **Read the story and discuss. Go back to a few of the pictures and revisit the children's predictions. Were they correct?**

3. **Reread some of the pages using dialogic or interactive read-alouds.**

4. **Use story cards to help the children understand the idea of sequencing a story. Reproduce a few of the key pictures from the story that help the children to understand the story. Make sure you have pictures from the beginning, middle, and end of the story. Have the children take turns sequencing the story cards and checking them against the original book. Are they correct? Use sequencing terminology or transition words and phrases, such as *in the beginning, first, then, next, after, finally, in the end.***

5. Retell the story using a story map (see Reproducible 6.10: Story Map 1; Reproducible 6.11: Story Map 2; and Reproducible 6.12: Story Board, on the CD).

6. Create a story board of the book or act out the story. Use the completed story map from step 5 as a guide.

Follow these steps to teach the children how to create a story board:

- Draw a number of squares (six to eight) on a blank sheet of chart paper.

- Think aloud as you sketch pictures in each box that remind you of important events from the story.

- Orally retell the story using the story board.

- Write a caption, a sentence, or even a word under each picture.

7. Change the ending. Children love to rewrite the story by changing the ending. Not all endings have to be happy as they generally are in picture books.

MINI-LESSONS 6.2
Using Wordless Picture Books to Teach Story Writing

1. Introduce a wordless picture book. Follow steps 1 through 6 of the previous mini-lessons. Suggested prompts to discuss the book include the following:

    ○ The title is _____. What do you predict the story will be about?

    ○ Tell me about this picture; what is happening in this picture?

    ○ How do you think the characters in this picture feel? Why do you think that? How would you be feeling?

    ○ If this page had words, what would they be?

    ○ What do you think the character is saying? What would you be saying if you were the character?

A great benefit of the wordless books is that the pictures provide the scaffolding that helps young authors to begin writing. This makes getting started easy.

2. Create a line of text to go with each page to support the storyline. Use modeled or shared writing. Create simple text using high-frequency words to make it easier for the children to reread. Consider writing the text on large sticky notes and attaching them to the pictures in the book.

3. Reread the shared writing of the wordless picture book.

4. Create another version of the story using dialogue bubbles. Children love it when dialogue bubbles are used to show what the characters are thinking, feeling, and saying. This is a great activity as it helps the children to understand at least subconsciously that when they are reading, whether it is words or pictures only, they can interpret or make sense of the text in more than one way. The same is true, of course, of watching movies or listening to music.

Figure 6.5

Source: Mayer (2003).

Use speech or dialogue bubbles to show a character's thoughts, feelings, or words.

5. Copy the pictures from wordless picture books and paste them on letter-size sheets of cardboard, leaving plenty of room for the children to write. Laminate each page and bind them in book form using rings. The children can then take turns writing the text using dry-erase markers. A photocopy of each story can be made before the pages are wiped clean. Alternatively, the pictures could be copied and made into individual

booklets for each child. Each child would then have his or her own wordless picture book and story to share with the class and to take home.

6. Brainstorm with the children topics for their own picture books. Write down the topics as a shared writing (see Chapter 4, page 82).

7. Have the children create their own picture books. Use six or eight sheets of blank, letter-sized paper stapled together or purchase prestapled booklets. The books may start out as wordless picture books in which the children simply draw the pictures and then tell the story orally. Alternatively, you might scribe the story for some emergent writers. More advanced writers may choose to draw pictures and then label each with a word, a phrase, or a sentence. This activity leads the children from oral to written storytelling.

GREAT TRADITIONAL AND WORDLESS STORYBOOKS

Friendship

Briggs, Raymond. *The Snowman*. New York: Penguin Group (USA) Incorporated, 2002.

Carle, Eric. *Do You Want to Be My Friend?* New York: Penguin Group (USA) Incorporated, 2002.

Mayer, Mercer. *A Boy, a Dog, a Frog and a Friend*. New York: Penguin Group (USA) Incorporated, 2003.

Mayer, Mercer. *Frog on His Own*. New York: Penguin Group (USA) Incorporated, 2003.

Mayer, Mercer. *One Frog Too Many*. New York: Penguin Group (USA) Incorporated, 2003.

McDonnell, Patrick. *South*. London, England: Little Brown & Company, 2008.

Rogers, Gregory. *The Boy, the Bear, the Baron, the Bard*. New York: Roaring Brook Press, 2007.

Rohmann, Eric. *My Friend Rabbit*. New York: Square Fish, 2007.

Wiesner, David. *Sector 7*. Boston: Houghton Mifflin Harcourt Publishing Company, 1999.

Family

Alborough, Jez. *Hug*. Somerville, MA: Candlewick Press, 2005.

Baker, Jeannie. *Home*. Toronto, ON: HarperCollins Canada, Limited, 2004.

"By writing down the stories that children compose as they 'read' wordless books, then assisting these young authors in turning their stories into books, teachers nourish children's sense of themselves as readers and writers." (Neuman, Copple, and Bredekamp 2000, 54)

Check It Out!

See the lesson "Draw a Story: Stepping From Pictures to Writing" at ReadWriteThink (www.readwritethink.org). In this activity, children draw a series of pictures that tell a simple sequential story. They read their story to others, transcribe their oral story into writing, and create an accordion book with drawings on the front side and writing on the back. Also check out this article from the United Kingdom Literacy Association titled "Storytelling: The Missing Link in Story Writing" by Teresa Cremin (2002). Go to www.ukla.org, "Spotlight on Writing in the Early Years."

McCully, Emily Arnold. *First Snow*. Toronto, ON: HarperCollins Canada, Limited, 2003.

Ormerod, Jan. *Sunshine*. London, England: Frances Lincoln Limited, 2005.

Turkle, Brinton. *Deep in the Forest*. New York: Penguin Group (USA) Incorporated, 1992.

Social Skills (Sharing, Bullying, Behavior)

dePaola, Tomie. *The Knight and the Dragon*. New York: Penguin Group (USA) Incorporated, 2002.

Dewey, Ariane. *The Last Laugh*. New York: Penguin Group (USA) Incorporated, 2006.

McGrath, Meggan. *My Grapes*. Toronto, ON: Scholastic Canada, Limited, 2001.

Popov, Nikolai. *Why?* New York: North-South Books, Incorporated, 1998.

Routines (Bedtime, Getting Dressed)

Geisert, Arther. *Hogwash*. Boston: Houghton Mifflin Harcourt Publishing Company, 2008.

Ormerod, Jan. *Moonlight*. London, England: Frances Lincoln Limited, 2005

Rathmann, Peggy. *Good Night, Gorilla*. New York: Penguin Group (USA) Incorporated, 2004.

Schories, Pat. *Breakfast for Jack*. Honesdale, PA: Boyds Mills Press, 2004.

Wiesner, David. *Free Fall*. Toronto, ON: HarperCollins Canada, Limited, 2008.

Wiesner, David. *Tuesday*. Boston: Houghton Mifflin Harcourt Publishing Company, 1997.

Humorous

Hutchins, Pat. *Rosie's Walk*. New York: Simon & Schuster Children's Publishing, 1998.

Yoo, Tae-Eun. *The Little Red Fish*. New York: Penguin Group (USA) Incorporated, 2007.

Stories (General)

Alborough, Jez. *Tall*. Somerville, MA: Candlewick Press, 2007.

Aliki. Tabby: *A Story in Pictures*. Toronto, ON: HarperCollins Canada, Limited, 1995.

Anno, Mitsumasa. *Anno's Journey*. New York: Penguin Group (USA) Incorporated, 2002.

Baker, Jeannie. *Window*. New York: HarperCollins Publishers, 1991.

Bang, Molly. *The Grey Lady and the Strawberry Snatcher*. New York: Simon & Schuster Children's Publishing , 1996.

Banyai, Istvan. *Re-Zoom*. New York: Penguin Group (USA) Incorporated, 1998.

Check It Out!

Check out these wonderful wordless picture books by Canadian authors:

Finding Kate's Shoes by Erica Dornbusch (Toronto, ON: Annick Press Limited, 2001).

Picturescape by Elisa Gutierrez (Vancouver: Simply Read Books, 2005).

Under the Sea by Liza Baker (Toronto, ON: HarperCollins Canada, Limited, 2003).

Zoe's Sunny Day by Barbara Reid (Toronto, ON: Scholastic Canada, Limited, 2002).

Banyai, Istvan. *Zoom*. New York: Penguin Group (USA) Incorporated, 1998.

Blake, Quentin. *Clown*. New York: Henry Holt & Company, 1998.

Crews, Donald. *Truck Board Book*. New York: HarperCollins Publishers, 1997.

Day, Alexandra. *Carl's Masquerade*. New York: Farrar, Straus & Giroux, 1992.

Day, Alexandra. *You're a Good Dog, Carl*. New York: Square Fish, 2007.

Dematons, Charlotte. *Yellow Balloon*. Honesdale, PA: Boyds Mills Press, 2004.

dePaola, Tomie. *Pancakes for Breakfast*. New York: Houghton Mifflin Harcourt Trade & Reference Publishers, 1978.

Edens, Cooper. *The Christmas We Moved to the Barn*. Toronto, ON: HarperCollins Canada, Limited, 1997.

Enderle, Judith Ross. *Six Creepy Sheep*. Honesdale, PA: Boyds Mills Press, 2003.

Faller, Regis. *Polo: The Runaway Book*. New York: Henry Holt & Company, 2007.

Faller, Regis. *The Adventures of Polo*. New York: Henry Holt & Company, 2006.

Fleischman, Paul. *Sidewalk Circus*. Somerville, MA: Candlewick Press, 2004.

Geisert, Arther. *Oops*. Boston: Houghton Mifflin Harcourt Publishing Company, 2006.

Guilloppé, Antoine. *One Scary Night*. Jericho, NY: ibooks, Incorporated, 2005.

Hutchins, Pat. *Changes, Changes*. New York: Simon & Schuster Children's Publishing, 1987.

Jenkins, Steve. *Looking Down*. Boston: Houghton Mifflin Harcourt Publishing Company, 2003.

Keats, Ezra Jack. *Clementina's Cactus*. New York: Penguin Group (USA) Incorporated, 1999.

Krahn, Fernando. *Amanda and the Mysterious Carpet*. Boston: Houghton Mifflin Harcourt Publishing Company, 1985.

Lee, Suzy. *Wave*. San Francisco: Chronicle Books LLC, 2008.

Lehman, Barbara. *Museum Trip*. Boston: Houghton Mifflin Harcourt Publishing Company, 2006.

Lehman, Barbara. *Rainstorm*. Boston: Houghton Mifflin Harcourt Publishing Company, 2007.

Lehman, Barbara. *The Red Book*. Boston: Houghton Mifflin Harcourt Publishing Company, 2004.

Lehman, Barbara. *Trainstop*. Boston: Houghton Mifflin Harcourt Publishing Company, 2008.

Liu, Jae Soo. *Yellow Umbrella*. La Jolla, CA: Kane/Miller Book Publishers, Incorporated, 2006.

Mayer, Mercer. *A Boy, a Dog and a Frog*. New York: Penguin Group (USA) Incorporated, 2003.

Mayer, Mercer. *Frog Goes to Dinner*. New York: Penguin Group (USA) Incorporated, 2003.

Mayer, Mercer. *Frog, Where Are You?* New York: Penguin Group (USA) Incorporated, 2003.

McCully, Emily Arnold. *Picnic*. Toronto, ON: HarperCollins Canada, Limited, 2003.

McCully, Emily Arnold. *School*. Toronto, ON: HarperCollins Canada, Limited, 2005.

Polhemus, Coleman. *The Crocodile Blues*. Somerville, MA: Candlewick Press, 2007.

Rohmann, Eric. *Time Flies*. New York: Random House Children's Books, 1997.

Schories, Pat. *Jack and the Missing Piece*. Honesdale, PA: Boyds Mills Press, 2004.

Schories, Pat. *Jack and the Night Visitors*. Honesdale, PA: Boyds Mills Press, 2006.

Schories, Pat. *Jack Wants a Snack*. Honesdale, PA: Boyds Mills Press, 2008.

Schubert, Dieter. *Where's My Monkey?* Honesdale, PA: Boyds Mills Press, 2004.

Sis, Peter. *Dinosaur!* Toronto, ON: HarperCollins Canada, Limited, 2000.

Sis, Peter. *Ship Ahoy!* Toronto, ON: HarperCollins Canada, Limited, 1999.

Sis, Peter. *Trucks, Trucks, Trucks*. Toronto, ON: HarperCollins Canada, Limited, 2004.

Van Ommen, Sylvia. *The Surprise*. Honesdale, PA: Boyds Mills Press, 2007.

Weitzman, Jacqueline Preiss. *You Can't Take a Balloon into the Metropolitan Museum*. New York: Penguin Group (USA) Incorporated, 2001.

Wiesner, David. *Flotsam*. New York: Houghton Mifflin Harcourt Trade & Reference Publishers, 2006.

Wildsmith, Brian. *The Apple Bird*. Don Mills, ON: Oxford University Press, 1983.

Yum, Hyewon. *Last Night*. New York: Farrar, Straus & Giroux, 2008.

For nonfiction wordless concept books, see page 155.

Wall Stories

Wall stories are typically 8- to 12-page stories created as a shared or interactive writing (see pages 82–86 of Chapter 4). They are displayed on the wall, a form of environmental print, for children to revisit as they read around the room. Additionally, wall stories can be used as a center activity and when taken down can be made into class Big Books.

Wall stories are based on the class's shared experiences. First, the children have to have an experience about which they can write and draw, such as a field trip, their observations of the life cycle of a classroom butterfly that emerges from the chrysalis, or the story of a sick classroom pet that visits a veterinarian's office. The experience may also be the retelling of a read-aloud or a movie they have watched together. Or, it may be an innovation of a story via changes to the character(s), the setting, some of the events, or even the ending. Children love it when they, through their names or pictures, become part of the story.

Use a familiar pattern or refrain from books such as *Rosie's Walk* by Pat Hutchins or *Brown Bear* by Bill Martin Jr. and Eric Carle. Innovate by changing the animal *(Black stallion, Black stallion, Who do you see?)* or adding the children's names.

Other Eric Carle books that lend themselves to innovations are *The Very Grouchy Ladybug, The Very Hungry Caterpillar,* and *The Very Busy Spider.* Stories that have patterns or repeated phrases also work well.

WINDOW ON THE CLASSROOM

One very creative teacher did a story innovation on Brian Wildsmith's Cat on the Mat. *Her shared writing innovations and letter home encouraging the children's families to participate follow.*

> **Magic Creatures on the Mat**
>
> Long, silly S.S. sat on the ugly, blue mat.
> Tricky, black Elizabeth sat on the ugly blue mat.
> Hairy, brown Spook sat on the ugly blue mat.
> Little, striped Baby sat on the ugly blue mat.
> Pretty, slithery Sara sat on the ugly blue mat.
> S - S - S - S !!   .
> Long, silly S.S. sat on the ugly, blue mat.

Now, it's your turn! Surprise us!

Figure 6.6

Magic creatures in this teacher's class are stuffed animals whom the children have named. They also write to the magic creatures (see "Writing Letters to magic creatures" on page 222 of Chapter 9).

> Kids on the Table
>
> Shandy jumped on the table.
> Ben jumped on the table.
> Rachel jumped on the table.
> Brandyn jumped on the table.
> Kristen jumped on the table.
> STOP!!!
>
> Shandy sat on a chair!

Figure 6.7

"These are rewritings we did of *Cat on the Mat*. I also made it into a magnetic story, which the children love to move around (words and pictures). You should see the rewriting (innovations) sent from home, done with me at school, and done independently! This story often helps the emerging readers/writers really take off!!"—Clarice Bloomenthal

Dear family,

We enjoyed reading Cat on the Mat *by Brian Wildsmith. It is a simple story that begins "The cat sat on the mat" and then follows using the same pattern with the dog, the goat, the cow, the elephant, and then Ssspsstt! And finally the story ends with the first line being repeated. Have your child read it to you. On the back of this letter are three original versions we had fun writing. We changed the characters, the action word (verb), and/or the location (noun). In one version we added some interesting words (adjectives) to tell about the characters. Have fun rewriting your own version at home using pets, family members' names, or familiar objects. Do several and send them to school for us to enjoy. Add illustrations and color too! Do the printing for your child if needed. Try this with Home Reading books too. It's good practice for spelling, reading, and writing.*

Mrs. Bloomenthal

Check It Out!

Story innovation is a way for children to enjoy talking, writing, and reading and develop vocabulary with support. The new text is easy to read because of the familiar patterns from the original story. See "Teaching Tips Story Innovation: An Instructional Strategy for Developing Vocabulary and Fluency" by Priscilla L. Griffith and Jiening Ruan (*The Reading Teacher* (December 2007): 334–38).

Wall-story text is supported with real photos (often of the children), pictures cut out of magazines, and/or illustrations drawn by both you and/or the children. (It is important to note that although wall stories have the word story in the title, they may also be a retelling of a nonfiction text or experience.) The real strength of the wall story is that the text is meaningful to the children since it is based on a shared experience. This makes the text inviting and engaging. The children want to revisit it often.

Wall stories serve many purposes. As the children experience shared, independent, and small-group reading as well as modeled, shared, and interactive writing, they develop their knowledge of the concepts of print (including punctuation), high-frequency words, letters, letter–sound correspondence and word-family knowledge, phonological awareness, and increased fluency. Wall stories can also be used to develop fine motor skills as the children develop their ability to sketch and write. The ability of the wall story to encourage the use of environmental print (including the word wall) is an additional strength. Just having environmental print around the room does not guarantee its use. The weakest literacy learners typically regard environmental print as wallpaper and rarely use it. But having the children make use of it through engaging activities that promote reading and writing is a real strength of the wall story.

There are two main types of wall stories: those that support writing by having the children sketch the illustrations that go with the stories and those that have the children write or retell the stories using letters, words, and punctuation.

MINI-LESSONS 6.3

Developing Wall Stories Mainly Through Children Sketching

The easiest wall story to undertake at the beginning of the year involves the children creating the pictures to accompany a story. A read-aloud works well.

1. After the read-aloud, create the script of a retelling with and/or for the children. The retelling may be a modeled writing if you want to have control over the difficulty level and quantity of text. If the wall story is going to be used by the children for reading around the room and/or center activities, then the text needs to be written at a just-right level. It cannot be too difficult or the children will not experience success, but it must not be too easy or the children will learn very little. There must be both challenges and supports to scaffold the learning. Too difficult or too easy means that the children will not remain engaged in the activity.

2. How you plan to use the wall story after it is written will affect how it is written and who does the actual writing. An interactive writing session in which the children share the pen is one approach. But if the plan is to create a wall story that is going to be revisited often on the wall or as a class Big Book, then legibility is extremely important. Preschool and kindergarten children need to see letters printed correctly, spaces between words, capitalization, and punctuation where appropriate. Emerging literacy learners also need to see consistent placement of print

Occasionally, you may choose to have the wall story already up in the classroom when the children arrive. Allow them time to work together to make sense of what it says. What excitement there is when a new wall story simply appears!

Teachers who choose to create the text by sharing the pen with the children find that using opaque tape allows the children to be successfully involved in the actual writing of the wall story. When a child makes a mistake by writing a wrong letter or writing some letters backwards, the tape covers the errors and provides space for corrections to be made.

on the page and strong print–picture matching. In other words, the picture has to provide very strong support to help the children decipher the print. (For example, if you are using an innovation on Eric Carle's *The Very Hungry Caterpillar,* you might have a picture of many apples and the sentence under the picture would read, *On Monday we ate apples.* The next page might show grapes and read, *On Tuesday we ate grapes.*)

3. After the text is created, assign illustrations for each panel or give the children the choice as to what panel of the story they want to illustrate.

4. When the illustrations are complete, ask the children to share their illustrations and to show where in the sequence of the wall story each illustration would fit. Prompt children by asking, "Does your picture belong near the beginning, the middle, or the end of the story?"

5. Not all of the illustrations can be used for each wall story; however, the illustrations that are not included in the wall story can be displayed elsewhere in the classroom. They may also be sent home with a note to families asking them to have their children retell the story using the illustration from school as a stimulus. Individual copies of wall stories may also be sent home. (See Reproducible 5.2: Wall Stories, on the CD.)

MINI-LESSONS 6.4

Developing Wall Stories Mainly Through Children Writing

At the beginning of the year, it is best to create the wall story as a modeled writing experience with the children creating the illustrations. As the year goes on and as the children's writing skill levels and enthusiasm for writing increase, involve them more in creating the text using paper and pencil, markers, or a computer and/or an interactive whiteboard.

1. Provide photos of the children in action (for example, building a snow fort, getting dressed in winter, or enjoying a mud experience) or illustrations taken from

magazines or copied from a wordless picture book. Have the children generate the text through modeled, shared, and/or interactive writing.

Figure 6.8

Figure 6.9

A personal recount: getting dressed
for winter recess!

If the wall story is created using a computer and/or an interactive whiteboard (such as a SMART Board), then it can be printed for each child to put in his or her individual book box of familiar text for revisiting. If the children have access to an iMac computer, the iMovies program will allow them to create movies using photos, short video clips, their own voices, and Garage Band music to create stories connected to important ideas or events. This is a perfect way to extend wall stories.

Use iMovies on an iMac to extend a wall story.

Check It Out!

- Gareth Lancaster has published numerous fun poems for children, including "I'm in Love with Mud" (see his website www.fizzyfunnyfuzzy.com).

- "Spring Will Be Pretty" by Dave Crawley is a wonderful poem about mud in the springtime. It can be found in *Rolling in the Aisles: A Collection of Laugh-Out-Loud Poems* edited by Bruce Lansky (Minnetonka, MN: Meadowbrook Creations, 2004). The poem is also available at http://www.poetry4kids.com/modules.php?name=News&file=article&sid=67.

2. Once the wall story has been used for several weeks for shared reading and reading around the room, then it can be made into a class Big Book to be used for the rest of the year or perhaps years to come. What a great way to develop reading fluency!

WINDOW ON THE CLASSROOM

Here is how one very creative kindergarten teacher extended a wall story:

We had been talking about springtime and how rainy and muddy it was. I used two short read-alouds to stimulate our mud conversation. The first was Mud *by Mary Lyn Ray (illustrated by Lauren Stringer), which has wonderful language ("Winter will Squish Squck Sop Splat Slurp melt in mud" and "Gooey, gloppy, mucky, magnificent mud"). The second book, also titled* Mud, *is by Wendy Cheyette Lewison (illustrated by Bill Basso). It is a simple text but has wonderful rhyme ("Mud in the puddle. Mud on the shoe. Mud on the socks. Mud on you!"), which was the language we adapted to our version of mud. The next day I read the poem "I'm in Love with Mud" by Gareth Lancaster (2003) as a modeled read. I took a smaller section of the poem (four lines) and rewrote them on my large easel, accompanied by picture clues. Over a number of days that followed, lessons addressed a variety of concepts about print (all focused on the same piece of text) coupled with a shared reading of the text each time. Each day I added another section to the poem. We would start by rereading what was familiar, and then move to the new page that would have a couple of changes (accompanied by picture clues). The actual framework of the poem remained the same, however.*

Photos that were taken when we had once made "mud" were connected to the actual writing of our own version of the mud story. The children helped decide exactly what would be said on each page (wall story created together) in which they made an obvious connection to the original poem. But they were also helped by the use of interactive writing based on, for example, their own letter–sound knowledge, high-frequency word knowledge, spacing, and what they learned from revisiting the text a number of times (i.e., knowing where to access in the poem such challenging words as mouth and nose). We then took the wall story and made it into a movie on the iMac computer for all to see.

Figure 6.10

Teacher Testimonial

A very talented kindergarten teacher, Heather Jelley, uses the wall stories frequently and very successfully with her 3-, 4-, and 5-year olds. "The power of wall stories cannot be overlooked in the gradual release of responsibility. As we take the time to focus on modeled and shared reading and writing, the wall story becomes a tool to connect children to what writers do. Returning again and again to the idea of helping children make the connection from "If I can think it, I can say it" to "If I can think it, I can say it, and it can be written down (to be read again at another time)," the wall story becomes the perfect vehicle.

Wall stories are used to intentionally focus on unraveling the mystery of what writers do. My wall stories begin with a photo or picture connected to an idea taken from the reading of a text (modeled, shared, or read aloud) or from a connection to some inquiry in science or math. I begin with the question, "What are you thinking?" The children are given lots of time to think/pair/share ideas. The teacher and/or the children will then write the script.

The focus of instruction can extend from simply understanding that an idea can be written down (say your idea and say it again so you are absolutely clear what you are going to write before you begin), to addressing numerous concepts of print, to a focus on high frequency words. Students help with developing the idea (shared) and then can help

- Find poems about rocks, sand, and mud, at http://www.canteach.ca/elementary/songspoems81.html.

- The children will love to hear you read the story *Mud Puddle* by Robert Munsch (Toronto, ON: Annick Press, 1996), or they can hear the author reading it aloud at his website (www.robertmunsch.com). Munsch's website also features art sent to him by children from all over the world, as well as poems he has written back to children.

- Children also love having their own copy of a wall story to take home and share with their families. (See Reproducible 5.2: Wall Stories, on the CD.) Involve the children in creating their own mini-wall stories by adding words, letters, punctuation, and drawings.

interactively with the writing. Wall stories provide another familiar read for children throughout the day when they engage in reading around the room (even in the restroom!).

Cody had to go so badly.

Figure 6.11

(When he was done...) he washed with soap.

Figure 6.12

He is drying his hands.

Figure 6.13

This wall story was created very early in the year when the teacher had the children talk about what to do when they go to the restroom. The message was constructed by the children. The story was posted in the restroom for all to revisit, whether looking at the pictures and/or the text. The smudged writing indicates that it was touched by "wet hands" in the restroom!

Writing Nonfiction

Most people, no matter what age, write nonfiction daily, but very few are frequent writers of fiction. Nonfiction writing is often functional; typically, it helps us in life. Young children often naturally turn to nonfiction writing, so it makes sense to teach nonfiction writing in kindergarten.

Young children often write labels, lists, personal recounts, notes, letters, cards, messages, memos, invitations, news items, reports, books, entries in their writer's notebook, plans, tickets, surveys, and interviews. These examples of nonfiction writing exemplify different text structures (for example, a letter has a different structure than a label, a memo, or an invitation). Some of these forms of nonfiction writing, such as writing a report or creating and conducting a survey or an interview, involve more creativity and composing when compared to making a list.

Nonfiction writing supports writing in social studies and science (writing across the curriculum) and supports reading and writing to learn curriculum content. Finally, nonfiction writing is typically much easier to write than fiction. So why not start with nonfiction and promote writing success early?

Thomas Newkirk and many other researchers have provided compelling evidence that children not only can write non-narrative text, including informational text such as lists, but they often do so quite naturally, spontaneously, and even *before* writing narrative text (Duke and Bennett-Armistead 2003).

Mini-Lessons and Activities to Support Writing Nonfiction

The work of Katie Wood Ray and Matt Glover (2008) among others promote children writing their own books. Emerging and early writers understand and appreciate purposeful writing. Provide them with engaging mini-lessons and activities to support not only the writing of books and personal recounts but also lists, plans, messages, invitations, surveys, and other forms of nonfiction. This will enhance their understanding of the nonfiction genre. They see that the writing is really purposeful!

Supporting Organization in Writing Personal Recounts and Developing Storylines

Children have to understand that when writing a story, the events have to follow a specific sequence, otherwise the story will not make sense. This is organization. Help the children to understand this concept by creating personal recounts, which are not really stories although many young children think that they are.

When we invite students to make something with writing instead of just asking them to write, they go about their work differently.

(Ray, 2004, 15)

Providing children with many oral language activities that involve following simple directions using terms such as *first*, *then*, *next*, and *last* helps scaffold the writing of personal recounts.

MINI-LESSONS 6.5

Using Everyday Experiences (Personal Recounts)

1. Prompt the children by creating story boards of personal recounts using their own experiences.

2. Sketch an illustration on each page and write one line of text under each illustration. Prompt the children with such themes as

   o getting ready for kindergarten

   o getting ready for bed

   o what they do on Saturday morning

   o how they help their dad, grandma, a friend . . .

Personal recounts for some children may turn into stories.

MINI-LESSONS 6.6

Using a Photo or Postcard to Prompt Writing

1. **Bring in a photo or a postcard showing somewhere you have visited. Talk about the image. Share**

   o   where the photo was taken

   o   who is in the photo

   o   what the people in the photo are doing

   o   how they look (happy, sad, confused . . .)

   o   when you visited the place where the photo was taken

   o   who you went there with

   o   why you went there

   o   what you did there

   o   what you think about the visit

   o   what happened before the photo was taken

   o   what happened after the photo was taken

2. **Create sketches to depict the experience. Think aloud as you sketch. Use transition words and phrases to indicate sequence. Write a caption, a word, or a sentence under each sketch (for example, *First* I found my skates. *Then* we walked to the rink . . .).**

3. **Have each of the children bring in a photo or postcard depicting somewhere they have been. It can be a photo of a grocery store, a park, or an event at grandma's house. It does not have to be a visit to an exotic place (see Reproducible 6.5: Writing From a Photo or Postcard, on the CD). Have the children talk about their photo or postcard. If necessary, use the prompts above to stimulate discussion. Encourage other children to ask questions about the photos or postcards of their classmates.**

The interactive whiteboard is a tool that often helps engage children in writing. By accessing pictures from the gallery, inserting pictures of a favorite topic downloaded from clip art, or inserting onto a notebook page a photo of the child engaged in a favorite activity in the classroom or at home, a teacher can make the activity meaningful to the child, thereby activating the engagement component. The writing process forms around the ideas the child wants to write about on a particular topic. The result can then be printed for the child to take home and/or saved in a folder labeled with the child's name. You can record the date and any notes regarding strengths, needs, or next steps directly on the saved work.

4. **Give each child a stapled booklet for the purpose of creating a personal recount of the experience. Direct them to start with sketching each page, but encourage the addition of text as well. Again, some personal recounts may turn into stories.**

Using Scrapbook Photo Albums to Prompt Writing

Figure 6.14

We made the letter X.

Taking photographs of children involved in activities and creating a scrapbook photo album for each child provides another authentic reason to write. Using interactive writing (see Chapter 4, page 84), the children are supported as they write their thoughts about the photos. Eileen Feldgus and Isabell Cardonick (1999) recommend waiting until the spring to glue photos into each child's scrapbook, leaving space for them to write. The children can then be given until the end of the year to write about the experiences. Other teachers prefer to have the children write when the experience is still fresh in their minds. Rereading the scrapbook photo albums might prompt some children to write a personal recount or even a story about the event. Whether the children are in the gym or on a field trip, the scrapbook photo album, usually sent home at the end of the year, provides memories for both the children and their families.

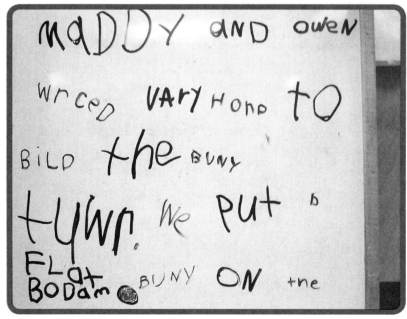

Figure 6.15
Maddy and Owen worked very hard to build the bunny tower.
We put a flat bunny on the bottom.

Scrapbooks that include pictures of the students showing emotions really motivate the students to write.

Figure 6.16

Figure 6.17

Using Wordless Concept Books

Concept picture books support nonfiction writing. They explain an idea or concept by providing examples. There are many concept books that deal with the alphabet, colors, numbers, dinosaurs, transportation, shapes, weather, living things, and nonliving things. These books typically stimulate great conversations and help to develop vocabulary. Since there is generally no storyline in concept picture books, sequence is not crucial. Two exceptions, of course, are alphabet books and number books. Wordless concept books often lead children into making their own informational texts such as *All About . . . Books* (see page 172). They learn that they can teach others information through the books they write. They have a real reason to write with an audience in mind.

GREAT NONFICTION WORDLESS CONCEPT BOOKS

Alphabet Books

Alda, Arlene. *Arlene Alda's ABC.* Berkeley, CA: Ten Speed Press, 2004.

Baker, Alan. *Black and White Rabbit's ABC.* New York: Kingfisher, 1999.

Baker, Leslie A. *The Animal ABC.* New York: Henry Holt & Company, 2003.

DK Publishing. *Farm ABC.* New York: Dorling Kindersley Publishing, Incorporated, 2006.

The Dog Artlist Collection. *The Dog from Arf! Arf! To Zzzzzz.* Toronto, ON: HarperCollins Canada, Limited, 2007.

Emberley, Ed. *Ed Emberley's ABC.* New York: Little, Brown & Company, 1978.

Fain, Kathleen. *Handsigns: A Sign Language Alphabet.* San Francisco: Chronicle Books LLC, 1995.

Jay, Alison. *ABC: A Child's First Alphabet Book.* New York: Penguin Group (USA) Incorporated, 2005.

MacKinnon, Debbie. *My First ABC.* London, England: Frances Lincoln Limited, 2007.

Marshall, Janet Perry. *Look Once Look Twice.* Boston: Houghton Mifflin Harcourt Publishing Company, 1995.

Miller, Jane. *Farm Alphabet Book.* New York: Scholastic Paperbacks, 1987.

Wells, Rosemary. *Max's ABC.* New York: Penguin Group (USA) Incorporated, 2008.

Counting/Numbers

Alda, Arlene. *Arlene Alda's 123: What Do You See?* Berkeley, CA: Ten Speed Press, 2004.

Anno, Mitsumasa. *Anno's Counting Book.* Toronto, ON: HarperCollins Canada, Limited, 1986.

Anno, Mitsumasa. *Anno's Counting House.* New York: Penguin Group (USA) Incorporated, 1982.

Boynton, Sandra. *Doggies: A Counting and Barking Book.* New York: Simon & Schuster Children's Publishing, 1984.

Carle, Eric. *1, 2, 3 to the Zoo.* New York: Penguin Group (USA) Incorporated, 2007.

Fleming, Denise. *Count.* New York: Henry Holt & Company, 1997.

Hands-On Crafts for Kids. *Count the Animals on the Farm.* New York: Sterling Publishing Co., Inc., 2002.

McMillan, Bruce. *Counting Wildflowers.* New York: HarperCollins Publishers, 1995.

Olson, K.C. and David Gordon. *Construction Countdown.* New York: Henry Holt & Company, 2004.

Sabuda, Robert. *Cookie Count: A Tasty Pop-Up.* New York: Simon & Schuster Children's Publishing, 1997.

Taylor-Butler, Christine. *Ah-Choo.* Danbury, CT: Scholastic Library Publishing, 2005.

Walsh, Ellen Stoll. *Mouse Count.* New York: Harcourt Children's Books, 2006.

Shapes

Hoban, Tana. *Is It Larger? Is It Smaller?* New York: HarperCollins Publishers, 1997.

Hoban, Tana. *Shapes, Shapes, Shapes.* New York: HarperCollins Publishers, 1996.

Colors

Ehlert, Lois. *Color Zoo*. New York: HarperCollins Publishers, 1997.

Hoban, Tana. *Is It Red? Is It Yellow? Is It Blue?* New York: HarperCollins Publishers, 1987.

Seeger, Laura Vaccaro. *Lemons Are Not Red*. New York: Henry Holt & Company, 2006.

Tafuri, Nancy. *Blue Goose*. New York: Simon & Schuster Children's Publishing, 2008.

Using and Writing Alphabet Books

Sharing published alphabet books (or ABC books) supports children in writing their own alphabet books. Published alphabet books help young children understand the concept of the alphabet and the concept of a letter. They also help the children to learn the letter names and sometimes their sounds as they encounter pictures or illustrations and familiar and not-so-familiar words that start with that specific alphabet letter. In addition, many alphabet books stress alliteration while some are also written in rhyme. Both alliteration and rhyme support phonological awareness development.

Some ABC books exhibit one picture or illustration and one word or label per page. Others include a complete sentence or several sentences. Often the books with more text also develop great new vocabulary, million-dollar words, or yummy words. Many of the books are themed-based. The themes may relate to food, geography, animals, numbers, history, or culture. Marie Clay's research (1993b) and the work of others support the importance of having children write their own alphabet books.

Writing I Am Kind Books

In Hudson Public Schools Kindergarten Center, Hudson, Massachusetts, the children create *I Am Kind* books. They are used to celebrate the 100th day of school and to support social emotional learning; in this case, the concept of kindness is stressed. The children interview family members and friends to identify acts of kindness that the children can perform. They record their acts in a heart shape on the paper provided. Before the pages are assembled into a class book, each child takes his or her page home so that family members can add comments. The teacher, with the assistance of volunteers or paraprofessionals, assembles the pages and each child receives a copy of the book to take home. It becomes one of the child's and family's favorite books to read (Mindess, Chen, and Brenner 2008). (See Reproducible 6.6: I Am Kind Book and Reproducible 6.7: I Am Kind! on the CD.)

Check It Out!

A great read aloud to support your writing of the I am Kind Books is *Emily's First 100 Days of School* by Rosemary Wells (author and illustrator; New York: Hyperion, 2005). A supporting DVD is *Emily's First 100 Days of School* (2006; closed captioned) with teachers, guide is produced by JZ Media and Weston Woods and is distributed by Weston Woods.

Using Environmental Print

Environmental print refers to print found in everyday contexts: signs, billboards, logos, and other functional print. Engaging reading and writing activities using environmental print help young children to understand how language is organized and used. Through these activities they learn that such print is meaningful and serves a purpose. Such activities also help children to develop print awareness (for example, what a letter is, what a word is, directionality) and phonics knowledge.

You can involve children in motivating and playful activities using environmental print at centers, including writing environmental print books, taking meaningful surveys, and creating and playing environmental print bingo.

Figure 6.18
From our science study of living things.

Children who are aware of environmental print and can "read" it see themselves as readers and writers and are more proactive in seeking out print (Prior and Gerard 2004). Unless they are encouraged to use environmental print, many children simply ignore it.

Check It Out!

You can download many examples of environmental print by keying the name of the sign, product, or company into your Internet search engine. You can also use the following links to access great signs, logos, and coupons. Be sure to print a good variety.

www.burgerking.com

www.campbellsoup.com

www.crayola.com

www.grocer.com

www.hubbardscupboard.org/Environmental_Print_A-F.PDF

www.hubbardscupboard.org/Environmental_Print_G-R.PDF

www.hubbardscupboard.
org/Environmental_
Print_S-Z.PDF

www.kelloggs.com

www.mcdonalds.com

www.mysavings.com/
coupons.asp

www.nabisco.com

www.pepsi.com

www.pizzahut.com

www.thesolutionsite.com/
lpnew/lesson/11903/
streetsign.doc

Magazines, newspapers,
and advertising flyers
are also great sources of
environmental print.

MINI-LESSONS 6.7

Writing Environmental Print Books

1. There are many types of environmental print books that children can make. To begin, familiarize the children with different types of environmental print by bringing into the classroom grocery bags, bread bags, pizza boxes, cereal boxes, juice and milk containers, coupons, T-shirts, logos, and pictures of signs. Encourage the children to bring in examples of environmental print from home. Duplicates are welcome! (See Reproducible 6.3: Environmental Print, on the CD.) Eventually, the samples can be used to create a *wall of print* bulletin-board display. It is helpful if the print can be affixed to the display using Velcro so that the children can sort it and use it in different ways. Children are more likely to use the print if it is familiar to them and if they have some ownership for bringing it in. Seeing similar forms of print both at home and at school helps to bridge literacy for children. It also helps them to understand that they can read and write using environmental print outside the classroom and school.

Figure 6.19

Figure 6.20

Figure 6.21

We can read this wall of print.
This makes a great center activity.

2. Have the children share and "read" the print that they bring from home before the print is put on the wall. Encourage the children to sort the items in different ways (for example, environmental print related to food or toys, signs, and so on).

3. Create a class *Words and Signs in Our World* Big Book. Discuss with the children all of the environmental print that has been collected. Model creating an environmental print page by selecting a piece of environmental print, gluing it onto a sheet of paper, and writing a caption or sentence under it as you think aloud. For example, you might have a picture of a pop bottle and under it write the word recycle.

4. Have each child select one piece of environmental print. Have him or her glue the sample onto a sheet of paper to be bound into a class Big Book or a scrapbook, one item per page. Direct the children to write a caption or sentence on each page they create and to add their name. Invite individuals to share their pages with the class and with other members of the school community. The conversation is even more important than the product created!

5. Encourage the children to revisit their Big Book of environmental print often.

6. Encourage the children to create their own environmental print books. Have them determine the purpose of their book first (for example, logos, signs, ABC books, and so on). Again, make time for the children to share their books with others.

Using Environmental Print to Play Bingo

1. Introduce environmental print to the children by following the steps in Mini-Lessons 6.7: Writing Environmental Print Books (see page 158).

2. Provide the children with copies of different logos and distribute about ten markers (such as tokens or counters) to each child. Make sure the caller has a copy of each of the logos as well.

3. Provide the children with blank bingo cards. The grid should consist of five columns (one for each letter in the word *bingo*) with three squares in each column. Support the children as they write the letters B-I-N-G-O in the top row of squares.

4. Have the children glue a logo in each of the ten blank squares remaining on their bingo cards. Each child will end up with a different card. To win the game, a player simply has to have ten logos called that are on his or her card in any place.

5. Model how the game works. Begin by calling out a logo. Instruct the children to scan their card for that logo. Demonstrate how to place a marker on the logo, if found, and how a winner is declared. Others may take turns acting as the caller once the concept of playing bingo and reading the logos is familiar to the children. The winner becomes the caller.

6. Increase the difficulty by having the children add more rows of logos to their bingo cards. Alternatively, play traditional bingo. For traditional bingo, the caller's logos will first need to be labeled with one of the five letters in the word *bingo*. Winners must have one complete line of logos marked on their card.

7. Once the children are familiar with the concept, they may prefer to create different environmental bingo cards using simple sketches, labels, or symbols.

Check It Out!

Environmental Print in the Classroom: Meaningful Connections for Learning to Read by Jennifer Prior and Maureen R. Gerard (Newark, DE: International Reading Association, 2004) is a practical resource to support using environmental print in the classroom. Also see the lesson "Stop Signs, McDonald's, and Cheerios: Writing with Environmental Print" at ReadWriteThink (www.readwritethink.org). This lesson is designed for K–2 children.

Check It Out!

See the lesson "Bingo! Using Environmental Print to Practice Reading" by Jennifer Prior and Maureen R. Gerard at ReadWriteThink (www.readwritethink.org).

List Making

Check It Out!

Here are some other great books to introduce list making:

Don't Forget the Bacon by Pat Hutchins (New York: HarperCollins, 1989).

Rosie's Walk by Pat Hutchins (New York: Simon & Schuster Children's Publishing, 1998).

Scaredy Squirrel at the Beach by Mélanie Watt (Toronto, ON: Kids Can Press, 2008).

Making lists is one of the easiest, most common, and authentic forms of writing. Because young children often see their parents/caregivers and teachers making lists, they are familiar with the concept. Some may even have had the opportunity to contribute to a grocery or to-do list at home. Furthermore, once the children are introduced to making lists, they will start to notice lists all around them (for example, menu boards, sports-team standings, train and bus schedules, television listings, and even search engine results).

The organizational pattern for lists is very simple. Writing a single word is much easier than writing a sentence. When asked to write in their journals, beginning writers often spontaneously choose to create lists of words, such as the names of friends or family members or even a list of the letters of the alphabet. In addition, making lists supports critical thinking. It is a form of classification—sorting things into groups based on common traits. This critical-thinking skill is used in math, science, and social studies, all across the day.

MINI-LESSONS 6.9
Writing Lists

1. **A great way to introduce the concept of writing lists is through children's literature. There are many entertaining list books, both new and old. An all-time favorite with children that is available in most school libraries is the Newberry Award–winning collection of short stories titled *Frog and Toad Together* by Arnold Lobel. In the story titled "A List," Toad says, "I have many things to do. I will write them all down on a list so that I can remember them" (1979, 4). This book is useful for introducing children to the concept that people frequently write lists to help them remember things. The adventure begins as Toad writes a long list and then loses it.**

A newer list book that stands out from the rest is *Wallace's Lists* by Barbara Bottner and Gerald Kruglik. Nearly every page has a different list, including the Arrivals and Departure monitor at the airport! A great Canadian list book is *Scaredy Squirrel* (2006) by Mélanie Watt. Scaredy Squirrel writes lists of his greatest fears, the advantages

and disadvantages of change, his daily routine, the contents of an emergency kit, and an exit plan for an emergency. This is also a great book to promote a discussion around risk taking.

2. Model making a shopping list. Explain that you are making the list so that you do not forget anything that you need to buy.

3. Ask the class what a rule is? Why do people have rules? Brainstorm and list some rules, such as rules for crossing the street. Point out to the children that you are making a list, and then ask the children why they come to school. Make a list of reasons, which will likely include learning to read, write, do math, and play with their friends. Again, point out that this is a list.

4. Ask the children what kinds of classroom rules would help them to learn and have fun. Again, through shared and interactive writing, create a list of classroom rules.

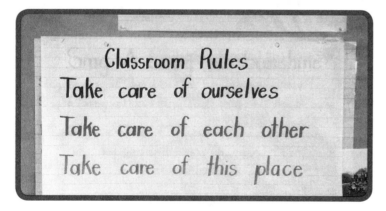

Figure 6.22

5. Introduce the concept of wishes. What is a wish? Why do people wish? Ask the children to think of three things that they might wish for. Have them turn to a partner and talk about their wishes. Model drawing a balloon for the children. Tell them that this is a "wish" balloon. Write two wishes in your balloon, one below the other. Think aloud as you write your list. Explain that lists are generally written in rows from top to bottom.

Scaredy Squirrel at Night by Mélanie Watt (Toronto, ON: Kids Can Press, 2009).

Scaredy Squirrel Makes a Friend by Mélanie Watt (Toronto, ON: Kids Can Press, 2007).

The Very Hungry Caterpillar by Eric Carle (New York: Philomel, 1994).

Check It Out!

See the lesson "Creating Class Rules: A Beginning to Creating Community" at ReadWriteThink (www.readwritethink.org).

6. **Have the children each draw a wish balloon. Have them fill their balloons with a list of wishes.**

Figure 6.23

7. **Have the children each share at least one item from their lists of wishes.**

8. **As a shared writing, brainstorm other lists that the children could write. This list may look something like this:**

Lists

o Numbers
o Things to do
o Waiting lists
o Foods that are good for you
o Junk foods
o Dinosaurs
o Things you love
o Sports
o Favorite things to do
o Teachers in the school
o Names of classmates
o Family members
o Pets
o Weather words

A waiting list helps children take turns and solve problems when a center is full. Have the children write their name next to a number on a list posted at the center. When one child leaves the center, he tells the next child on the list. That child then places a check mark beside her name to show she is taking her turn in the area. Problem solved! Great for establishing classroom routines while at the same time supporting early literacy learning.

- ○ TV shows
- ○ Letters of the alphabet
- ○ *A, B, C* words

Lists may begin with the children creating a collage of photos.

Figure 6.24

9. **Include lists during science.**

Figure 6.25
iron, paper clip, metal, knife . . .

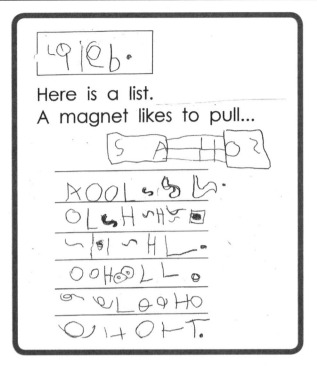

Figure 6.26

This child has definitely written a list, emphatically using periods. The list exhibits the precommunicative stage of spelling (see Chapter 3, page 42).

10. Explain to the children that they are going to make a Big Book of lists and that each child will create a list for the book. Have each child make up a list on any topic. Share the lists. Have the children copy their lists onto chart paper and add illustrations.

For other ways to encourage children to write lists, see Reproducible 2.4: Writing Lists, on the CD. See also Writing a List Poem: Step by Step on page 201 in Chapter 7.

A traditional kindergarten word wall typically includes only the children's names and some high-frequency words. Other word wall lists also appear in kindergarten classrooms.

MINI-LESSONS 6.10

Using Word Walls and Other Environmental Print to Demonstrate and Write Lists

1. Help the children to understand that word walls represent lists and that the words on the walls are useful for writing.

2. Brainstorm with the children what types of lists can be written from the traditional word wall. For example, words in alphabetical order, words that have double letters together (*hill*), short words of one to three

letters (*and*), medium-length words of four to six letters (*here*), and long words of seven or more letters (likely only the word *because* or perhaps a name). Additionally, word walls can be used to make lists of word-family words (for example, *-ake, -an, -at, -in, -it, -all*) and words that are made up of two little words (*into*).

3. Word wall words and other environmental words can also be written as word chains. Using strips of different colored heavy construction paper, have the children copy words from the word wall and, later in the year, from any other environmental print. But there is a catch. To make the activity more challenging for those up to it, each word following the first must start with the last letter of the previous one. The words are then joined together (glued or stapled) to make a word chain. The chain is complete when there are at least 10 words.

4. Keep the word chains in the classroom to use with small groups for the purpose of reading or sharing with guests. As the chain is passed from person to person, the next word is read. The more chains, the better!

Figure 6.27

List Making to Develop Skill in Classification and Vocabulary

1. Introduce the concept of list making to help sort or classify/categorize things. Show the children a list made of all of their names sorted in alphabetical order. Ask an *I wonder* question (for example, *I wonder why I might want to put your names in alphabetical order?*). Provide a second example, such as *I wonder why some people sort their clothes into different piles before they do the laundry?* (color—light vs. dark, fabric—cotton vs. wool, water temperature—hot vs. cold). Bringing in a laundry label to show the children provides concrete evidence to show how reading, including reading signs and symbols, helps with sorting.

2. Show them how a list can be used to help solve a problem. You may want to use the example that follows or one of your own. (Note that whichever example you use, it is important to remain sensitive to the personal experiences and individual circumstances of the children in your class.) *I am thinking of taking my family on a holiday to someplace warm next winter, but I am not sure if it is a good idea. Let's see if I can figure this out.* Next, use modeled writing (see Chapter 4, page 82) to make two lists: one showing the advantages (pros) and the other the disadvantages (cons) of going somewhere warm over the winter holidays. Think aloud as you complete the lists of pros and cons. (Ensure that the con list shows that it will cost too much money.) Solve the problem based on the two lists created.

3. Use the wonderful book *Sort It Out!* by Barbara Mariconda to develop the concept of writing a list to help sort and classify in order to clean up and put things away. This book, written in delightful rhyme, is wonderful for developing phonological awareness.

Figure 6.28

The book begins: "Pack rat collected a whole bag of stuff.

His mother said, "Packy, enough is enough!

Empty that stuff you've collected today!

Then sort it all out and put it away!"

Source: Image and Poem from Mariconda (2008).

Packy sorts his collection of things by color, feel (hard vs. soft, smooth vs. rough), what they are made of, their shape, and how they are used. What great ways to develop vocabulary! In the end, someone takes much of his collection and the mystery of the missing possessions has to be solved.

For more information on using concept and word sorts to develop vocabulary see Reproducible 6.2: Developing Your Child's Vocabulary by Sorting, on the CD.

There are also many authentic reasons for writing lists at centers.

Check It Out!

Visit the Sylvan Dell Publishing website (www .SylvanDellPublishing.com) and click on the book cover *Sort it Out!* by Barbara Mariconda for further cross-curricular teaching activities to support the concept of sorting, classifying, and categorizing. This book is rich in vocabulary, an important factor to consider when picking any read-aloud.

Word Sorts

A natural progression from list making and classifying would be to engage the children in several word-sort activities next. This will help the children to understand that sorting can also help them with their reading and writing.

Have the children create their own word cards, and then have them actively engage in sorting cards by

- first letter
- length (shortest to longest words)
- rime (words in the same word family)
- attribute, such as color words, number words, weather words, transition words (*first, then, next, after, finally*)

Children love sorting. But they also love having their own pack of word cards that they have created.

MINI-LESSONS 6.12

Sorting Sentence Strips and Words From Sentences

Sorting sentence strips and words from sentences helps to develop concepts of print, high-frequency word knowledge, fluency, and comprehension.

1. Sorting sentence strips supports retelling, and retelling supports vocabulary development and comprehension. Provide the children with sentence strips from either a published story or one created in class, and then work together to retell the story using transition words.

Figure 6.29
Working with a partner
using a familiar song.

---

2. Sorting words from sentences helps the children to understand the concepts of first word, last word, the importance of word order in a sentence, directionality when writing a sentence, and wraparound or return sweep (when you get to the end of the line, you return to the far left of the sheet to continue writing). It also helps the children to understand capitalization at the beginning of a sentence and punctuation at the end, and develops high-frequency word knowledge. Provide the children with cards on which individual words from a sentence are written and work together to re-create the sentence.

3. A fun game to play is Be a Sentence. Create a sentence on a sentence strip as a modeled or shared writing activity. Stress the uppercase letter at the beginning of the sentence and the punctuation at the end as you write. Cut up the sentence strip into individual word cards and a punctuation card. Mix up the cards and have the children take turns helping to reconstruct the sentence. Once the cards are all in order, invite the children to take turns coming up and holding the word and punctuation cards in order to *Be a Sentence.* It is possible that the word cards can be arranged in different ways to create different sentences. This is an important concept for young children to learn. Each time they mix up the cards and reorder them, they are developing concepts of print, high-frequency word knowledge, fluency, and comprehension.

Figure 6.30

Writing *All About . . . Books:* You're an Expert!

Gail Tompkins (2000) describes *All About . . . Books* as child-created books written on a single topic. Children are often very interested in certain topics and feel that they know a lot about that topic. They feel like they are experts! Children need to learn that one of the purposes of writing is to write informational text to help others to learn. So, they too are encouraged to share what they know about a topic they find interesting.

I do it!

Check It Out!

Check out these wonderful additions to Jim Arnosky's All about series:

All about Frogs (New York: Scholastic, 2008).

All about Manatees (New York: Scholastic, 2008).

All about Turkeys (New York: Scholastic, 2008).

All about Turtles (New York: Scholastic, 2008).

MINI-LESSONS 6.13
Writing Informational Text
(*All About . . . Books*)

1. Model the writing of an *All About . . . Book*. Explain to the children that an *All About . . . Book* is a book full of information on a topic. (You may have to explain the terms *information* and *topic*.) Tell them you are writing this book so that you can share this information with them.

2. Demonstrate how to get started. Share a read-aloud on the topic, if available. This helps to provide more background knowledge on the topic. For example, if you are writing a book about trees, you might read aloud Caldecott Medal winner *A Tree Is Nice* by Janice May Udry. It has minimal text and detailed illustrations, some in black and white and some in color. This book is often part of school library collections. (Other great read-alouds about trees include *Are Trees Alive?* by Debbie Miller, *Tell Me, Tree: All About Trees for Kids* by Gail Gibbons, and *The Big Tree* by Bruce Hiscock.)

3. Make a list of all of the things you know about the topic. You may include more information than was provided in the book.

4. Start by drawing a picture for the cover page. For a book about trees, draw a tree and label the cover page *All about Trees*. Write your name on the cover as a real author would. Choose eight points from the list of things you know about the topic and use a different page to create a quick sketch for each point.

5. Add a label, caption, or even a sentence at the bottom of each page to support the sketch. Think aloud as you write, but be sure to go back and reread what you have written before adding new text. This is an important thinking and writing strategy to teach.

6. As the children develop as writers, show them how to create a first page that introduces the concept and a final page that provides closure or indicates that the end of the book has been reached. The writing sample that follows demonstrates this understanding. For emerging writers, an illustration that they can describe or an illustration and a label or caption is sufficient for book writing. In fact, it is something to celebrate.

7. Share your completed *All About . . . Book.*

The following book was created by an inquisitive end-of-year kindergartner, who had been writing in preschool and who was read to a great deal at home.

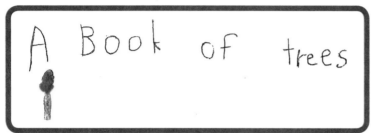

A Book of trees

trees
Are nice

But what do they
Give us ?
Paper and
wood

whar other
things
Do we get
from trees?
Fruit And
nuts

How do we
Use trees?
we can use
It for shade,
And calimbing
And sswinging
On

You can
Make a
House
Would you
like one?

Do you like trees
I do?
trees are
Nice

Figure 6.31
A book of trees: Note all the details (facts) shared
and the voice!

8. Create a class *All About . . . Book* (shared writing) using a class topic or theme. Brainstorm and make a list of all of the facts the children have learned about the topic. Remind the children that you have just made a list. Assign a fact to each child by writing his or her name beside one of the facts on the list. Alternatively, allow the children to choose a fact about which they will draw and write. This may mean that 20 children will write about the same fact, but this is acceptable since engagement and choice are keys to good writing.

9. Have the children share their class *All About . . . Book* with another class. Ensure each child is able to share his or her page.

10. Brainstorm topics about which the children feel they are experts, such as certain mammals, birds, fish, insects, sports, or planets.

11. Have each child pick a topic and then turn and tell a partner at least three things they know about that topic.

12. Distribute blank *All About . . . Booklets* (six or eight letter-size sheets of blank paper, stapled together). Always refer to these as books when discussing them with the children.

13. Explain to the children that they will be sharing their *All About . . . Book* with an audience: first with one another, then with others in the school, and finally with their families. Knowing that their writing will have an audience makes children more motivated to write.

14. Encourage the children to illustrate each page and to write at least something about each illustration. By the spring, if not before, every child should be attempting to write at least one sentence on each page.

15. Have the children share their books with one another and then with others in the school.

16. Hold a special evening during which the children share their knowledge and their *All About . . . Books*

with family members and friends. Send home a letter inviting family members to the celebration of writing and learning. (See Reproducible 6.1: Come and Celebrate Your Child's Book Writing, on the CD.)

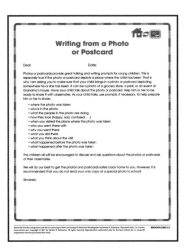

WINDOW ON THE CLASSROOM

Jo Simpson from Oswego, Illinois, has her class write individual books while studying birds in her kindergarten classroom. It is no accident that Jo develops strong kindergarten writers. Jo motivates her class to write, goes deeply into a topic so that the children have the background knowledge and vocabulary and have something that they want to share, provides writing mini-lessons involving modeled and shared writing, connects their writing to read-alouds and gets them writing a great deal from day 1. They are taught that their art is also very important. They are taught to look carefully so that they can include lots of details when they draw. Figures 6.32 and 6.33 that reveal wonderful nonfiction writing. Jo explains: "These were part of individual student books that students wrote. We worked on a page a day while we were studying birds. We were also hatching chicks at the same time which ties in well with the bird unit. We read many nonfiction books about birds. One of them had a format where it asked a question and then answered it. We discussed how that was one interesting format for a book. I modeled one on the LCD. Some students did try it in their writing, which I thought was very fun. At that point of the year, we are more able to look at a style of writing as they are more mature. Since we were reading nonfiction, we all worked on trying to tell facts about birds and illustrating them with many details.

In my class we tend to delve into a topic enough that the students are pretty excited about writing on it."

Birds laiy egg and they
  (lay) (eggs)
Fliy riy hiy. Wy
(fly) (very) (high.) (Why)
are babey Birds pingk?
      (baby)
I doot now be kus
(don't) (know)   (because)
they wer just
       (were)
born. Ow Now I
       (Oh,)
no!
(know)

Figure 6.32
Can't you hear the great voice in this piece!! Due to Jo's selection of read-alouds and modeled writing mini-lessons, this child has learned how to ask and answer questions when writing.

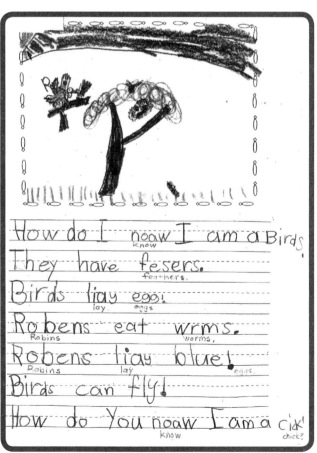

How do I noaw I am a Birds
        (know)
They have fesers.
        (feathers.)
Birds liay egg!
      (lay) (eggs)
Robens eat wrms.
(Robins)   (worms,)
Robens liay blue!
(Robins) (lay) (eggs.)
Birds can fly!
How do You noaw I am a cik!
           (know)   (chick?)

Figure 6.33

Check It Out!

Here are some wonderful question-and-answer books to read aloud:

Do Bees Sneeze? And Other Questions Kids Ask about Insects by J.K. Wangberg (Golden, CO: Fulcrum Publishing, 1998).

How Do Flies Walk Upside Down? Questions and Answers About Insects by Melvin and Gilda Berger (New York: Scholastic Reference, 1999).

I Wonder Why Snakes Shed Their Skin and Other Questions about Reptiles by Amanda O'Neill (Boston: Kingfisher, 1996).

I Wonder Why Triceratops Had Horns and Other Questions about Dinosaurs by Rod Theodorou (Boston: Kingfisher, 1994).

Why Do Dogs Have Wet Noses? by Stanley Coren (Toronto, ON: Kids Can Press, 2006).

Why Do Volcanoes Blow Their Tops? Questions & Answers about Volcanoes & Earthquakes by Melvin and Gilda Berger (New York: Scholastic Reference, 2000).

Why Don't Haircuts Hurt? Questions and Answers About Your Body by Melvin and Gilda Berger (New York: Scholastic Reference, 1999).

You Asked for It! Strange but True Answers to 99 Wacky Questions by Marg Meikle and Tina Holdcroft (Toronto, ON: Scholastic, 2000).

For even more question-and-answer book titles, see the Early Literacy Telecollaborative Project (www.earlyliterature.ecsd.net) and click on Predictable Books.

Writing Reports: Supporting Inquiry and the Project Approach

The terms "the project approach" and "inquiry" are not new terms, but they are presently popular terms used to describe approaches to learning in many early childhood classrooms. One term supports the other. The project approach is described by Katz as a method of teaching in which an in-depth study of a particular topic is conducted by a child or a group of children. The children investigate a topic that they are interested in. The investigation focuses on finding answers to questions posed by a child, a group of children or the teacher and children together. Each project or investigation provides a meaningful context to promote language and literacy learning as the children learn about a particular topic. There is an inquiry, a wondering. What approach could cause the children to be more engaged than this?

It is important to note that the Project Approach is incorporated across the curriculum but does not likely constitute the entire curriculum.

Emerging and early writers can write simple reports that support their wonderings, their inquiries. A question-and-answer report (or book) and a culminating unit report are but two examples.

Check It Out!

To learn more about the Project Approach or the Inquiry approach explore Helms' and Katz's Second edition of *Young Investigators The Project Approach in the Early Years* Teachers College Press 2011 or the *Illinois Projects in Practice* online at http://illinoispip.org/

MINI-LESSONS 6.14

Writing a Question-and-Answer or Inquiry Report

Reports are often a response to a question or wondering a child or an adult has. What more authentic reason to write can there be than to pick a topic of interest to investigate?

1. Introduce the activity by sharing a question-and-answer book with the children as a read-aloud.

2. Model the activity. The following example, which has been used successfully with a kindergarten class, is a report about Velcro.

   o Select a topic about which you know at least two facts (in this case, Velcro).

   o Draw and label the topic.

Figure 6.34

○ Encourage the children to examine the Velcro on their shoes.

Figure 6.35

○ List at least two facts you know about the topic. Write the facts in list form. You may choose to include the facts in "Did you know that. . . " bubbles just for fun. For example,

　○ Velcro is made of two pieces of material.

　○ The two pieces of material stick to each other.

　○ When you pull the pieces apart they make a ripping sound.

　○ Velcro is used on many things, including shoes.

○ Write a question related to the topic that you want to answer. (*I wonder how Velcro works?*)

○ Research answers to the question at home or at school.

○ Write the answer in the same place you wrote the facts and the question. *Velcro consists of two parts—a hook side and a loop side. They fasten together. The hook side is covered with tiny hooks, and the loop side is covered with small, hairy loops.*

You may also want to share the following interesting facts with the children. When the two sides are pressed together, the hooks catch in the loops and hold the pieces together. The idea for Velcro came from a man whose dog became covered with burs (the prickly seed-sacs of some plants) while on a walk. The man studied the burs under a microscope and decided to create a similar material that could be used to keep something closed, like a coat or a purse.

Do not write down all of these facts as too much information might overwhelm the children. You do not want them to think that a report has to be long. They have to believe that they too can write a report. Drawings and labels or captions make a great preschool or kindergarten report.

3. **Share your report and an example, if appropriate. (For example, show the children some Velcro on a running shoe and examine the material together.)**

4. **Brainstorm topics about which the children have questions. Create the list as a shared writing.**

5. **Provide the children with a framework for writing a report (see Reproducible 6.8: My Report, on the CD).**

Beyond *All About . . . Books*, children can write simple reports as a culmination to a unit. They often require your support or that of a buddy, a volunteer, or a paraprofessional. Reports often occur at the end of a social studies or science unit.

WINDOW ON THE CLASSROOM

A Wonder Center: Recently I visited a classroom where the children were enjoying the wonder center. The idea for the center came from a book by Georgia Heard and Jennifer McDonough, A Place for Wonder: Reading and Writing Nonfiction in the Primary Grades *(2009). The concept is a simple one. The children are encouraged to write any questions or wondering they have on sticky notes which are then stuck on a wonder center board (chart paper works just as well).The children are also encouraged to put their names beside their wondering (just in case the printing is hard to decipher). Once or twice a week the children and teacher review the questions or the wonderings looking for topics to investigate. Topics can also be investigated at home and the results then shared at school. What a great reason to write!*

Writing a Class Riddle Book

A great follow-up to learning about a topic or theme is to develop a class Big Book of riddles. Children enjoy trying to solve riddles, so why not have each child contribute to a class riddle book?

MINI-LESSONS 6.15
Writing a Class Riddle Book

1. **Explain to the children that a riddle is like having a puzzle or mystery to solve. All riddles use clues, which may involve a trick or some simple facts. Explain that you will show them both types of riddles.**

2. **I do it. Model some "trick" riddles for the children to try and solve. For example:**
   o What kind of keys can't open a door? (piano)
   o I have teeth but I cannot eat. What am I? (comb)
   o I can run but I don't have legs. What am I? (water)
   o I have a nose but I am not on a face. What am I? (airplane)
   o I have hands but no fingers. What am I? (clock)

Check It Out!

For three step-by-step lessons that engage children in research, writing, and sharing their knowledge about a topic, see "Writing Reports in Kindergarten? Yes!" at ReadWriteThink (www.readwritethink.org).

Check It Out!

Kindergarten Kids: Riddles, Rebuses, Wiggles, Giggles, and More! by Stephanie Calmenson (New York: HarperCollins, 2005).

3. Read a number of riddle books to the class.

4. Now share some "fact" riddles with the children (see the examples below).

5. Use pictures to stimulate riddle writing (Feldgus and Cardonick 1999). Hold up a picture and model writing clues that would help someone figure out what is being discussed.

I taste good.
I ran away.
What am I?

6. We do it. Provide a stack of photos or illustrations and allow each child to select one. Have the children then work with a partner to create clues for their pictures. Once they have written clues for each of their pictures, have each pair challenge other pairs in the class to solve their riddles. Children may write the clues on the covers of riddle cards (like greeting cards). The answers (which may include photos or illustrations) are written inside.

EXAMPLES OF CLASS RIDDLES DEVELOPED AFTER A UNIT ON INSECTS

(Questions on front) I make people sick. I also suck blood. I am a _____.

(Answer inside) flea

(Questions on front) I have 6 legs and 2 wings. I make a noise when I flap my wings. My mouth is like a sharp needle. I am a _____.

(Answer inside) mosquito

7. You do it. Have each child use a picture prompt to create a riddle page for a class Big Book. Direct the children

to write their clues on the front of the page and to put their illustrations and written answers on the back.

8. Once a social studies or science unit has been completed, have the children take that knowledge and create a class Big Book of riddles. Ask each child to

   ○ pick a topic from the unit (for example, a fly from the insect unit)

   ○ list three facts they have learned about the topic (for example, flies have six legs, two wings, and huge eyes)

   ○ create a riddle

Each child's riddle may be word processed by you and illustrated by the child. Or the children could work on their own or with a partner to create a page. Note, however, that the children will need a great deal of support. Older buddies, volunteers, or paraprofessionals might be used to support interactive writing.

Using Surveys to Support Writing, Reading, and Talk

Another real reason to write involves taking surveys. Conducting surveys is one of the richest literacy activities that young children can do. To conduct a survey they have to

- determine a survey question that they want answered
- write down the survey question
- find someone to survey
- record the response
- share the results orally with the rest of the class

Coming up with questions can be tricky as not all children understand the concept of what a question actually is.

MINI-LESSONS 6.16
Conducting a Survey in Kindergarten

1. Model coming up with a survey question. You may want to start with an example. Think aloud: "I have a question that I need answered. I am inviting all of the teachers over to my house on Sunday for lunch. I need to know if any of them are allergic to dogs."

Discuss the term *allergy* and determine if any of the children can make a personal connection. Continue with, "I need to find out this information because I have a dog named Sprinter. If there are people who are allergic to dogs, then Sprinter will stay at my neighbor's house on Sunday so that none of my guests become sick. If no one has an allergy, then Sprinter can stay at home."

2. Model writing the question on chart paper.

3. Model giving the Yes/No survey by asking a few children the survey question and recording the survey results on chart paper.

Are you allergic to dogs?	
Yes	*No*
Tony	Kirsten
	Atsuko

Figure 6.36

4. Share the survey results with the children as you think aloud.

5. Brainstorm a number of possible survey questions for which the children might like to find the answers. List them on a chart. Start them off with the sentence stem, *Do you like . . . ?* (See Reproducible: 6.9: My Survey, on the CD).

6. Have the children work with a partner to help each other create a Yes/No survey question and write it down. Remind them to include space to record the names of people who respond *Yes* and those who respond *No*.

WINDOW ON THE CLASSROOM

Recently, I was in a kindergarten class in which the teacher was teaching the children how to conduct surveys. One child surveyed the principal, the custodian, the secretary, and the librarian with the question, "Do you like your job? Yes or No?"

7. Have the children conduct their own surveys of several classmates. Using clipboards works well. Remind the children to write down the names of the people they survey under the appropriate response.

8. Have the children share their survey results.

WINDOW ON THE CLASSROOM

Critical literacy results in high-level comprehension. It is a way of thinking that challenges texts (read, heard, or viewed) and life as we know it. It helps to uncover social inequalities and injustices, develops empathy, and helps children to act, often resulting in social change and social justice. This seems a bit heavy for 3-, 4-, and 5-year-olds, but they will rise to the occasion. Vivian Vasquez's magical book Negotiating Critical Literacies in Young Children *(2004) provides many such examples. It recounts the author's experiences working with 3- to 5-year-old children in kindergarten classrooms in Ontario, Canada.*

Chapter 4 is titled "Our Friend Is a Vegetarian." It tells the story of what happened the day after a school barbeque was held for staff, students, and parents. The children, as would be expected, arrived at school excited about what happened at the barbeque the night before. One child asked if she could do a hand-count survey to see how many people had eaten hot dogs or hamburgers. She wanted to know their preferences. As the survey was being taken, the children learned that one of their classmates could not be part of the survey because he was a vegetarian and could eat neither hot dogs nor hamburgers. The children asked whose idea it was to serve only hamburgers and hot dogs and found out that it was a committee decision, which included parents, teachers, and the assistant principal as chair. The children decided to write a letter to the committee, which their teacher scribed.

The letter read, "If we don't eat food we'll die. We have to get new hot dogs and hamburgers. You can ask Anthony's daddy what you can buy because Anthony is a vegetarian" (p. 105). The children thought seriously about the wording: We (meaning all of us) and have to (meaning this is not negotiable).

When the children did not receive a response after two weeks, they wrote a second letter, which was even more forceful. This time they did get a response and were invited down to the assistant principal's office to share their thoughts as to what food they could serve next time. They then decided that they also needed to make all the school principals in the area aware of this issue so that no other children would be left out. This letter included a survey for the principals to complete (see below).

ABOUT VEGETARIANS SURVEY

What is the name of your school? _____

Do you have a school barbeque?   Yes ☐   No ☐

Do you know if you have vegetarians
at your school?   Yes ☐   No ☐

Do you think it is fair not to have
food for vegetarians?   Yes ☐   No ☐

Are you going to have vegetarian food
if you have vegetarians?   Yes ☐   No ☐

(Vasquez 2004, 109)

These children found a real reason to write. Their writing has voice because they have found something worthwhile to write about and they have an audience in mind. By reading the survey above, using their own words, you can hear the wheels turning, their thoughts being formed. Think of all that they learned in the process, all the mini-lessons on word choice and persuasive writing that came out of a teachable moment. No commercial program could have provided such a meaningful experience.

1. Begin with Mini-Lessons 6.16: Conducting a Survey in Kindergarten on page 185.

2. Make copies of each of five food-item logos or simply pictures of the products for each child.

3. Share the logos, read them together several times, and then distribute them to the children.

4. Ask each child to indicate his or her favorite food item out of the five by holding up the corresponding logo or picture.

5. Graph or chart the results.

6. Discuss the results.

7. Provide an important vocabulary lesson. Explain that *prefer* means you like one thing more than another. Provide examples. Hold up two pictures, one of a cat and the other of a dog. Say, "I prefer to have a dog, not a cat, as a pet." Survey the class using a hand-count survey. "How many of you prefer cats? How many prefer dogs?" Provide one more example. Ask, "How many of you prefer the color red and how many prefer the color blue?" Have the children turn to a partner and share their preference. Prompt them with "Start your sentence with *I prefer the color....*"

8. Hold up two more logos or pictures. Survey the class by asking, "*Do you prefer* to eat____ or____?"

9. Chart and share the results.

10. Have each child pick two food logos or pictures, or photos of other types of environmental print. The pictures of foods must be labeled. Encouraging children to cut out the images from magazines or newspapers works well.

11. Have the children write a survey question based on the two environmental print samples they chose (for example, *Do you prefer____ or____?*). Encourage the

The following reproducibles referenced in Chapter 6 are available on the *Learning to Write and Loving It!* CD:

Reproducible 2.4: Writing Lists

Reproducible 5.2: Wall Stories

Reproducible 6.1: Come and Celebrate Your Child's Book Writing

Reproducible 6.2: Developing Your Child's Vocabulary by Sorting

Reproducible 6.3: Environmental Print

Reproducible 6.4: Use Wordless Picture Books With Your Child

Reproducible 6.5: Writing From a Photo or Postcard

children to copy the words directly from the samples. Have them glue the logo, the picture, or the photo on to the survey sheet.

12. Have the children conduct their survey and record the results. They may either put a check mark in the appropriate column or write their classmates' names in the Yes or No column. The latter ensures that each person is surveyed only once.

13. Provide the children with the opportunity to share their results.

Chapter **7**

Writing Songs and Poetry

Singing and poetry are both important in kindergarten. Both promote active student engagement. Both can be used to develop print awareness, phonological awareness, alphabet knowledge, and oral language. Children can be supported in developing all of these skills in a joyful way as they sing and write songs and poetry with support.

Writing Songs in Preschool and Kindergarten

A great deal of singing is important in kindergarten. Songs support phonological awareness, which is an important skill used when reading and writing. Memorized songs when supported by music and the written words can be a valuable resource for learning to read and write (Jalongo 1997). Furthermore, singing is fun and promotes the active participation of all. Children typically love songs and they love to create and sing their own versions. A song picture book is an ideal way to motivate the children to read, write, sing, and draw. Song picture books are typically illustrated versions of well-known songs, chants, and musical finger plays. Most use rhyme, repetition such as a chorus or refrain, and predictable structures such as the days of the week or numbers (for example, *There were 10 in the bed and the little one said roll over, roll over . . . There were 9 in the bed and the little one said . . .*).

> "One particular type of book, the song picture book, is uniquely well suited for supporting children's growth in art, music, literature and language."
> (Jalongo 1997, 1)

Using Songs as Writing Models

There is much research to support the links between music and emergent literacy development. "Song picture books support emergent literacy by
- building on familiarity and enjoyment
- providing repetition and predictability
- expanding vocabulary and knowledge of story structures
- promoting critical thinking and problem solving
- fostering creative expression and language play"

(Jalongo 1997, 2)

CHILDREN'S SONG PICTURE BOOKS

Adams, P. *There was an Old Lady Who Swallowed a Fly*. Auburn ME: Child's Play-International, 2003.

Aliki. *Go Tell Aunt Rhody*. New York: Simon & Schuster Children's Publishing, 1996.

Aylesworth, J. *Old Black Fly*. New York: Henry Holt & Company for Young Readers, 1995.

Beck, I. *Five Little Ducks*. London: Orchard Books, 1992.

Binch, Caroline, et al. *Down by the River: Afro-Carribean Rhymes, Games, and Songs for Children*. Toronto, ON: Scholastic Canada Ltd. (Illustrated song collection), 1996.

Brett, J. *The Twelve Days of Christmas*. New York: Penguin Group (USA) Inc., 2004.

Carle, E. *Today Is Monday*. New York: Penguin Group (USA) Inc., 2007.

Christelow, E. *Five Little Monkeys Jumping on the Bed*. Boston: Houghton Mifflin Harcourt Publishing Company, 2006.

Dale, P. *Ten in the Bed*. Somerville, MA: Candlewick Press, 2007.

Glazer, T. *On Top of Spaghetti*. New York: Scholastic, Inc., 2006.

Hammerstein, O., and R. Rodgers. *My Favorite Things*. Toronto, ON: HarperCollins Canada Ltd., 2001.

Hale, S. J. *Mary Had a Little Lamb*. New York: Penguin Group (USA) Inc., 2004.

Ho, M. *Hush! A Thai Lullaby*. New York: Scholastic Inc., 2000.

Hoberman, M. A. *A House Is a House for Me*. New York: Penguin Group (USA) Inc., 2007.

Hudson, W., and C. Hudson. *How Sweet the Sound: African–American Songs for Children*. (Illustrated song collection). Toronto, ON: Scholastic Canada Ltd., 1997.

Hurd, T. *Mama Don't Allow*. Pine Plains, NY: Live Oak Media, 2004.

Ivimey, J. *Three Blind Mice*. New York: Little Brown & Company, 1990.

Jones, C. *This Old Man*. Boston: Houghton Mifflin Harcourt Publishing, 1998.

Jorgensen, G. *Crocodile Beat*. New York: Simon & Schuster Children's Publishing, 1989.

Keats, E. J. *Over in the Meadow*. New York: Penguin Group (USA) Inc., 1999.

Kellogg, S. *There Was an Old Woman*. New York: Simon & Schuster Children's Publishing, 1984.

Kennedy, J. *The Teddy Bears' Picnic*. New York: Simon & Schuster Children's Publishing, 2000.

Kovalski, M. *Jingle Bells*. Markham, ON: Fitzhenry & Whiteside, 1998.

La Prise, L. *The Hokey Pokey*. New York: Simon & Schuster Children's Publishing, 1997.

Langstaff, J. *Frog Went A-Courtin.'* New York: Harcourt Children's Books, 1955.

Langstaff, J. *Oh, A-Hunting We Will Go*. New York: Simon & Schuster Children's Publishing, 1991.

Mallet, D. *Inch by Inch: The Garden Song*. Toronto, ON: HarperCollins Canada, 1997.

Paparone, P. *Five Little Ducks: An Old Rhyme*. New York: North-South Books, 1995.

Parton, D. *Coat of Many Colors*. Toronto, ON: HarperCollins Canada Ltd., 1996.

Peek, M. *Mary Wore Her Red Dress and Henry Wore His Green Sneakers*. Boston: Houghton Mifflin Harcourt Trade & Reference Publishers, 2006.

Raffi. *Baby Beluga*. New York: Random House Children's Books, 1992.

Raffi. *Down by the Bay*. New York: Random House Children's Books, 1988.

Raffi. *Shake My Sillies Out*. New York: Random House Children's Books, 1988.

Raffi. *Everything Grows*. Burlington, MA: Rounder Books, 2004.

Reid, B. *Two by Two*. Toronto, ON: Scholastic Canada Ltd., 2002.

Seeger, P. *Abiyoyo*. New York: Simon & Schuster Children's Publishing, 2001.

Soto, G. *The Old Man and His Door*. New York: Penguin Group (USA) Inc., 2002.

Spier, P. *The Fox Went Out on a Chilly Night*. New York: Random House Children's Books, 1994.

Thiele, B., and G. D. Weiss. *What a Wonderful World*. New York: Simon & Schuster Children's Publishing, 1995.

Wadsworth, O. A. *Over in the Meadow*. New York: North-South Books Inc., 2003.

Weiss, N. *If You're Happy and You Know It*. New York: HarperCollins Publishers, 1987.

Westcott, N. B. *Peanut Butter and Jelly: A Play Rhyme*. Toronto, ON: Penguin Group Canada, 1992.

Westcott, N. B. *Skip to My Lou*. New York: Little, Brown Books for Young Readers, 2000.

Winter, J. *Follow the Drinking Gourd*. New York: Random House Children's Books, 1992.

Zelinsky, P. O. *The Wheels on the Bus*. New York: Penguin Group (USA) Ltd., 2001.

Writing Using Songs

1. **Use a song picture book if available. If the song is not in Big Book form, copy the song onto chart paper or SMART Board or on the computer and use an LCD projector. Alternatively, write your own song on chart paper and set it to a familiar tune. First read the song to the children and discuss it.**

2. **Teach the children how to sing the song. This should be easy since they may already know the familiar tune.**

3. **Provide the children with the opportunity to take turns tracking the print while they sing the song.**

4. **Write the words to the song on sentence strips. Have the children reconstruct (order) the sentence strips at center time (optional).**

5. **Word process the song and give each child a copy to illustrate. (Some children may prefer to copy the song and illustrate it.)**

6. **Model creating a variation on the song. For example, using the song picture book *This Is the Way We Eat Our Lunch: A Book about Children around the World* by Edith Baer, create a variation such as *This is the way we play at recess.* . . . Print the words at the bottom of the chart paper and brainstorm with the children what illustrations might work.**

7. **Brainstorm with the children other variations, such as *This is the way we brush our teeth* . . . , *help at home* . . . , *have a bath* . . . , *play at school* . . .**

VARIATIONS ON THIS IS THE WAY WE . . .

- *. . . come to school*
- *. . . make our books*
- *. . . look at words*
- *. . . read a book*
- *. . . sit in a circle*
- *. . . eat our lunch*
- *. . . cut and paste*
- *. . . raise our hands*

Check It Out!

One of the most amazing song picture books ever written is *Hey, Little Ant* by Phillip and Hannah Hoose (Berkeley, CA: Tricycle Press, 1998). The book includes the musical score and is written in rhyme, which is great for phonological awareness. The story tells of an ant that is about to be squished by a little boy. The ant and the boy argue back and forth. The story is left open-ended with the question, "What do you think that kid should do?" This question leads to great and sometimes heated discussions and ultimately to predictions. The illustrations support visual and critical literacy, interpreting perspective. (You can access a free teacher's guide or listen to the song at the Hey, Little Ant website: www.heylittleant.com.)

8. Scribe each child's variation if it is near the beginning of the year. Early writers should be able to copy the pattern *This is the way we . . .* and then use invented spelling to complete the line.

9. Have the children illustrate their own song page and share it with a partner or a group.

10. Bind the song pages to create a class book. For a class book, however, it is preferable for the invented spelling to be made conventional. This enables others to read it over and over again and to be exposed to conventional spelling.

Figure 7.1

This kindergartener made use of environmental print. She simply looked at the words to the song "The Itsy-Bitsy Spider" as she sang. This then motivated her to write and to draw a picture of the itsy-bitsy spider.

Check It Out!

Take a look at the website Songs for Teaching: Using Music to Promote Learning (www.songsforteaching .com). Click on Early Childhood Songs, Preschool and Kindergarten to listen to some song clips.

Writing Poetry in Preschool and Kindergarten

Regie Routman (2000) has shown through her work with numerous kindergarten teachers that with scaffolding, young children are very successful with writing poetry. Not only are they successful, but they also love it!

Although children enjoy rhyme and need to be able to identify and create rhymes, creating poetry that rhymes is difficult and very limiting for kindergarten writers. Instead, free verse is the answer. In free verse everyone is successful. There is no right or wrong. Children are free to use words, phrases, sentences, or any combination thereof.

It is important to begin by reading aloud lots of poetry to the children on a daily basis. Some of it can rhyme, but the children also need to be immersed in a great deal of free-verse poetry. Some teachers like to include formula poems or frames, such as the frame from Margaret Wise Brown's read-aloud poem books *I Like Bugs* and *I Like Stars*. The frame is easy for the children to follow: "I like bugs. Black bugs, Green bugs, Bad bugs, Mean bugs, Any kind of bug. A bug in a rug, A bug in the grass. . . ."

> Horses
> I like horses!
> Black horses, brown horses,
> Jumping horses, running horses,
> Any kind of horses.
> I like horses!
> A horse on the grass
> A horse in a stable,
> A horse on a road
> A horse in a barn.
> I like horses!
> Happy horses, sad horses,
> Funny horses, mad horses,
> I like horses!
> by Div. 13
> (Mrs. B. and the kids)

Figure 7.2
"You should see the bulletin board fill up with versions from home (done with parents) and from school."
—Mrs. B.

Formula poems do give a nudge for some young writers who need to get started and experience success (see Reproducible 7.1: Using Patterns to Write, on the CD).

Katie Wood Ray and Lisa Cleaveland do not promote formula poems, however. "These formulas may help someone write a single poem (albeit a poem a lot like everyone else's poem), but they don't help children come to understand the genre of poetry and all the techniques writers use to write in this form" (2004, 218).

Writers of poetry are free to write about anything. It is important for kindergarteners to understand that many poets write about very little things in their lives. Some of the poems in the book *all the small poems and fourteen more* by Valerie Worth provide the children with concrete examples of simple topics through the poem titles: "pig," "grass," "cow," "mud," "doll," "book," "kitten," "pie," "sun," "raw carrots," "marbles."

"We want to immerse them (the children) in poems about ordinary things and experiences and, in doing so, help them see that potential poems are all around them." (Ray and Cleaveland 2004, 214)

Mini-Lessons for Writing Poetry

Mini-lessons for writing poetry in kindergarten include
- picking a topic
- introducing different formats for writing poetry, such as poems that rhyme and those that do not, list poems, and so on (see below)
- word choice
- spacing on the page, including line breaks and white spaces
- the ending
- rhythm
- composing a title
- rereading while composing

Introducing Different Formats

Help the children to understand that there are different formats for writing poetry. Start by reading two poems on the same topic to the children, one that rhymes and one that does not. Ask them how the two poems are

Demonstrate

List poems are simply a list of words about a topic or subject. Rhyming is not required. List poems include a pattern and may have some repetition. These poems are very easy to write.

different. There likely will be many answers to this question that make sense. You may have to prompt them with, "How do the poems sound different?" to get at the concept of rhyme. This is a great opportunity to develop the concept of rhyme and the children's skill in phonological awareness.

It is also important for the children to understand that most poems could be written as paragraphs. But poems, using just a few words (such as with list poems), often express the same content in a more effective way. Model writing a list poem.

Check out Georgia Heard's new collection of list poems: *Falling Down the Page: A Book of List Poems* (New York: Macmillan Publishing, 2009).

WINDOW ON THE CLASSROOM

Figure 7.3

I modeled writing two list poems for a kindergarten class. The mini-lesson began with my explaining to the class that my dog Miko died a few months prior and that I missed her so. I explained that we had Miko as part of our family for 15 years, and I showed them a picture of her with our son Colin (above) when he was 5 years young. I explained that I really wanted another dog and had been looking at ads in the newspapers. I read them a couple of examples of ads, and we had a conversation as the children made connections to my story. I modeled the writing of the list poem below and thought aloud as I wrote:

Dogs

Cute

Soft

Friendly

Loving

Dogs

I also wrote the poem out as a sentence (a nonpoem).

Dogs are cute, soft, friendly, and loving.

Give the children poetry paper in different shapes (long and narrow for a list poem) to encourage writing other than sentences.

We compared the two formats for the same content, and the children preferred the poem format. Another day I took the same poem and extended it.

Dogs

Cute as a baby

Soft as a tissue

Friendly as Sarah

Loving as my mother

Dogs

We compared both poems, and the children voted on the one they preferred. We then discussed why they chose one poem over another.

I also illustrated both poems. It is important for the children to see that I am no artist but that I am still willing to "give it a go." In fact, I asked one child to come up and give me a hand with the sketch.

Writing a List Poem: Step by Step

1. Brainstorm a shared-writing chart of topics that interest the children. Write their names beside the topics they contribute. Add a couple of topics that interest you and write your name beside them.

Figure 7.4

2. Model the creation of a list poem using one of the topics that appears beside your name on the shared-writing chart.

3. Create another list poem, this time with the children as a shared writing. Use your other topic on the chart as the basis for this poem.

4. Review the topics brainstormed with the children. Have them find their name on the chart and share the topic listed beside it. Some children may need prompting.

5. Have the children create their own list poem using their topic from the chart. Encourage them to illustrate the poem. This will enable them to more easily read their poem back.

6. Encourage the children to celebrate each of their poems, first with a partner and eventually, over several days, with the whole class.

Brainstorm

I do it.

We do it.

You do it.

....

Check It Out!

See the lesson framework for teaching poetry in kindergarten in *Kids' Poems: Teaching Kindergartners to Love Writing Poetry* by Regie Routman (New York: Scholastic, 2000). The book explains how to make each section of the lesson framework successful, step by step! It also includes a delightful selection of poems written by kindergarteners, which can be used to show the children that they too can write poetry. Both the original handwritten poems with much invented spelling and backwards letters, and the word-processed, published copies are included. Celebrating kindergarten poems, which may come from a published book or be collected over time, is extremely powerful.

Celebrate!

Poetry-Writing Lesson Format			
Step 1: Demonstrate poetry writing	• Share and discuss several children's poems. You might use poems written by children in previous years or samples from Regie Routman's *Kids' Poems: Teaching Kindergartners to Love Writing Poetry* (New York: Scholastic, 2000). Nothing motivates kindergarteners like the writing of other kindergarteners. They begin to believe that they too can write like that!	10–15 minutes
	• Write a poem in front of the children (modeled writing).	5–7 minutes
	• Write a poem together (shared writing).	10 minutes
Step 2: Brainstorm with the children before they write.	• This oral stage is extremely important. Encourage the children not only to share their ideas for the poem, but also to say the whole poem or as much of it as they can. • Saying it aloud helps them to remember what they want to put down. Some children will be ready to start more quickly while others will need more rehearsal time with an adult.	5–7 minutes
Step 3: Write (and illustrate) a poem independently.	• Regie Routman among others recommends lightly pencilling-in words that the child has written but that you cannot read so that it can be read again at a later date.	15 minutes
Step 4: Share and celebrate the children's poems.	• Occasionally, children may prefer not to share or may prefer to have you read the poem for them. Sometimes the latter can be tricky!	10 minutes

Source: Adapted from Routman 2000, 9.

All poetry-writing sessions or lessons based on the Routman lesson format above provides great scaffolding: demonstration followed by oral

"I encourage them to compose out loud, on the spot with the whole class listening in." (Routman 2000, 19)

Some children will initially need to dictate their poems, which they can then illustrate.

brainstorming, independent writing and illustrating, sharing, and then celebrating. With this approach, every child will be a successful writer of poetry.

Writing Fact Poems

A fact poem is full of facts. After a social studies or science unit, create a shared-writing fact poem with the children. Give each child a copy to illustrate. Encourage the children to create their own fact poems on any topic.

Here is a fact poem about flies, written in the form of a list poem:

6 legs

2 wings

huge eyes

live everywhere

Flies

Advantages of Poetry Writing in Kindergarten

There are many advantages to writing poetry in kindergarten:
- Poetry writing does not require children to write a great deal or even to write a sentence or worry about punctuation.
- Every child can "write" a poem.
- Poems can be written about any topic and are powerful to use to help the children to remember facts they learned in social studies and science.
- Writing in kindergarten should be fun, and writing poems such as fact poems are fun to write.

"Amazing as it seems, kindergartners can easily write free-verse poems (poems without rhymes) about their lives and interests. When released from the structure of 'school writing' and shown poems by other kindergartners in their original handwriting, developing writers quickly experience the fun and possibilities that poetry writing provides." (Routman 2000, 5)

Reproducible 7.1: Using Patterns to Write, referenced in Chapter 7, is available on the *Learning to Write and Loving It!* CD.

- Kindergarteners can generally read back a poem they have written, even after several days.
- Many of the shared-writing poems created with the children during mini-lessons become shared-reading Big Books of poetry that the children love to read and reread. They also enjoy having small copies that they can illustrate and keep in their book bags or book boxes of familiar texts for rereading.
- Poems created by the children can be published as a Big Book of poems and shared with other classes and with families.

Chapter 8

Play Plans Before and After Centers

Check It Out!

"Chopsticks and Counting Chips: Do Play and Foundational Skills Need to Compete for the Teacher's Attention in an Early Childhood Classroom?" by Elena Bodrova and Deborah J. Leong in *Beyond the Journal: Young Children on the Web*, ed. Derry Koralek (Washington, DC: National Association for the Education of Young Children, 2004), 1–7. Also see *Spotlight on Young Children and Play*, edited by Derry Koralek (Washington, DC: National Association for the Education of Young Children, 2004).

"The Importance of Being Playful," by Elena Bodrova and Deborah J. Leong in *Educational Leadership* 60, no. 7 (2003): 50–53.

Children learn literacy as they play at the many centers and outdoors. Studies by Bodrova, Leong, and others show the links between play and the development of both literacy and social skills, including self-regulation. Many examples of literacy developed through play, such as the doctor's office, the restaurant and the camping centers, have been shared throughout this book. But how can teachers effectively scaffold this learning to support both imaginative play and writing?

Elena Bodrova and Deborah Leong have written extensively about the concept of play in kindergarten. In their article "Chopsticks and Counting Chips: Do Play and Foundational Skills Need to Compete for the Teacher's Attention in an Early Childhood Classroom?" Bodrova and Leong (2004) share research that indicates that many young children today appear less imaginative during pretend play. For example, when children are involved in socio-dramatic play (role-playing) at the Home Center, many perform the same routines day after day, such as feeding the baby or cooking on the stove. Bodrova and Leong describe these repetitive actions as immature play.

A play plan is a way for children to incubate ideas.

"Nowadays young children spend less time playing with their peers and more time playing alone, graduating from educational toys to video and computer games." (Bodrova and Leong 2004, 4)

Immature play is often evident with preschoolers; however, more creative, imaginative, and sophisticated or mature play should be happening both in preschool and in kindergarten. Research with preschool and kindergarten teachers (Bodrova and Leong 2001) found that the teachers in these classrooms achieved the best results when they focused on supporting mature play. The children in these classrooms not only mastered literacy skills and concepts at a higher rate, but they also developed better language and social skills (Bodrova and Leong 2004).

There are many ways to develop mature play. One strategy that works well is to engage the children in creating written play plans as a group or with a partner before beginning their center play.

So, why do kindergarten children need a plan to play? After all, generally they just pick up the props and begin to play. But how often do they repeat the same scenario over and over? How often is there parallel play at the centers rather than cooperative play? What about two children who want to play the same role?

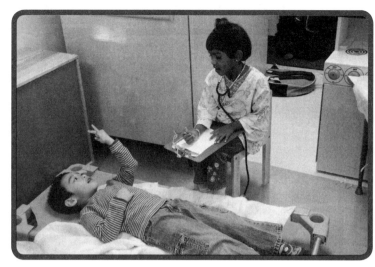

Figure 8.1
Play plans help to establish the role of the doctor, the patient and others such as a lab technician or an ambulance driver.

When the children work together to plan their play, they incubate their ideas. They have to decide on roles, props, and scenarios. To make these decisions together, they have to discuss their impending play, come to some agreement, and get the props ready by gathering or making them. They then work together to sketch the plan, which includes the roles, props, and scenarios. The end result is improved oral language (including vocabulary), stronger writing and social skills, and more imaginative (mature) play. The play plans may simply be drawings with or without letters or words.

Writing Before Centers: Creating Play Plans

It takes time and effective mini-lessons for young children to understand the concept of a play plan and how to create one. The following mini-lessons demonstrate a possible five-day process for introducing and scaffolding the writing of play plans.

Showing the children blueprints for a building makes the concept of written plans at the Block/Building Center come to life.

MINI-LESSONS 8.1
Scaffolding Play Plans

1. **Day 1: First of all, play plans have to be modeled by you and then by a few children. Explain to the children that a play plan helps them to think about what they will play before their play begins. Introduce the concept by explaining that an architect makes plans to help construction workers understand what a building should look like and how to build it. The plan is made before they start to build the building. From the plan,**

the builder knows what kinds of workers and materials will be needed and what role each worker will play in making the building.

2. Read aloud *Building a House* by Byron Barton (New York: Greenwillow Books, 1981). This is a perfect book to read to young children to help them realize how important a plan is and how important order is to the plan. Each two-page spread consists of a picture and one line of print. The book begins with, "On a green hill a machine digs a big hole." This indicates that you cannot start the building until the hole is dug. Builders then create the frame, a cement mixer pours the cement, bricklayers lay large white bricks, carpenters build the wooden floor, the walls are built, the roof is put on, the fireplace and chimney are made, the plumber and the electrician do their work, the carpenters put on the windows and the doors, and the painters paint inside and out. Finally, the family moves in.

Generally, read through the text with minimal stopping. Let the children feel the flow and the sequencing.

3. Revisit the story. Review with the children who all the players (construction workers) were and what their roles were: digger operator, cement pourers, carpenters, bricklayers, painters, plumbers, electricians. Discuss the materials and the machinery that each worker used to build the house. Help the children to notice that bricks of different sizes and shapes were needed for different parts of the construction. After rereading the story go back and actively involve the children in retelling the story using transition words such as *first, then, next, after,* and *finally.* These words emphasize that there is a sequence to this plan. Transition words are important for the children to learn. Discuss the plan and encourage children to make personal connections to the story.

4. Now retell the story starting on the last page—the family moves in—and see if the children think that it still works. Next, try retelling the story beginning with the carpenters hanging the windows and doors. Again, elicit from the children why this would not work and why there had to be a plan before building could begin.

5. Model for the whole class how to create a construction play plan using shared or interactive writing at the Block/Building Center. Pick two or three children to work with you. Explain to the children that the three or four of you are going to build a gas station. Discuss with the whole class what a gas station is. What buildings make up a gas station? What items do you see at a gas station? Who works at a gas station? Discuss each role. This is so important! Draw and label the people, the buildings, and the items (props) on chart paper. On another sheet, show the children how to plan the building of the gas station by drawing the steps, beginning with the digger and showing what will be needed to make the building. (See Reproducible 8.1: Here is my play plan for blocks, on the CD)

Name _____ Date _____

Here is my play plan for blocks.

Here is my play plan for <u>Blocks.</u>

C. Drew

Figure 8.2

6. Ask your helpers what roles they will play at the gas station once it is built? One might be a mechanic, another might pump gas, a third might work the cash, and a fourth might be a customer.

7. Have all the children imagine different scenarios that might happen at a gas station. Have them turn and talk, sharing possible scenarios.

8. Model sketching a few scenarios.

9. Day 2: Review the building plans from the previous day and work with your helpers to model for the whole class the construction of the gas station. As different blocks are selected, describe their sizes and shapes by thinking aloud. Gather the props or make them. Model the labeling of different items (for example, create signs for the gas station name and the cost of the gas, labels for the pumps, and so on). Review some of the play scenarios from the previous day. Have your helpers pick their roles and role-play one of the scenarios.

10. Day 3: Pick another center, such as the Home Center. Select four other children and ask them what roles they might play at the Home Center. Ask them to then share with the class what scenarios they might play at the center. Have them each sketch and label their roles. Sketch the scenarios on chart paper with the heading "My Play Plan." Have the children decide what props they will need to make or find. Draw and label the props.

11. Day 4: Review yesterday's play plan. At the end of the day, have the children at the center model their play based on the play plan. Discuss the result as a class. What roles and props did the children actually use from the play plan? Did they change their minds as they were playing; that is, did they deviate from the plan? Help the children to understand that the plan is to help them, especially to help them get started. But deviating is just fine too because when we start to play, we don't know exactly how it will all turn out!

The Block/Building Center is one of the best centers to support very imaginative (mature) play. It also supports the creation of a construction play plan.

Make building plans come to life by inviting an architect to your class to show some of his or her plans. Arrange for the architect to spend just a few minutes explaining to the children in appropriately simple language how important construction planning is. Leave plenty of time for the children to ask questions and share their thoughts with your guest.

Create a play plan journal for each center. Have the children write or stamp the date and their names on the top of a fresh page for each new play plan. This will promote the rereading or revisiting of others' plans. This may also help others to incubate ideas.

12. **Day 5: Assign small groups of children (three or four) to different centers. Have each group work to create a play plan. They will remain at the assigned center for several days and will review their play plan each day before beginning to play. Every child must write or draw something on the play plan. Use the following prompts to support the children in creating their group's play plan:**

o What will your role be? Draw and label it.

o What do you imagine will happen during your play? Draw and label it.

o What props will you need? Draw and label them.

Some teachers question the possible downside of a play plan. After all, does it not destroy spontaneity of play? Yes, it may. That is why it is not recommended that children always be required to create play plans at centers. However, incorporating play plans in support of kindergarten literacy is highly recommended. Play plans provide the children with a real reason to write, and encourage discussion, cooperation, interactive rather than parallel play and self regulation. The end result is more imaginative thinking, vocabulary development, and richer play.

WINDOW ON THE CLASSROOM

I recently received a great idea from Kathy Steele, Surrey School District, Surrey, British Columbia, that demonstrates how teachers can effectively link literacy and play, both at home and at school. It is a takeoff on the idea of sending home a stuffed animal and a journal, one child at a time. The child then brings the stuffed animal and the journal back to school and shares the adventures with the group. I had wanted to change it up, so I brought in a copy of the Architectural Digest *magazine. We talked about designing and building structures. I then put some pattern blocks into a bag along with a large scrapbook/class journal called "Architectural Digest." On the inside cover I included a letter to parents to let them know their child could keep the materials for a couple of days, build a structure with the blocks, and represent it in some way in the "digest" — diagram, writing, photo. . . . "Everyone enjoyed his or her time in adding to the book, and some students found it particularly engaging. Of course there were the added benefits of more writing at the block center and the parents understanding a little more about the learning and application of children working with blocks."*

Writing After Centers: Reporting

After center time, you may find it helpful to have the children write and/or draw a report. In their report, the children reflect on what happened at the centers and what they learned (perhaps in the areas of science, math, and art). It also encourages metacognition—thinking about their own thinking.

Reporting provides a real reason to write. The children write to share their thoughts with you. What did they do at the center? What did they learn? What did they like? What did they dislike? Some of the reports may also be shared with a partner, a small group, or the rest of the class. Children are motivated to write when they know that they have an audience in mind. The reporting may also appear in the play plan journal.

Reproducible 8.1: Here is my play plan for blocks, referenced in Chapter 8, is available on the *Learning to Write and Loving It!* CD.

Chapter 9

Writing Messages and Using Interactive Journals

Writing messages and using interactive journals are two of the most engaging forms of writing for young children. Both provide the children with an audience. When writers have an audience their voices are more likely to shine through.

Writing Messages in Preschool and Kindergarten

Messages and notes are among the most common forms of writing for very young children. Messages provide the children with authentic and meaningful reasons to write. You probably routinely write messages to children on the chalkboard, a whiteboard, chart paper, or an interactive whiteboard, such as a SMART Board. Why not then encourage the children to also write messages to the whole class? Research shows that message boards are very motivating for young children, even preschoolers. Once the use of message boards is established, the children write more both at home and at school (Laster and Conte 1998/99).

"One of the early skills that Message Boards facilitate is recognition of the relationship between written symbols and spoken words. This is an essential first step in learning to read." (Laster and Conte 2000, 104)

MINI-LESSONS 9.1

Implementing a Message Board

A message board is a written show and tell. There are three stages in implementing a successful message board in the classroom. First, explain to the children the purpose of a message board and various message models. Second, give the children opportunities to write messages, and support them in their message writing. Finally, encourage the children to share their messages.

1. From the first day of preschool, it is important to write messages to the children. The messages will often include a combination of conventional print and pictures. You might begin the day with a morning message, which communicates something special that is happening that

day, such as a field trip, birthday, or visitor. You might also write a message before recess or home time reminding the children to wear their mittens, to take home their home reading, or to avoid the mud on the playground (the latter message might be adhered to by some!). The goal is for the children to learn that people use a message board to communicate for authentic reasons.

Of course you can also make good use of the message board for finding and noting high-frequency words, beginning and ending consonants, and making a rhyming word. However, the main reason for the written communication is to share a message with the whole class. Additionally, the principal, parents/caregivers, and students from other grades are also encouraged to come into the classroom and share their messages on the message board. How motivating it is for the children to get messages from other adults and peers. (See Writing Mystery Messages, page 217.)

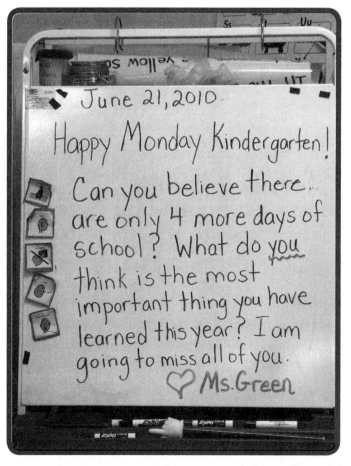

Figure 9.1
A message from the principal to the kindergarten students.

Learning to read and write messages gives children information about common words from slightly different perspectives, which seems to help them to understand more about the ways in which written words work (Clay 1991).

Recently, I was in a kindergarten classroom in which the message board was used to solve a major problem. The children at the Block/Building Center often take their construction very seriously and spend a great deal of time and effort trying to get their buildings, roads, and other features just so. In a half-day kindergarten class, the children may get upset when they have to dismantle their creations so that the children in the next group can use the materials. The teacher solved the problem by encouraging the children to draw their creations on the message board and to share their ideas with the class before their creation was dismantled. This also left a message for the next group to read (with the teacher's help).

The message board can also be used to solve personal problems. In one kindergarten class, a little boy named Samuel used the message board to enlist the help of others in finding his cat.

Figure 9.2

2. Encourage the children to write messages such as news from home on the message board (see Writing News-Based Messages, page 218). A good time to prompt children to write is first thing in the morning while you are engaged in greeting other children, collecting signed forms from home, and so on. A number of children can be kept meaningfully engaged by writing on the message board while others take out their book bags or book boxes and look at books alone or with a partner.

Another option to using the message board to solve problems is to use photos as permanent records of the children's experiences. The photos are then stored in a scrapbook or photo album. The children often write under the pictures, describing their accomplishments. The result: fewer children become upset when they have to dismantle their creations at centers. The pictures preserve their work indefinitely. (See Using Scrapbook Photo Albums to Prompt Writing on page 152 of Chapter 6.)

An after-recess news board is another motivating and authentic variation on a message board (see After-Recess News Board, page 218).

3. Another good time to encourage writing on the message board is at the end of the day. Prompt the children to write about something they did that day at school that they might then share with their families when they get home. This may help to reduce the number of times that children respond with the word *nothing* when asked by a family member, "What did you do in school today?"

4. Provide the time and the encouragement to have the children share their writing with the class. The major caution here is to try to make the sharing as interesting and meaningful as possible without spending a lot of time having the other children sit passively and listen. Encourage the children to share their writing, encourage the rest of the class to participate by creating a conversational tone, and model how to extend the conversation for the rest of the class.

For example, when Samuel shared his message about his cat (see Window on the Classroom, page 215), the teacher may have used this wonderful opportunity to help the other children make text-to-self connections by asking, "Has anyone ever lost anything? How did you find it? What else might Samuel do to find his cat?" This could have led to others helping Samuel create posters to put up around the school or to create a shared-writing letter to send home to inform others of the lost pet.

When there are too many messages to share in one sitting, draw a line under the messages that have already been shared. At other times throughout the day, you might share one or two other messages until all the messages from that day have been shared. The time used writing and sharing, if supported by you, is time well spent in scaffolding skills in writing, reading, and oral language.

Not only does the message board encourage young children to write, but it also encourages other teachers and parents/caregivers to come into the classroom to write. Some also choose to stay for a few minutes and share their message with the class. This method of communication should be promoted at home as well (see Reproducible 9.2: Writing Messages or Notes, on the CD).

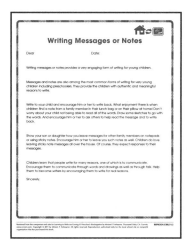

Writing Mystery Messages

Mystery messages are fun for young children. The messages may provide information, such as *Today we go to the farm,* or they may be just for fun, such as a riddle. Consider starting with a mystery message in September that you create as a modeled writing with the children watching (see page 82 of Chapter 4 for more information on modeled writing). Next, read the message together as a shared reading. The message may comprise both conventional letters and pictures.

Beginning in January, you might write a very simple message, but rather than read it with the children, have them work together to solve the mystery message. At the end of the day, read the message together as a group and the mystery is solved.

Barbara Laster and Betty Conte describe a 4-year-old who began by writing messages on the refrigerator notepad in September. In April, the same child took sticky notes and wrote messages all the way up the staircase at home. Each sticky note had a word or phrase: *Mom, Dad, sister, Tanya, I love you!* (2000).

Figure 9.3

Writing News-Based Messages

Children always have lots of news they want to share, such as experiences that have happened to them during recess or outside of school. Why not create a News Center or even a news board where they can write and illustrate the news?

Figure 9.4

Some children extend their news from day to day. The personal recount goes on . . . a saga develops.

After-Recess News Board

An after-recess news board is another authentic way to encourage the children to write and can be a very motivating writing experience.

> ## WINDOW ON THE CLASSROOM
>
> *I learned about the after-recess news board approach after one of my workshops. A teacher (who regrettably did not leave a name) left me this note:*
>
> After recess children are always anxious to tell you what happened on the playground—there are too many to listen to. I have them write what happened and put it on the "news board." I use real newspaper as a border and put a blank sheet in the middle for them to tell their story.

Providing the children with an opportunity to verbally share their recess news after they have written it makes the activity more engaging because the children know that they will share their writing with an audience. The audience may be another student, an adult, or the whole class.

Writing Notes, Memos, Cards, Invitations, Tickets, and Letters

Notes, memos, cards, invitations, tickets, and letters provide additional authentic reasons to write. The children will have an audience in mind, which means that they will be more motivated to write and will write with more voice. Creating a Post Center in the classroom is one way to encourage the children to write notes to one another.

Smile Notes

Smile notes are notes that will make someone feel happy. Discuss with the children how a note can make someone smile. How special it is to say or write something that makes others feel great. Sharing appreciation verbally is wonderful, but writing a special note allows the person to keep the note and read it over and over again.

WINDOW ON THE CLASSROOM

When I introduced the concept of writing notes to make someone smile, I brought a few special notes to school to share with the class. There was a note from a parent and a very simple note from a kindergarten child. I explained to the children how I had had these notes for many years and that I had kept them because they still made me happy each time I read them. I went on to say that most teachers keep such special notes for a very long time.

Next, I modeled writing a smile note to the custodian.

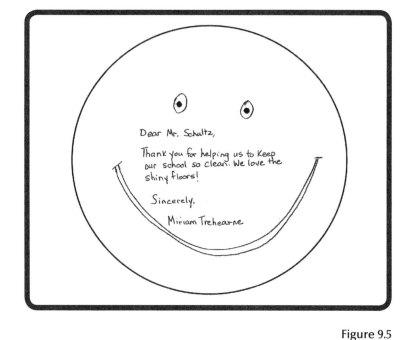

Figure 9.5

Another day we brainstormed how we should write a smile note as a shared writing experience. The children felt the principal deserved a thank you for helping us find the money we needed to rent a bus to visit a farm. They felt that note would make him happy and make him smile. I drew a happy face on poster paper and we decided as a group to write "Dear Mr. Smith, Thank you for helping us go to the farm. It was fun." All of the children then signed the note and presented it to Mr. Smith.

The next day the children identified many people they wanted to make smile. They also explained why. Each child drew a happy face and wrote a note to make one of the people on their list happy. The children then sent or hand-delivered their notes.

Writing Memos

Many children may be aware that both teachers and parents/caregivers send and receive memos. Explain that memos are used for many different purposes, such as to request or provide information (*On Friday, May 5, we will have a safety presentation in the gym.*), to give instructions, (*Please send home interview forms today.*), or to explain a decision (*The Parent Council has decided to have only healthful foods in the snack machine.*).

MINI-LESSONS 9.2
Writing a Memo in Kindergarten

1. **Show the class a memo you may have received from the office. Explain the purpose of it. Describe the components that make up a memo.**
    - To
    - From
    - Date
    - Message

2. **Model writing a memo. Drawing a picture in the message section assures all children that they too can write memos.**

3. **Use a shared writing to create a memo to send to someone in the school (perhaps the secretary or the**

principal). Alert the individual ahead of time so that she or he will know to write back if possible!

4. Brainstorm a list of people in the school, including other students (learning buddies) or siblings, to whom the children might send memos.

5. Suggest that the children turn and talk about who will receive their memo.

6. Have the children write a memo to their chosen recipient.

7. Have them hand-deliver their memos (so that they can explain what the memo says).

Writing Cards, Invitations, and Tickets

Sending out birthday cards, thank-you cards, postcards, and invitations give the children more authentic reasons to write. Having the children create personalized cards inviting families to attend a school open house, an assembly, or a field trip, goes a long way to enhancing the home–school connection. Creating personalized tickets for a special event, which can be created and sent home, may motivate more family members to attend the event. Letters to the tooth fairy work too!

Figure 9.6

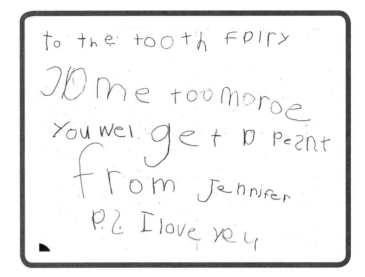

to the tooth fairy

JOme toomoroe

You wel get a peznt

from Jennifer

P.2 I love yeu

Figure 9.7

Figure 9.8

Writing Letters to Magic Creatures: The Most Motivating Kind of Letter Writing

Nothing develops a young writer's voice like writing a letter to a real audience, especially when there is the expectation that the recipient will write back. Writing friendly letters enables the children to develop a personal relationship with the people to whom they are writing and allows them to share information. Children love to write to their friends, their families, and their teachers. However, the ultimate letter-writing experience for young children is usually writing to a magic creature. This magic creature is, in reality, simply a stuffed toy, but to the children, the creature is truly magical.

Introduce the magic creature at any time during the year and explain that the creature loves to write letters. It is a great idea to begin by giving the children a letter from the magic creatures (see example below, Figure 9.9). It is also helpful to send a letter home as well, explaining to families who the creature is and requesting their encouragement in getting their child to write to the creature at home as well as at school. (See Reproducible 9.3: Writing to Magic Creatures, on the CD.)

January 18, 2010

Dear Boys and Girls,

We are the *Magic Creatures*. We have come to live in your class, to be your friends. We love getting letters from you. Tell us all about you. What is your favorite color? What do you like to eat? What is your favorite thing to do? Do you like the summer more than the winter? What center at school do you think is the most fun?

Your teacher tells us that you are very good illustrators too so please draw us some pictures to go with your writing.

We promise to write back to you. So, please write to us soon!

Love,

The Magic Creatures

Figure 9.9

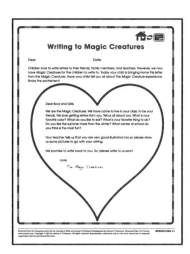

Check It Out!

Try these great read-alouds to support letter writing:

Dear Mr. Blueberry by James Simon (New York: Simon and Schuster, 1991).

Dear Peter Rabbit by Beatrix Potter (New York: Frederick Warne, 1995).

Frog and Toad Are Friends by Arnold Lobel (New York: HarperCollins, 1970).

I Wanna Iguana by Karen Kaufman Orloff and David Catcrow (New York: G.P. Putnam's Sons, 2004).

The Jolly Postman or Other People's Letters by Janet and Allan Ahlberg (Boston: Little Brown, 1986).

Lilly's Purple Plastic Purse by Kevin Henkes (New York: Greenwillow Books, 1996).

Mouse Letters by Michelle Cartlidge (New York: Dutton, 1993).

Mouse's Scrapbook by Michelle Cartlidge (New York: Dutton, 1995).

WINDOW ON THE CLASSROOM

I saw engagement in writing firsthand when my daughter and, three years later, my son were in first grade. Their teacher introduced a stuffed cat named Zink the Pink to the class. Both children wrote letter after letter to Zink, and both were thrilled every time they received a response. My daughter was saddened in January when she came home and informed me that Zink was moving to Australia. Any experienced teacher would understand why Zink needed a holiday!

At a kindergarten workshop in Toronto, I described to the group how my children's teacher, to a large extent using Zink, made them into motivated and skilled writers. Diana Bruni, a kindergarten teacher in Toronto, took the idea back to her class. Soon after, she e-mailed me with the subject line "Zink the Pink idea big success in my class." It is through her voice and photographs that magic creatures come to life for teachers.

Dear Miriam,

I attended a kindergarten workshop you gave on October 1 in Toronto. I enjoyed your seminar immensely and walked out of there with a book full of ideas I was eager to try implementing in my JK/SK class. One idea struck me in particular. You mentioned that your daughter's grade 1 teacher used Zink the Pink to motivate her class to write. Well, that night I happened to be shopping when I saw this huge huggable dog that I immediately fell in love with. As soon as I saw it, I knew that this was my Zink the Pink. I spoke to the manager of the store and he was very kind and agreed to donate the dog to my class. I have no shame about begging when it comes to my kids!

I had read a story (The Puppy Who Went to School by Gail Herman and Betina Ogden) early on in the year about a dog that followed his owner to school and got into all kinds of trouble. The dog's name in the story was Wags so I decided to name our dog after him. I had already taken my own dog, Candy, to school for the day a couple of times and my kids loved her, so I knew they were going to love Wags too. You should have seen their faces when they saw this beautiful 6-foot-long dog. Their smiles could not have gotten any bigger!

Figure 9.10

Wags wrote the class letters telling them how much he loved to read and write and asked them to write letters to him. I had made a special mailbox for Wags in the shape of a doghouse and I made up his own set of "doggy" stationery on the computer as well. The response from my kids was beyond my wildest dreams. They are writing Wags letters at school and writing him letters from home without any prompting from me whatsoever. I try to make sure that every child gets at least one letter from Wags each week but now I can understand why Zink had to go to Australia! The kids are loving it, I'm loving it, the parents are loving it too. Thank you so much for the great idea. In 20 years of teaching, I have never seen kindergarten kids so eager to write.

Figure 9.11
Wags in his reading tent. Also notice his mailbox.

I bought a special play tent (Wags's Reading Tent) for Wags to live in and the kids love taking turns visiting him there where they read him their letters or stories. Even the older kids in the school will stop by for a hug from Wags now and then. My Grade 6 kindergarten helpers even asked me why I hadn't done this when they were in my class!

I have lots of future plans for Wags. The possibilities are endless really. I would also like to host an early literacy night for parents called Reading and Writing with Wags. We sing songs about Wags, we are going to write stories about Wags, and we'll even attempt to make up our own book about Wags and his adventures. Perhaps Wags will be the next Clifford! I just had to write and let you know how one of your stories has sparked such a writing frenzy in my classroom. Many thanks again.

Sincerely,

Diana Bruni, JK/SK Teacher,
Transfiguration School,
Toronto, ON

P.S. Your idea was so successful that I decided to make up my own special teacher mailbox as well. Now the kids mail me letters and drawings too, and I write back on my own stationery.

Diana also sent a letter home so that family members might support their children's writing.

A year later, I received the following e-mail from Diana. Just feel the excitement in her class!

Hi Miriam,

I'm not sure if you remember me or not but I think you'll probably remember my classroom mascot dog Wags. I just wanted to let you know that I've gone to the next level (or 2!) with your idea. Wags got a girlfriend as a present from Santa this year named Wiggles. Wags proposed to Wiggles on Valentine's Day, they got married with a full Italian doggy wedding and they just had six gorgeous puppies a couple of weeks ago! It has been the most amazing experience . . . interesting and fun for me and my parent volunteers and the kids just love it. My reading and writing scores are much, much higher and I'm pretty sure I can attribute that to Wags and Wiggles. Thanks yet again for sparking the whole idea!

Diana Bruni
Transfiguration School

Dear Kindergarten Parents,

Please allow me to introduce myself. My name is Wags. I am a big, floppy dog that lives in your child's Kindergarten class. I am very happy to be their special friend. The children sing their Hello Song and come up and give me a big hug every day at the beginning of class.

One of my favourite things to do is write letters to my new friends in Mrs. Bruni's class. I hope you will encourage them to write letters back to me too, because I love getting letters even more than I like writing them! Sometimes my friends will write letters to me at school but please help them to write me letters from home too. Then they can bring them to school and mail them in my special "doggy" mailbox in the classroom. I will read their letters and write back to them.

Today I gave each of my new friends a sheet of my special doggy paper that I hope they will use to write me a letter. Please encourage your child to ask me questions and to write their own words if they can. I love when they draw me pictures too.

It was very nice talking to you. Please come in and visit me at school anytime.

Love,

Figure 9.12

Dear Wags and Wiggles
Have a fun summer. What are you doing
for yor VACASHN? I will mis you.
Love Siera

Figure 9.13

Figure 9.14

Wags, Wiggles, and a puppy!

Figure 9.15
Sierra creates a wedding book. She wrote and wrote and wrote!

Wags and Wiggles went to Hawaii for their honeymoon.

Figure 9.16
A page from Sierra's wedding book—the honeymoon.

Interactive Journal Writing in Preschool and Kindergarten

In her article "A Sense of Story: Interactive Journal Writing in Kindergarten," Susan White Cress (1998) describes how using interactive journals in kindergarten can encourage young children to write, help them to understand the writing process, and at the same time develop a sense of story. Cress describes some research findings with regard to journal writing in kindergarten classes. Typically, kindergarten children draw pictures, may label something in the picture, and sometimes write or dictate short sentences. But there is rarely any connection from one day's writing to the next. Each piece of writing becomes its own entity. Since there is usually only a line or two of writing, rarely is there a sense of story. However, according to Cress's research, children do learn about the writing process and story writing through interactive journal writing. They are also motivated to write because they are writing to someone (in this case, you) who will write back.

Cress outlines an effective step-by-step process for implementing interactive writing journals.

MINI-LESSONS 9.3
Implementing Interactive Journal Writing

1. Place 10 pages of blank paper into a booklet format. Cover each booklet with colored construction paper. Instruct the children to use one page of their booklet per day so that the journal lasts about two weeks, assuming daily writing. Two weeks typically also works well in developing" stories" as their writing on the same topic extends day to day. For each subsequent booklet created, use different colored covers. For example, make the first set of booklet covers blue, the second red, and so on. This will help you to keep track of how much each child is writing. Although finishing a booklet is not the goal, we know that to develop the skill and the will to write, young children need to write a great deal.

Model and think aloud to demonstrate how the children are to draw and write on each page. Some children might need to be shown how to divide their page with a line so that there is room for both writing and drawing.

2. Have a heterogeneous group of children sit together at a table on Day 1 so that they can learn from and support one another. The children will be at different writing skill levels. Some may be scribbling, others may be writing words to go with their pictures.

3. Instruct the children to draw and write about whatever they want on the first page of the journal. Explain to the children that you will speak with them about what they wrote and that you will write back to them.

4. As the children finish their work, speak with them about their writing. It is best not to ask them what they wrote as some may not actually know or remember what they wrote. Instead, ask each child to tell you about his or her writing and drawing. Some children may read what they wrote while others might make up something or simply describe their drawing. To remember the child's message, underwrite in conventional script or write the conventional script on a sticky note. (For more information on underwriting, see Chapter 2 on page 43.) Be sure to write back before the next day. For example, if the child drew a picture of a cat and wrote *M CT* (*my cat*), write back by asking a question at the top of the next page (page 2) such as, *What does your cat like to do?* It is important that your response is at the top of the next page. This enables the child to copy some of the words from your response in his or her response if desired.

5. The next day (Day 2), review what the child wrote on Day 1 and read your question response to the child. Have the child point to each word as you read. Next, direct the child to respond in words and pictures below your question on the second page. The dialogue about the cat might go on for two full weeks. In the end, the child may create a story about the cat or simply describe the cat. Each day, the child is encouraged to start at the beginning of the book and review what has been written (and drawn). They are reminded that this is what published adult authors like Eric Carle and Kevin Henkes do.

6. Once a booklet is completed, the finished product is sent home with a note to parents/caregivers explaining the interactive journal-writing process and ways that they can support the process (see Reproducible 9.1: Interactive Journal Writing, on the CD).

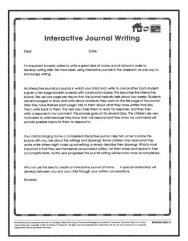

Although interactive journal writing may seem like a great deal of work for you, it is worth it. Young children are *very* motivated to write because they know you will respond the next day. No child can logically respond with "I don't know what to write" if you have provided something specific to respond to in the form of a question. Additionally, the children are encouraged to read and reread (or even remember) what they have written as well as what you have written. This is, of course, part of the writing process. Writers are constantly rereading in order to revise and to continue writing. Rereading also helps young writers develop skill in reading, including phonics and sight-word knowledge and skill.

Consider having a group of four or five writers sit together to share their interactive journal entries. This provides another real audience: their peers. Because the writing on any one topic goes on for several days (usually 10 days or 2 weeks), there is writing continuity from day to day. This is preferable to daily journal entries on different topics. The children see how to develop a simple story or report over a number of days. Finally, a special relationship develops between you and the child through your written conversations.

The following reproducibles referenced in Chapter 9 are available on the *Learning to Write and Loving It!* CD:

Reproducible 9.1: Interactive Journal Writing

Reproducible 9.2: Writing Messages or Notes

Reproducible 9.3: Writing to Magic Creatures

Closing Thoughts

Bea Johnson feels that it is *never too early to write*. Katie Wood Ray feels that children are *already ready to write* when they walk through the preschool door. I would agree. Most children have been scribbling, drawing, and creating letterlike formations long before arriving in preschool or kindergarten. It is this "writing" that supports and reveals their knowledge and skills in the areas of print awareness, phonological awareness, alphabet knowledge, phonics, and oral language. Writing supports reading just as reading supports writing. Furthermore, both reading and writing help stimulate thinking. However, the most important reason for learning to write is to provide children with another way to communicate.

Nothing improves writing like writing. Children need to write across the preschool and kindergarten day for many different reasons and using many different writing forms and genres. They soon begin to understand the value and purposes that writing serves. Nonfiction writing often provides that real purpose. Whether children are creating a poster about their lost cat, making a sign or label for the Block/Building Center, writing a letter or note, or making a page for a shared writing book, their writing is purposeful. Whenever they write, there is an audience in mind. Writing is always meant to be shared. As the year progresses, the children become more confident writers and more willing to share.

Although engaging children in writing from the first day of preschool or kindergarten is important, it is not enough. Read-alouds using good literature and mentor texts, shared reading, vocabulary building, and lots of focused talk support writing. To write, children also need to develop skill in alphabet letter knowledge, word work, phonics, and phonological awareness. Whole-class, small-group, and sometimes one-on-one writing mini-lessons teach writing in meaningful contexts. The best way to take the mystery out of writing is to demonstrate by writing both for (modeled) and with (shared, interactive, and guided) the children. Finally, it is crucial that families are supported in encouraging their children to write at home. Much of this writing, such as adding the letter *m* for milk on the grocery list or drawing and labeling a picture for grandma, takes only a few seconds.

Preschool and kindergarten: there is no more magical time. It is so clearly evident in their writing. Watching a child learn to write is like watching a rosebud slowly open. It takes time, but each step is exciting and the end result is amazing.

When I look at my son Colin's progress since September of kindergarten, I marvel at and celebrate how far he had come by the end of the year! Dated writing samples show great progress over time (see Figures CT.2 and CT.3). In September he was scribbling, although he could print his name. In March, he was clearly communicating an apology to me. He even learned that a letter has a greeting (salutation) and a closing. More importantly, he had figured out that writing serves a purpose and a written apology can be even more powerful than just saying "sorry."

Figure CT.1
This is Colin on his first
day of kindergarten!

Figure CT.2
Colin's writing, September:
scribbling and name

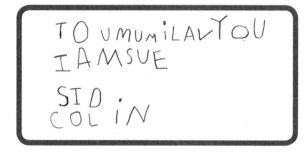

Figure CT.3
Colin's writing, March: *To you mum,*
I love you. I am sorry. Signed, Colin

As kindergarten teacher Jo Simpson from Oswego Illinois stated: "I just love watching them become writers!" It is not always easy . . . but well worth the effort!

Find Out More About Writing in Preschool and Kindergarten

Writing in preschool and kindergarten has just begun to take its rightful place in a comprehensive literacy program. Authors, teachers, and researchers such as Donald Graves, Dorothy Strickland, Lesley Mandel Morrow, Regie Routman, Lucy Calkins, Shelley Harwayne, Katie Wood Ray, and Georgia Heard, among others, have led the charge.

In addition to the solid research base, developmentally appropriate and easy-to-implement assessment tools, and practical and engaging activities for both school and home that are provided in this resource, the following books, reports, CDs, and DVDs are also recommended:

Calkins, Lucy, Amanda Hartman, and Zoë White. *Conferring with Primary Writers*. CD-ROM. Portsmouth, NH: Heinemann, 2005.

Calkins, Lucy, Amanda Hartman, and Zoë White. *One to One: The Art of Conferring with Young Writers*. Portsmouth, NH: Heinemann, 2005.

Calkins, Lucy, and The Teachers College Reading and Writing Project Community. *Big Lessons from Small Writers*. DVD. Portsmouth, NH: Heinemann, 2005.

Copple, Carol, and Sue Bredekamp, eds. *Developmentally Appropriate Practice in Early Childhood Programs: Serving Children from Birth through Age 8*. 3rd ed. Washington, DC: National Association for the Education of Young Children, 2009.

Dorfman, Lynne R., and Rose Cappelli. *Mentor Texts: Teaching Writing through Children's Literature, K–6*. Portland, ME: Stenhouse Publishers, 2007.

Feldgus, Eileen G., and Isabell Cardonick. *Kid Writing: A Systematic Approach to Phonics, Journals, and Writing Workshop*. DeSoto, TX: Wright Group/McGraw-Hill, 1999.

Freeman, Marcia S. *Teaching the Youngest Writers: A Practical Guide*. Gainesville, FL: Maupin House Publishing, Inc., 1998.

Graham, Steve, and Michael Hebert. *Writing to Read: Evidence of How Writing Can Improve Reading*. New York: Alliance for Excellent Education, 2010.

Harwayne, Shelley. *Writing Through Childhood: Rethinking Process and Product*. Portsmouth, NH: Heinemann, 2001.

Heard, Georgia. *Falling Down the Page: A Book of List Poems*. New York, Macmillan Publishing, 2009.

Heard, Georgia, and Jennifer McDonough. *A Place for Wonder*. Portland, ME: Stenhouse Publishers, 2009.

Horn, Martha, and Mary Ellen Giacobbe. *Talking, Drawing, Writing Lessons for Our Youngest Writers.* Portland, ME: Stenhouse Publishers, 2007.

Johnson, Bea. *Never Too Early to Write: Adventures in the K–1 Writing Workshop.* Gainesville, FL: Maupin House Publishing, Inc., 1999.

National Institute for Literacy. *Developing Early Literacy: Report of the National Early Literacy Panel.* Jessup, MD, 2008.

Ray, Katie Wood, and Lisa B. Cleaveland. *About the Authors: Writing Workshop with Our Youngest Writers.* Portsmouth, NH: Heinemann, 2004.

Ray, Katie Wood, and Matt Glover. *Already Ready: Nurturing Writers in Preschool and Kindergarten.* Portsmouth, NH: Heinemann, 2008.

Routman, Regie. *Writing Essentials: Raising Expectations and Results While Simplifying Teaching.* Portsmouth, NH: Heinemann, 2005.

Routman, Regie. http://www.regieroutman.com/inresidence/default.aspx, 2008.

Schulze, Arlene C. *Helping Children Become Readers through Writing: A Guide to Writing Workshop in Kindergarten.* Newark, DE: International Reading Association, 2006.

Spandel, Vicki, and Jeff Hicks. *Write Traits Kindergarten: Bringing the Traits to Kinderwriters.* Wilmington, MA: Great Source Education Group, 2008.

Stead, Tony. *Is that a Fact? Teaching Nonfiction Writing K-3.* Portland, ME: Stenhouse Publishers, 2001.

Strickland, Dorothy S., and Lesley Mandel Morrow, eds. *Beginning Reading and Writing.* Newark, DE: International Reading Association, 2000.

References

Adams, Marilyn Jager. *Beginning to Read: Thinking and Learning about Print A Summary.* Champaign: University of Illinois, 1990.

Allington, Richard, ed. *Teaching Struggling Readers.* Newark, DE: International Reading Association, 1998.

Allington, Richard. "What I've Learned about Effective Reading Instruction from a Decade of Studying Exemplary Elementary Classroom Teachers." *Phi Delta Kappan* 83 (2002): 740–47.

Allington, Richard. *What Really Matters for Struggling Readers: Designing Research-Based Programs.* Boston: Pearson Education, 2006.

Allington, Richard. "What At-Risk Readers Need." *Educational Leadership* (March 2011): 40–45.

Anderson, Nancy L., and Connie Briggs. "Reciprocity between Reading and Writing: Strategic Processing as Common Ground." *The Reading Teacher* 64, no. 7 (2011): 546–49.

Barnett, W. S., and J. T. Hustedt. "Preschool: The Most Important Grade." *Educational Leadership* 60, no. 7 (2003): 54–57.

Bennett-Armistead, V. Susan, Nell K. Duke, and Annie M. Moses. *Literacy and the Youngest Learner: Best Practices for Educators of Children from Birth to Five.* New York: Scholastic, 2005.

Bergen, Randee. *Teaching Writing in Kindergarten.* New York: Scholastic, 2008.

Bodrova, Elena, and D. J. Leong. *The Tools of the Mind Project: A Case Study of Implementing the Vygotskian Approach in American Early Childhood and Primary Classrooms.* Geneva: International Bureau of Education, UNESCO, 2001.

Bodrova, Elena, and Deborah J. Leong. "The Importance of Being Playful." *Educational Leadership* 60, no. 7 (2003): 50–53. ASCD: Alexandria, VA.

Bodrova, Elena, and Deborah J. Leong. "Chopsticks and Counting Chips: Do Play and Foundational Skills Need to Compete for the Teacher's Attention in an Early Childhood Classroom?" In *Beyond the Journal: Young Children on the Web*, ed. Derry Koralek, 1–7. Washington, DC: National Association for the Education of Young Children, 2004.

Booth, David. *Whatever Happened to Language Arts?* Markham, Ontario, Canada: Pembroke Publishers, 2009.

Booth, David, and Bill Moore. *Poems Please! Sharing Poetry with Children* (2nd ed.). Markham, Ontario, Canada: Pembroke Publishers, 2003

Bredekamp, S., and C. Copple. *Developmentally Appropriate in Early Childhood Programs*. Washington, DC: NAEYC, 1997.

Brown, Margaret Wise. *I Like Bugs*. New York: Random House for Young Readers, 1999.

Brown, Margaret Wise. *I Like Stars*. New York: Random House Books for Young Readers, 2007

Buss, Kathleen, and Lee Karnowski. *Reading and Writing Nonfiction Genres*. Newark, DE: International Reading Association, 2002.

Calkins, Lucy, Amanda Hartman, and Zoë White. *Conferring with Primary Writers*, CD ROM, International Reading Association, 2002.

Calkins, Lucy, Amanda Hartman, and Zoë White. *One to One: The Art of Conferring with Young Writers*. Portsmouth, NH: Heinemann, 2005.

Calkins, Lucy and the teachers College Reading and Writing Project Community. *Big Lessons from Small Writers*. DVD, Portsmouth, NH: Heinemann, 2005.

Carroll, Maureen. *Cartwheels on the Keyboard: Computer-Based Literacy Instruction in an Elementary Classroom*. Newark, DE: International Reading Association, Inc., 2004.

Centre for the Improvement of Early Reading Achievement (CIERA). *Every Child a Reader, Topic 2 Concepts of Print, Letter Naming and Phonemic Awareness*. Ann Arbor: University of Michigan, 1998a.

Centre for the Improvement of Early Reading Achievement (CIERA). *Every Child a Reader, Topic 6 Reading and Writing*. Ann Arbor: University of Michigan, 1998b.

Choi, Yangsook. *The Name Jar*. New York: Dragonfly Books, 2003.

Clay, M. "Emergent Reading Behaviour." PhD diss., University of Auckland, New Zealand, 1966.

Clay, M. *Becoming Literate: The Construction of Inner Control*. Portsmouth, NH: Heinemann, 1991.

Clay, M. *An Observation Survey of Early Literacy Achievement*. Portsmouth, NH: Heinemann, 1993a.

Clay, M. *Reading Recovery: A Guidebook for Teachers in Training*. Portsmouth, NH: Heinemann, 1993b.

Copple, Carol, and Sue Bredekamp. *Basics of Developmentally Appropriate Practices: An Introduction for Teachers of Children 3–6*. Washington, DC: National Association for the Education of Young Children, 2006.

Copple, Carol, and Sue Bredekamp. *Basics of Developmentally Appropriate Practice: An Introduction for Teachers of Children 3 to 6* (4th ed.).

Washington, DC: National Association for the Education of Young Children, 2009a.

Copple, Carol, and Sue Bredekamp. *Developmentally Appropriate Practice in Early Childhood Programs: Serving Children from Birth through Age 8*. Washington, DC: National Association for the Education of Young Children, 2009b.

Cress, Susan White. "A Sense of Story: Interactive Journal writing in Kindergarten. *Early Childhood Education* 26, no. 1 (1998): 13–17.

Cunningham, P., and R. Allington. *Classrooms That Work: They Can All Read and Write*. New York: Harper Collins, 1994.

Cunningham, P.M. *Phonics They Use: Words for Reading and Writing* (3rd ed.). New York: Harper Collins, 2000.

DeMille, Ted. *Making Believe on Paper: Fiction Writing with Young Children*. Portsmouth, NH: Heinemann, 2008.

Dickinson, David K., and Susan B. Neuman, eds. *Handbook of Early Literacy Research* (vol. 2). New York: Guilford Press, 2006.

Dickinson, David K., and Kimberley E. Sprague. "The Nature and Impact of Early Childhood Care Environments on the Language and Early Literacy Development of Children from Low-Income Families." In *Handbook of Early Literacy Research*, ed. Susan B. Neuman and David K. Dickinson, 263–80. New York: Guildford Press, 2001.

Dorfman, Lynne R., and Rose Cappelli. *Mentor Texts: Teaching Writing through Children's Literature, K–6*. Portland, ME: Stenhouse Publishers, 2007.

Duke, Nell K. and V. Susan Bennett-Armistead, et al. *Reading and Writing Informational Text in the Primary Grades*. New York, NY: Scholastic Teaching Resources, 2003.

Durkin, Delores. *Children who Read Early*. New York: Teachers College Press, 1966.

Ehmann, Susan, and Kellyann Gayer. *I Can Write Like That! A Guide to Mentor Texts and Craft Studies for Writers' Workshop, K-6*. Newark, DE: International Reading Association, Inc., 2009.

Elementary Teachers' Federation of Ontario. *Thinking It Through: Teaching and Learning in the Kindergarten Classroom*, 2010. http://www.etfo.ca.

Elementary Teachers' Federation of Ontario. *Playing Is Learning*. Pamphlet. Toronto, Ontario, 2011. http://www.etfo.ca/ELKP/PlayingisLearning/Documents/PlayingisLearning.pdf.

Farstrup, Alan and S. Jay Samuels, eds. *What Research Has to Say about Reading Instruction*. Newark, DE: International Reading Association, 2002.

Feldgus, Eileen G., and Isabell Cardonick. *Kid Writing: A Systematic Approach to Phonics, Journals, and Writing Workshop*. DeSoto, TX: Wright Group/McGraw-Hill, 1999.

Fitzgerald, J., and T. Shanahan. Reading and Writing Relations and Their Development. *Educational Psychologist* 35, no. 1 (2000), 39–50.

Fletcher, Ralph, and JoAnn Portalupi. *Craft Lessons: Teaching Writing K–8*. York, ME: Stenhouse Publishers, 1998.

Fletcher, Ralph, and JoAnn Portalupi. *Non-Fiction Craft Lessons: Teaching Information Writing K–8*. Portland, ME: Stenhouse, 2001a.

Fletcher, Ralph, and JoAnn Portalupi. *Writing Workshop: The Essential Guide*. Portsmouth, NH: Heinemann, 2001b.

Freeman, Marcia S. *Teaching the Youngest Writers: A Practical Guide*. Gainesville, FL: Maupin House, 1998.

Fulghum, R. *All I Really Need to Know I Learned in Kindergarten*. New York: Random House, 1988.

Gentry, Richard, and Jean Wallace Gillet. *Teaching Kids to Spell*. Portsmouth, NH: Heinemann, 1993.

Gibbons, Gail, *Tell Me, Tree: All about Trees for Kids* New York: Little, Brown Books for Young Readers, 2002.

Glover, Matt. *Engaging Young Writers: Preschool–Grade 1*. Portsmouth, NH: Heinemann, 2009.

Good, Linda. *Teaching and Learning with Digital Photography Tips and Tools for Early Childhood Classrooms*. Thousand Oaks, CA: Corwin, 2009.

Graham, Steve, and Hebert, Michael. *Writing to Read: Evidence of How Writing Can Improve Reading*. New York: Alliance for Excellent Education, 2010.

Graves, D. *A Fresh Look at Writing*. Portsmouth, NH: Heinemann, 1994.

Gullo, Dominic, F. *K Today: Teaching and Learning in Kindergarten Year*. Washington, DC: National Association for the Education of Young Children, 2006.

Hanson, Ralph A., and Donna Farrell. "The Long-Term Effects on High School Seniors of Learning to Read in Kindergarten." *Reading Research Quarterly* 30, no. 4 (1995): 908–33.

Harris, Mauree Elizabeth. "Implementing Portfolio Assessment in Young Children." *The Journal of the National Association for the Education of Young Children* 64 no. 3 (2009), 82–85.

Harrison, Gina L., Keira Ogle, Laureen McIntyre, and Laurie Hellsten. "The Influence of Early Writing Instruction on Developing Literacy." Paper presented at the annual conference of the Canadian Society for the Study of Education, Canadian Association of Educational Psychologists, Vancouver, British Columbia, Canada, May 31, 2008.

Harste, J., K. G. Short, and C Burke. Creating Classrooms for Authors and Inquirers. Portsmouth, NH: Heinemann, 1998.

Harwayne, Shelley. *Going Public*. Portsmouth, NH: Heinemann, 1999.

Harwayne, Shelley. *Lifetime Guarantees*. Portsmouth, NH: Heinemann, 2000.

Harwayne, Shelley. *Writing through Childhood: Rethinking Process and Product*. Portsmouth, NH: Heinemann, 2001.

Harwayne, Shelley. *Learning to Confer*. Portsmouth, NH: Heinemann, 2004.

Heard, Georgia. *Falling Down the Page: A Book of List Poems*. New York: Macmillan, 2009.

Heard, Georgia and Jennifer McDonough. A Place for Wonder. Portland, Maine: Stenhouse Publishers, 2009.

Helm, Judy Harris and Lillian G. Katz. *Young Investigators: The Project Approach in the Early Years* (2nd ed.). New York: Teachers College Press, 2010.

Henkes, Kevin. *Chrysanthemum*. New York: Mulberry Books, 1996.

Hiscock, Bruce. *The Big Tree*. Honesdale, PA: Boyds Mills Press, 1999.

Holdaway, Don. *The Foundations of Literacy*. Portsmouth, NH: Heinemann, 1979.

Horn, Martha, and Mary Ellen Giacobbe. *Talking, Drawing, Writing Lessons for Our Youngest Writers*. Portland, ME: Stenhouse Publishers, 2007.

Illinois Projects in Practice. Available at the Illinois Early Learning Web site, http://illinoispip.org/ (accessed July 5, 2011).

Illinois Projects in Practice. Available at the Illinois Early Learning Web site, http://illinoispip.org/ (accessed July 5, 2011).

International Reading Association (IRA) and the National Association for the Education Of Young Children (NAEYC). "Learning To Read And Write: Developmentally Appropriate Practices For Young Children." *Young Children* 53.4 (1998): 30–46.

Jalongo, Mary Renck, and Deborah McDonald Ribblett. "Using Song Picture Books to Support Emergent Literacy." *Childhood Education* 74 (Fall 1997): 15–22.

Johnson, Bea. *Never Too Early to Write: Adventures in the K–1 Writing Workshop*. Gainesville, FL: Maupin House Publishing, Inc., 1999.

Katz, Lillian, and Sylvia Chard. "The Contribution of Documentation to the Quality of Early Childhood Education." ERIC ED393 608, April 1996. http://www.ericdigests.org/1996–4/quality.htm.

Koralek, Derry, ed. *Spotlight on Young Children and Play*. Washington, DC: National Association for the Education of Young Children, 2004.

Koralek, Derry, ed. *Spotlight on Young Children and Social Studies*. Washington, DC: National Association for the Education of Young Children, 2006.

Koralek, Derry, ed. *Spotlight on Teaching Preschoolers*. Washington, DC: National Association for the Education of Young Children, 2009.

Laster, Barbara, and Betty Conte. "Emerging Literacy: Message Boards in Preschool." In *Developing Reading-Writing Connections Strategies from the Reading Teacher,* ed. Timothy V. Rasinski, Nancy D. Padak, Brenda Weible Church, Gay Fawcett, Judith Hendershot, Justina M. Henry, Barbara G. Moss, Jacqueline K. Peck, Elizabeth (Betsy) Pryor, and Kathleen A. Roskos, 101–7. Newark, DE: The International Reading Association, 2000.

Lewis, M. and Wray,D. *Developing children's non-fiction writing: Working with writing frames*. Leamington, Spa. UK: Scholastic, 1995.

Lobel, Arnold. *Frog and Toad Together.* New York: HarperCollins, 1979.

Mariconda, Barbara. *Sort it Out!* Mount Pleasant, South Carolina: Sylvan Dell Publishing, 2008.

Mariconda, Barbara, and Dea Paoletta Auray. *Getting Ready to Write.* Trumbull, CT: Empowering Writers, 2007.

Mayer, Mercer. *Frog, Where Are You?* New York: Penguin Group (USA), 2003.

McGee, Lea M., and Donald J. Richgels. *Designing Early Literacy Programs: Strategies for At-Risk Preschool and Kindergarten Children*. New York: Guilford, 2003.

McGee, Lea M., and Lesley Mandel Morrow. *Teaching Literacy in Kindergarten*. New York: Guilford, 2005.

McGill-Frazen, Anne. *Kindergarten Literacy.* New York: Scholastic, 2006.

Miller, Debbie. *Are Trees Alive?* London: Walker Childrens, 2003.

Mindess, M., Min-hua Chen, and R. Brenner. "Social-emotional Learning in the Primary Curriculum." *Young Children* 63, no. 6 (2008): 56–59.

Morrow, Lesley Mandel, Dorothy Strickland, and Deborah Woo. *Literacy Instruction in Half- and Whole-Day Kindergarten*. Newark, DE: International Reading Association, 1998.

National Institute for Literacy. *Developing Early Literacy: Report of the National Early Literacy Panel.* Jessup, MD: National Institute for Literacy, 2008.

Neuman, Susan B. "Foreword." In *Literacy Instruction in Half- and Whole-Day Kindergarten*, ed. Lesley Mandel Morrow, Dorothy Strickland, and Deborah Woo, x-xi. Newark, DE: International Reading Association, 1998.

Neuman, Susan B., and David K. Dickinson, eds. *Handbook of Early Literacy Research*. New York: Guilford Press, 2001

Neuman, S. B. "How Can We Enable All Children to Achieve?" In *Children Achieving: Best Practices in Early Literacy*, ed. S. B. Neuman and K. A. Roskos, 18–32. Newark, DE: International Reading Association, 1998.

Neuman, S. B., C. Copple, and S. Bredekamp. *Learning to Read and Write: Developmentally Appropriate Practices for Young Children*. Washington, DC: National Association for the Education of Young Children, 2000.

Neuman, Susan B., and Kathleen Roskos with Tanya S. Wright and Lisa Lenhart. *Nurturing Knowledge Building a Foundation for School Success by Linking Early Literacy to Math, Science, Art and Social Studies*. New York: Scholastic, 2007.

Northwest Educational Technology Consortium (http://www.netc.org/software/index.html)

Olness, Rebecca. *Using Literature to Enhance Writing Instruction: A Guide for K–5 Teachers*. Newark, DE: International Reading Association, Inc., 2005.

The Ontario Ministry of Education. *A Guide to Effective Instruction in Writing, Kindergarten to Grade 3*. Toronto, Ontario, Canada: Ontario Education, 2005.

The Ontario Ministry of Education. *The Full-Day Early Learning Kindergarten Program*, Draft Version, 2010–2011, Toronto, Ontario, Canada, http://www.edu.gov.on.ca

Pascal, Charles E. "With Our Best Future in Mind: Implementing Early Learning in Ontario." Report to the Premier by the special Advisor on Early Learning, June 2009. Available at http://www.ontario.ca/en/initiatives/early_learning/ONT06_018865.

Polochanin, D. "Teacher as Author: Modeling the Writing Process." *Classroom Leadership* 8, no. 3 (2004). Available at http://www.ascd.org/publications/classroom-leadership/nov2004/Teacher-as-Author.aspx.

Prior, J., and M. R. Gerard. *Environmental Print in the Classroom: Meaningful Connections for Learning to Read*. Newark, DE: International Reading Association, 2004.

Rasinski, Timothy V., Nancy D. Padak, Brenda Welbie Church, Gay Fawcett Judith Hendershot, Justina M. Henry, Barbara G. Moss, Jacqueline K. Peck, Elizabeth (Betsy) Pryor, and Kathleen A. Roskos, eds. *Developing Reading-Writing Connections: Strategies from* The Reading Teacher. Newark, DE: International Reading Association, Inc. 2000.

Rasinski, Timothy V., Nancy D. Padak, Brenda Welbie Church, Gay Fawcett Judith Hendershot, Justina M. Henry, Barbara G. Moss, Jacqueline K. Peck, Elizabeth (Betsy) Pryor, and Kathleen A. Roskos, eds. *Motivating Recreational Reading and Promoting Home-School Connections: Strategies from* The Reading Teacher. Newark, DE: International Reading Association, Inc. 2000.

Ray, Katie Wood. "When Kids Make Books." *Educational Leadership* October 2004, 14–18.

Ray, Katie Wood, and Lisa B. Cleaveland. *About the Authors: Writing Workshop with Our Youngest Writers*. Portsmouth, NH: Heinemann, 2004.

Ray, Katie Wood, and Matt Glover. *Already Ready: Nurturing Writers in Preschool and Kindergarten*. Portsmouth, NH: Heinemann, 2008.

Reading, Writing and Technology. Newark, DE: The International Reading Association, http://www.reading.org/Libraries/Parents/pb1074_technology.sflb.ashx

Roskos, K., and J. Christie. "Examining the Play-Literacy Interface: A Critical Review and Future Directions." *Journal of Early Childhood Literacy* 1, no. 1 (2001): 59–89.

Routman, Regie. *Regie Routman in Residence*. Portsmouth, NH: Heinemann, 2008 and 2009. Retrieved from http://www.regieroutman.com/inresidence/default.aspx

Routman, Regie. *Kids' Poems: Teaching Kindergartners to Love Writing Poetry*. New York: Scholastic, 2000.

Routman, Regie. *Writing Essentials*: *Raising Expectations and Results while Simplifying Teaching*. Portsmouth, NH: Heinemann, 2005. http://www.regieroutman.com.

Schickedanz, J. A. "Early Childhood Education and School Reform: Consideration of Some Philosophical Barriers." *Journal of Education* 176, no. 1 (1994): 29–47.

Schickedanz, J. A. (1998). "What Is Developmentally Appropriate Practice in Early Literacy? Consider the Alphabet." In *Children Achieving: Best Practices in Early Literacy,* ed. S. B. Neuman and K. A. Roskos, 20–37. Newark, DE: International Reading Association.

Schickedanz, Judith A., and Renee M. Casbergue. *Writing in Preschool: Learning to Orchestrate Meaning and Marks*. Newark, DE: International Reading Association Inc., 2004.

Schickedanz, Judith A., and Renee M. Casbergue. *Writing in Preschool: Learning to Orchestrate Meaning and Marks* (2nd ed.). Newark, DE: International Reading Association Inc., 2009.

Schulze, Arlene C. *Helping Children Become Readers through Writing: A Guide to Writing Workshop in Kindergarten*. Newark, DE: International Reading Association, 2006.

Seitz, Hilary. *The Power of Documentation in the Early Childhood Classroom Young Children*. Washington DC, National Association for the Education of Young Children, 2008

Shanahan, Timothy. "Nature of the Reading-Writing Relation: An Exploratory Multivariate Analysis." *Journal of Educational Psychology* 76, no. 3 (1984): 466–77.

Shanahan, Timothy. "Where Does Writing Fit in Reading First." In *Understanding and Implementing Reading First Initiatives*, ed. Carrice Cummins, 106–115. Newark, DE: International Reading Association, 2006.

Snow, C., M. Susan Burns, and P. Griffin, eds. *Preventing Reading Difficulties in Young Children*. Washington, DC: National Academy Press, 1998.

Spandel, Vicki. *Creating Writers through 6-Trait Writing Assessment and Instruction* (3rd ed.). New York: Addison Wesley Longman, 2001.

Spandel, Vicki. *Creating Writers through 6—Trait Writing Assessment and Instruction* (4th ed.) Boston: Pearson Education Inc., 2005.

Spandel, Vicki. *Using the Six Traits to Enrich Writing Process in Primary Classrooms*. Boston: Allyn and Bacon, 2007.

Spandel, Vicki, and Jeff Hicks. *Write Traits Kindergarten: Bringing the Traits to Kinderwriters* (Teacher's Guide). Wilmington, MA: Great Source Education Group, 2008.

Stead, Tony. *Is That a Fact? Teaching Nonfiction Writing K–3*. Portland, ME: Stenhouse Publishers, 2002.

Strickland, Dorothy S. *Essential Readings on Early Literacy*. Newark, DE: International Reading Association, Inc., 2010.

Sulzby, Elizabeth. "Assessment of Emergent Writing and Children's Language while Writing." In *Assessment for Instruction in Early Literacy*, ed. L. Morrow and J.Smith, .Englewood Cliffs, . NJ: Prentice Hall, 1990.

Taberski, Sharon. *On Solid Ground*. Portsmouth, NH: Heinemann, 2000.

Technology and Young Children Interest Forum Members. *Meaningful Technology Integration in Early Learning Environments. Beyond the Journal. Young Children on the Web*. Washington, DC: National Association for the Education of Young Children, 2008

"Thinking about the Reading/Writing Connection with David Pearson." *The Voice* 7, no. 2 (2002): 6, 9. http://www.nwp.org/cs/public/print/resource/329.

Thomason, T., and C. York. *Write on Target: Preparing Young Writers to Succeed on State Writing Achievement Tests*. Norwood, MA: Christopher-Gordon, 2000.

Tomlinson, Carol Ann, and Marcia B. Imbeau. *Leading and Managing a Differentiated Classroom*. Alexandria, VA: ASCD, 2010.

Tompkins, Gail E. *Teaching Writing Balancing Process and Product*. Upper Saddle River, NJ: Prentice Hall, 2000.

Trehearne, Miriam P. Lynne Hemming Healy, Maria Cantalini-Williams, and Joan L. Moore. *Language Arts Kindergarten Teacher's Resource Book.* Toronto, Ontario, Canada: Nelson Thomson Learning, 2000

Trehearne, Miriam P., et al. *Comprehensive Literacy Resource for Kindergarten Teachers.* Vernon Hills, IL: ETA/Cuisenaire, 2003.

Trehearne, Miriam P., et al. *Comprehensive Literacy Resource for Preschool Teachers.* Vernon Hills, IL: ETA/Cuisenaire, 2005.

Turbill, Jan. "A Researcher Goes to School: Using Technology in the Kindergarten Literacy Curriculum." *Journal of Early Childhood Literacy* 1, no. 3 (2001): 255–79.

Udry, Janice May. *A Tree Is Nice.* New York: Harper & Row, 1956.

National Institute for Literacy. *Developing Early Literacy: Report of the National Early Literacy Panel.* Jessup, MD: National Institute for Literacy, 2008.

Van Scoter, J., D. Ellis, and J. Railsback. *Technology in Early Childhood Education: Finding the Balance.* Portland, OR: Northwest Regional Educational Laboratory, 2001. Retrieved July 25th, 2011, from http://www.netc.org/earlyconnections/pub.html

Van Scoter, Judy, and Suzie Boss. "Understanding Technology's Role in Literacy." In *Learners, Language, and Technology: Making Connections That Support Literacy.* Portland, OR: Northwest Regional Educational Laboratory, Child and Family, 2002. Retrieved July 25th, 2011, from http://www.netc.org/earlyconnections/pub/sec2.pdf

Vaszquez, Vivian. *Negotiating Critical Literacies in Young Children.* Mahwah, NJ: Lawrence Erlbaum, 2004.

Vukelich, Carol, and James Christie. *Building a Foundation for Preschool Literacy: Effective Instruction for Children's Development.* Newark, DE: International Reading Association, 2004.

Washington, V., and J.D. Andrews, eds. *Children of 2020 Creating a Better Tomorrow.* Washington, DC: Council for Professional Recognition and National Association for the Education for Young Children, 2010.

Worth, Valerie, *All the Small Poems and Fourteen More.* St. Louis, MO: Turtleback, 1996.

Wurm, Julianne P. *Working in the Reggio Way.* St. Paul, MN: Redleaf Press, 2005.

Index